Table of Contents

Introduction 7
Overview of Book Goals 7
Definition of "Risky" Investments 9
Psychology of Risk-Taking in Investing 11
Managing Risk While Seeking Returns 14
Chapter 1: Naked or Uncovered Options 17
Understanding Naked Options 17
Unlimited Loss Potential 20
Margin Requirements and Leverage 23
Case studies and worst-case outcomes 27
Risk Management Strategies 32
Chapter 2: Digital or Binary Options Trading 36
How Binary Options Work 36
Difficulty of Winning Consistently 41
Watch Out for Scams 47
Technical Analysis Limitations 53
Alternatives with Lower Risk 58
Chapter 3: FOREX Rollover Arbitrage 65
Understanding Rollover Arbitrage in Forex Trading 65
Risks of Unexpected Interest Rate Changes 69
Central Bank Policy Shifts 74
Currency Peg Instability 81
Margin Requirements 86
Chapter 4: Initial Coin Offerings (ICOs) 89
ICOs as an Alternative to IPOs 89
Lack of Regulation and Oversight 93
Evaluating White Papers 96
High Startup Failure Rate 99
Fraud Risk Warning Signs 103
Chapter 5: Futures Contracts 107

Understanding Futures and Leverage *107*
Volatility and Margin Calls *111*
Contango and Backwardation *114*
Hedging vs Speculation *119*
Limiting Outsized Losses *125*

Chapter 6: Options Trading **131**
Basics of Call and Put Options *131*
Leverage Amplifies Both Gains and Losses *135*
Implied Volatility and Pricing *140*
Pick Direction Correctly and Time It Right *145*
Advanced Strategies Briefly *150*

Chapter 7: Forex Trading **154**
What is Forex and its Size *154*
Volatility and Liquidity *160*
Technical vs. Fundamental Analysis *165*
Risk Management Essentials *171*
Watch Out for Scams *176*

Chapter 8: Newer Cryptocurrencies **180**
The Appeal of Altcoins *180*
Lack of Track Record *184*
Understanding White Papers *189*
Watch Out for Pump and Dumps *193*
Long-Term Adoption Still Uncertain *197*

Chapter 9: Microcap Stocks **202**
What Are Microcaps *202*
Risks of Low Liquidity and Regulation *207*
Susceptibility to Manipulation *211*
Financial Reporting Standards Lax *215*
Diversification Challenges *219*

Chapter 10: Ultra High-Yield Bonds **223**
What Are Junk Bonds *223*
Appeal of High Yields *227*

Copyright © 2023 by Jonathan T. Morgan (Author)

All rights reserved. No part of this book may be reproduced or utilized in any form or by any means, electronic or mechanical, including photocopying, recording or by any information storage and retrieval system, without permission in writing from the publisher, except for brief quotations in critical articles or reviews.

The content of this book is based on various sources and is intended for educational and entertainment purposes only. While the author has made every effort to ensure the accuracy, completeness, and reliability of the information provided, the information may be subject to errors, omissions, or inaccuracies. Therefore, the author makes no warranties, express or implied, regarding the content of this book.

Readers are advised to seek the guidance of a licensed professional before attempting any techniques or actions outlined in this book. The author is not responsible for any losses, damages, or injuries that may arise from the use of information contained within. The information provided in this book is not intended to be a substitute for professional advice, and readers should not rely solely on the information presented.

By reading this book, readers acknowledge that the author is not providing legal, financial, medical, or professional advice. Any reliance on the information contained in this book is solely at the reader's own risk.

Thank you for selecting this book as a valuable source of knowledge and inspiration. Our aim is to provide you with insights and information that will enrich your understanding and enhance your personal growth. We appreciate your decision to embark on this journey of discovery with us, and we hope that this book will exceed your expectations and leave a lasting impact on your life.

Title: Flirting With Financial Oblivion
Subtitle: Navigating the World's Riskiest Bets and Living to Tell the Tale

Author: Jonathan T. Morgan

Credit Risk and Default Likelihood 231
Bond Covenants Matter 235
Recession Impacts 239
Chapter 11: Penny Stocks 243
Definition of Penny Stocks 243
Risks of Newly Public Companies 247
Financial Reporting Reliability 251
Volatility and Liquidity Challenges 255
Avoiding Pump and Dumps 259
Chapter 12: NFTs 263
What Are NFTs 263
Digital Scarcity Model 267
Very Speculative Pricing 270
High Volatility 274
Long-term Value Uncertain 278
Chapter 13: Offshore Private Placements 281
Risks of Limited Information 281
Lack of Regulatory Oversight 285
Difficulty Evaluating Opportunities 288
Scams and Fraud Risk 292
Accessing Investments 295
Chapter 14: Unregulated Online Lending 298
How P2P Lending Platforms Work 298
Underwriting Standards Vary Widely 302
Default and Collection Challenges 305
Lack of FDIC Insurance 308
Secondary Market Opacity 311
Chapter 15: High Risk ETFs 314
Understanding Leveraged ETFs 314
Volatility Decay Over Time 317
Rebalancing Eats Returns 320
Sector Risks Like Biotech 323

Avoid Holding Long-Term *326*
Chapter 16: Junk Bonds **329**
What Are High-Yield Bonds? *329*
The Appeal of High Coupons *333*
Credit Risk Spectrum *336*
Recession Impacts on Defaults *339*
Bond Covenants Matter *342*
Chapter 17: Cryptocurrencies **346**
Blockchain and Crypto Basics *346*
Volatility Versus Stocks *350*
Debates Over Usefulness *353*
Cryptographic and Protocol Risks *357*
Evolving Regulatory Oversight *361*
Chapter 18: Startup Investing **365**
Evaluating Founders and Teams *365*
Difficulty of Valuing Pre-Revenue Startups *369*
High Failure and Loss Rates in Startup Investing *373*
Lack of Liquidity in Startup Investing *377*
Diversification Challenges in Startup Investing *381*
Conclusion **385**
Key Takeaways on Risky Investing *385*
Balancing Risks and Rewards *389*
Clear Goals and Risk Tolerance *393*
Limit Speculation to Small Allocations *396*
Conduct Proper Due Diligence *399*
Wordbook **403**
Supplementary Materials **406**

Introduction
Overview of Book Goals

Welcome to "Flirting With Financial Oblivion: Navigating the World's Riskiest Bets and Living to Tell the Tale." In this exploration of the perilous peaks and shadowy abysses of the financial world's highest risk ventures, we embark on a journey that will illuminate the intricacies of exotic investments. This introduction serves as a roadmap, providing you with an overview of the goals and aspirations of this book.

At the heart of this book lies a dual purpose: to inform and to caution. Our primary goal is to empower readers with a comprehensive understanding of the most audacious financial ventures, from naked options to offbeat cryptocurrencies. By delving into the mechanics, risks, and potential rewards of these high-stakes investments, we aim to equip you with the knowledge necessary to make informed decisions.

The secondary goal is to serve as a cautionary guide, emphasizing the potential perils that accompany the allure of extraordinary gains. While the financial world's riskiest bets may offer the prospect of outrageous fortunes, they also pose a substantial risk of financial obliteration. Throughout these pages, we'll unravel the stories of those who have flirted with financial oblivion, offering valuable lessons and insights gained from both triumphs and tribulations.

In pursuit of these goals, each chapter dissects a specific category of high-risk investment, presenting a detailed analysis of its intricacies, pitfalls, and risk management strategies. From the wild terrain of naked options to the uncharted waters of initial coin offerings (ICOs) and the speculative realm of NFTs, we leave no stone unturned in our quest to demystify the exhilarating yet treacherous landscape of high-risk finance.

This book also aims to foster a deeper understanding of the psychology behind risk-taking in investing. By exploring the motivations, biases, and cognitive traps that investors may encounter, we shed light on the intricate interplay between human psychology and financial decision-making.

As you navigate the chapters that follow, keep in mind that the insights provided are not intended to dissuade you from exploring these high-risk avenues but rather to guide you through the labyrinth of possibilities. Armed with knowledge, you can approach the world of risky investments with eyes wide open, ready to make calculated decisions and, ultimately, to live to tell the tale.

In the spirit of adventure, let us embark on this thrilling exploration of the financial world's most daring ventures, where fortunes are won and lost, and the line between success and financial oblivion is razor-thin.

Definition of "Risky" Investments

At its core, risk in the realm of finance is the uncertainty that an investment's actual returns will differ from its expected returns. The degree of this uncertainty varies across different types of investments, and the term "risky" encapsulates a spectrum of potential perils that investors may encounter. Let us dissect the components that contribute to the risky nature of an investment and how these factors shape the financial decisions we make.

1. Volatility and Market Fluctuations: One of the fundamental elements that categorize an investment as risky is its susceptibility to market fluctuations. Volatility, the degree of variation in trading prices over time, is a key metric in assessing risk. High volatility implies a greater likelihood of substantial price swings, presenting both opportunities and threats for investors.

2. Lack of Predictability: Investments deemed risky often lack predictability. This unpredictability can stem from factors such as economic conditions, geopolitical events, or shifts in market sentiment. In contrast to more stable and predictable assets, risky investments are characterized by their vulnerability to unforeseen developments.

3. Potential for Loss: The risk associated with an investment is closely tied to the potential for financial loss. Unlike low-risk investments, where the likelihood of losing a significant portion of the invested capital is minimal, risky investments expose investors to the prospect of substantial losses. This risk-return tradeoff forms the cornerstone of investment decision-making.

4. Liquidity Challenges: Another dimension of risk arises from liquidity constraints. Investments that lack

liquidity, meaning they cannot be easily bought or sold without affecting the asset's price, pose challenges for investors. Illiquid assets may lead to difficulty in exiting positions quickly, amplifying the impact of market downturns.

5. Regulatory and Legal Risks: The regulatory environment plays a crucial role in shaping the risk profile of an investment. Assets operating in less regulated or unregulated markets often carry higher levels of risk due to the potential for fraudulent activities, lack of investor protection, and susceptibility to sudden regulatory changes.

6. Financial Leverage: The use of financial leverage, or borrowed capital, introduces an additional layer of risk. While leverage can amplify returns, it also magnifies losses, potentially leading to a rapid erosion of invested capital. Investments that rely heavily on leverage are inherently riskier due to their sensitivity to market fluctuations.

7. Market Sentiment and Speculative Nature: The perceived value of certain investments is often influenced by market sentiment and speculation. Investments driven by hype, rather than underlying fundamentals, are prone to sudden shifts in value, introducing an element of risk for investors who may find themselves caught in market frenzies.

Understanding the multifaceted nature of risk is paramount as we embark on this exploration of the financial world's riskiest bets. In the chapters that follow, we will apply this understanding to dissect various high-risk investments, from naked options to unconventional cryptocurrencies, unraveling the complexities that make these ventures both alluring and hazardous. Join us as we navigate the nuances of risk in the pursuit of financial enlightenment and resilience in the face of uncertainty.

Psychology of Risk-Taking in Investing

As we embark on the thrilling odyssey through the world of high-risk investments, it is essential to unravel the intricate interplay between the human psyche and the financial decisions that shape our financial destinies. In this chapter, we delve into the fascinating realm of the psychology of risk-taking in investing. Understanding the psychological drivers behind our financial choices is paramount, as it not only illuminates the motivations that lead us to embrace risk but also unveils the cognitive biases that can cloud our judgment on this precarious journey.

1. The Urge for Reward: At the heart of risk-taking lies the innate human desire for reward. The potential for substantial gains can trigger a rush of euphoria, enticing investors to venture into riskier territories in pursuit of financial triumph. This pursuit of reward, however, is not always tempered by a sober assessment of potential risks.

2. Fear of Missing Out (FOMO): The fear of missing out on lucrative opportunities is a powerful psychological force that often propels investors into high-risk ventures. The allure of quick profits and the fear of being left behind in a rapidly evolving market can override caution, leading to impulsive decisions that may have profound consequences.

3. Overconfidence Bias: A pervasive cognitive bias in the realm of investing is overconfidence. Investors, buoyed by past successes or the illusion of control, may overestimate their ability to navigate high-risk waters successfully. This unwarranted confidence can lead to excessive risk-taking and a disregard for potential downsides.

4. Loss Aversion: Human psychology is wired to be averse to losses. The fear of losing hard-earned capital can

paralyze decision-making or, conversely, prompt investors to take greater risks in an attempt to recover losses quickly. Understanding the dynamics of loss aversion is crucial in deciphering the motivations behind certain risk-taking behaviors.

5. Herding Behavior: Investors often exhibit a herd mentality, following the crowd into high-risk investments during periods of exuberance. The collective belief that others possess superior knowledge or insight can result in a wave of speculative behavior, creating bubbles that eventually burst, leaving many investors in financial turmoil.

6. Recency Bias: The tendency to give greater weight to recent events when making decisions, known as recency bias, can significantly impact risk-taking behavior. Recent market successes may lead to a false sense of security, while recent failures can instill a heightened fear of risk, both of which can distort rational decision-making.

7. Cognitive Dissonance: The discomfort arising from holding conflicting beliefs or making decisions misaligned with one's self-image is termed cognitive dissonance. Investors may engage in risk-taking behaviors to reconcile conflicting views or to maintain consistency with their perceived identity as astute risk-takers.

8. Regret Aversion: Fear of regret can influence risk-taking decisions, with investors opting for safer choices to avoid potential remorse. Conversely, the fear of regret over missed opportunities may drive individuals to take risks they might otherwise eschew.

Understanding these psychological drivers is not intended to undermine the capacity for rational decision-making but rather to highlight the nuanced factors that influence our perception of risk. In the chapters that follow, we will witness how these psychological intricacies manifest in specific high-risk investments, shaping the narratives of success and failure that define the financial landscape. Join us as we navigate the labyrinth of the human mind in the pursuit of a deeper comprehension of risk-taking in the captivating world of high-stakes finance.

Managing Risk While Seeking Returns

In the exhilarating universe of high-risk investments, the pursuit of returns is inseparable from the imperative to manage risk effectively. As we embark on this exploration of the financial world's most daring ventures, understanding how to navigate the precarious balance between risk and reward is paramount. In this chapter, we delve into the intricacies of managing risk while seeking returns, dissecting the strategies and principles that can guide investors through the tumultuous waters of high-stakes finance.

1. Diversification as a Shield: Diversification stands as a cornerstone of risk management. By spreading investments across a diverse array of assets, sectors, or geographical regions, investors can mitigate the impact of a poor-performing investment on their overall portfolio. This strategy acts as a shield, reducing the potential for catastrophic losses while allowing for exposure to different sources of potential returns.

2. Risk Tolerance Assessment: Understanding one's risk tolerance is a fundamental step in managing risk. Investors must evaluate their ability and willingness to endure fluctuations in the value of their investments. By aligning investment choices with individual risk tolerance, investors can avoid the emotional pitfalls that often accompany volatile markets.

3. Setting Clear Goals: Establishing clear investment goals is crucial in the pursuit of returns while managing risk. Whether seeking capital appreciation, income generation, or a combination of both, having well-defined objectives helps investors make informed decisions that align with their financial aspirations and risk appetite.

4. Active Monitoring and Rebalancing: High-risk investments require vigilant oversight. Regularly monitoring the performance of investments allows investors to identify emerging risks or opportunities. Rebalancing the portfolio in response to changing market conditions ensures that the allocation aligns with the intended risk-return profile.

5. Utilizing Risk Management Tools: Employing risk management tools, such as stop-loss orders and limit orders, can help investors automate protective measures. These tools establish predetermined exit points or price limits, safeguarding against excessive losses and providing a disciplined approach to risk mitigation.

6. Stress Testing Portfolios: Stress testing involves simulating various adverse scenarios to assess how a portfolio would fare under challenging conditions. By subjecting the portfolio to hypothetical stresses, investors can identify vulnerabilities and refine their risk management strategies accordingly.

7. Understanding the Time Horizon: The time horizon for investment goals profoundly influences risk management strategies. While high-risk ventures may offer the potential for substantial returns, investors with shorter time horizons may need to adopt more conservative risk management approaches to protect capital when nearing their financial objectives.

8. Stay Informed and Adaptive: The financial landscape is dynamic, with market conditions and risk factors evolving continuously. Staying informed about economic indicators, geopolitical events, and industry trends enables investors to adapt their strategies proactively. Being adaptive in the face of changing circumstances is integral to effective risk management.

9. Leverage with Caution: While leverage can amplify returns, it also magnifies risks. Managing leverage with caution is paramount in high-risk investments. Understanding the potential consequences of leverage and incorporating it judiciously into an investment strategy can enhance returns without exposing the portfolio to undue risk.

10. Contingency Planning: No risk management strategy is foolproof, and unforeseen events can still impact portfolios. Developing contingency plans and considering the potential consequences of worst-case scenarios can help investors react swiftly and decisively in times of crisis, minimizing potential losses.

As we navigate the chapters that follow, these principles of managing risk while seeking returns will serve as our guiding compass. From the wild terrain of naked options to the speculative realm of cryptocurrencies, each high-risk venture will be dissected through the lens of effective risk management. Join us as we unravel the strategies that empower investors to dance on the edge of financial possibility while maintaining a vigilant guard against the perils that lurk beneath.

Chapter 1: Naked or Uncovered Options
Understanding Naked Options

Welcome to the intricate world of naked options, a financial terrain where the stakes are high, and the risks are as naked as the name suggests. In this chapter, we unravel the complexities of naked options, exploring what makes them a daring venture in the realm of high-risk investments.

At its core, a naked or uncovered option refers to a financial derivative contract that gives the holder the right, but not the obligation, to buy (call option) or sell (put option) a specific underlying asset at a predetermined price (strike price) within a specified time frame (expiration date). What sets naked options apart from their covered counterparts is the absence of an offsetting position in the underlying asset.

In the context of call options, an investor sells a call option without holding the underlying asset, essentially betting that the asset's price will not rise above the strike price before the option expires. On the flip side, with put options, an investor sells a put option without holding the underlying asset, anticipating that the asset's price will not fall below the strike price before expiration.

The Allure of Naked Options

Naked options lure investors with the promise of substantial returns, often outstripping those achievable through conventional investments. The appeal lies in the ability to leverage market movements without the need to invest in the actual asset, allowing for potentially significant gains with a relatively small upfront investment.

This strategy is not for the faint of heart, as it involves a high level of speculation and exposes the investor to unlimited risk. Unlike covered options, where the risk is mitigated by the ownership of the underlying asset, naked options leave the investor naked to the whims of the market.

Unlimited Loss Potential

The defining characteristic of naked options is their unlimited loss potential. When an investor sells a naked call option, the losses can theoretically be infinite if the underlying asset's price surges significantly above the strike price. Similarly, with naked put options, the potential losses are limitless if the underlying asset's price experiences a sharp decline below the strike price.

To illustrate, consider an investor who sells a naked call option on a stock at a strike price of $50. If the stock's price skyrockets to $100, the investor must purchase the stock at the current market price to fulfill the call option contract, resulting in a substantial loss.

Margin Requirements and Leverage

Engaging in naked options requires investors to deposit a margin with their brokerage to cover potential losses. Margin requirements for naked options are often higher than those for covered options due to the elevated risk associated with unlimited loss potential.

The allure of naked options lies in the leverage they provide. With a relatively small upfront investment, investors can control a more significant position in the underlying asset. However, this leverage is a double-edged sword, magnifying both gains and losses.

Case Studies and Worst-Case Outcomes

To truly grasp the risks associated with naked options, we delve into case studies that highlight real-world scenarios where investors faced both remarkable gains and catastrophic losses. These stories serve as cautionary tales, emphasizing the importance of thorough risk assessment and strategic decision-making when venturing into the world of naked options.

Risk Management Strategies

Despite the inherent risks, investors can employ various risk management strategies to navigate the precarious landscape of naked options. From setting stop-loss orders to implementing position-sizing techniques, we explore the tools available to investors to mitigate potential losses and safeguard their portfolios.

In the chapters that follow, we will continue our exploration of high-risk investments, each with its own set of challenges and potential rewards. Join us as we navigate the thrilling world of financial ventures where the line between success and financial peril is drawn with the intricacy of naked options.

Unlimited Loss Potential

In the daring world of naked or uncovered options, the allure of potentially extraordinary gains comes hand in hand with an ominous shadow — the specter of unlimited loss potential. This characteristic sets naked options apart from their covered counterparts and establishes them as one of the riskiest ventures in the financial landscape.

Understanding Unlimited Loss Potential

The concept of unlimited loss potential with naked options stems from the absence of an offsetting position in the underlying asset. In a traditional covered option strategy, where an investor holds the actual asset, the risk is somewhat mitigated. However, in the case of naked options, investors expose themselves to the full force of market movements without holding the security in question.

Consider a naked call option scenario. When an investor sells a naked call, they are essentially making a bet that the underlying asset's price will not surpass the strike price before the option expires. If the market moves against this prediction and the asset's price rises significantly, the investor may be forced to purchase the asset at the elevated market price to fulfill the call option contract. Since there is no cap on how high an asset's price can climb, the potential losses for the investor become theoretically unlimited.

Similarly, with naked put options, an investor sells a put option without holding the underlying asset, anticipating that the asset's price will not fall below the strike price before expiration. If the market moves unfavorably, and the asset's price takes a nosedive, the investor may be obligated to buy the asset at a price significantly higher than its market value, incurring substantial losses.

Risks Amplified by Market Volatility

The risk of unlimited losses with naked options is particularly pronounced in volatile markets. Sudden and drastic price movements can lead to unexpected and extreme outcomes. Market volatility, rather than acting as a mere fluctuation, becomes a potent force that can magnify the magnitude of losses for investors engaged in naked options.

Investors entering the realm of naked options should be acutely aware that market conditions can change rapidly and unpredictably. Factors such as economic indicators, geopolitical events, and sudden shifts in investor sentiment can trigger sharp and unexpected movements, accentuating the peril of unlimited loss potential.

Real-Life Examples of Unlimited Losses

To truly comprehend the gravity of unlimited loss potential, examining real-life examples is instructive. Historical cases of investors facing catastrophic losses due to unfavorable market movements underscore the risks associated with naked options. These cautionary tales serve as powerful reminders of the need for thorough risk assessment and prudent decision-making when navigating the landscape of high-risk investments.

Risk Mitigation Strategies

While the specter of unlimited losses looms large with naked options, investors can adopt various risk mitigation strategies to protect themselves. Setting stop-loss orders, which automatically trigger the sale of an option when it reaches a predetermined price, is a common technique to limit potential losses.

Additionally, investors may choose to implement position-sizing techniques, allocating only a small portion of their overall portfolio to naked options. This approach, combined with a diversified portfolio, helps mitigate the impact of a substantial loss on the overall wealth of the investor.

The Role of Margin Requirements

Understanding the implications of margin requirements is essential when dealing with naked options. Brokers often require investors to deposit a margin to cover potential losses, with the amount determined by the perceived risk of the investment. Investors should be diligent in managing their margin, as inadequate coverage could lead to margin calls and further losses.

Educating Investors on the Risks

As we navigate the world of naked options, it is imperative to emphasize the importance of investor education. The risks associated with unlimited loss potential demand a thorough understanding of the market, option strategies, and risk management techniques. Investors must be equipped with the knowledge and tools necessary to navigate the complexities of naked options responsibly.

In the subsequent chapters, we will continue our exploration of high-risk financial ventures, each presenting its unique challenges and rewards. Join us as we dissect the intricacies of financial markets and shed light on the fascinating, yet perilous, world of uncovered options.

Margin Requirements and Leverage

In the intricate realm of naked or uncovered options, the concept of margin requirements and leverage plays a pivotal role in shaping the dynamics of these high-risk financial instruments. As we explore the risks and potential rewards of naked options, understanding the nuances of margin trading and leverage becomes essential for investors daring enough to venture into this captivating but perilous territory.

Introduction to Margin Trading

Margin trading is a practice that allows investors to borrow funds from a broker to trade larger positions than their account balances would otherwise permit. This borrowing is facilitated through a margin account, where the investor puts up a certain amount of capital, known as the margin, while the broker provides the remaining funds needed to execute the trade.

In the context of naked options, margin trading becomes a fundamental aspect due to the unlimited loss potential associated with these instruments. Brokers impose margin requirements to ensure that investors have sufficient funds to cover potential losses, given the elevated risks inherent in trading options without holding the underlying asset.

Margin Requirements for Naked Options

Margin requirements for naked options are typically higher than those for covered options or other less risky trading strategies. The rationale behind this higher margin is straightforward — it serves as a protective buffer for the broker against the potential unlimited losses that can arise from adverse market movements.

When an investor sells a naked call option, the broker may require a margin to cover the potential obligation of purchasing the underlying asset at the market price if the option is exercised. Similarly, selling a naked put option may necessitate a margin to cover the potential obligation of buying the underlying asset at the strike price if the option is exercised.

The specific margin requirements can vary based on factors such as the underlying asset, the strike price, the time to expiration, and market volatility. Brokers employ risk models to calculate these requirements, ensuring that investors have adequate funds to weather adverse market conditions.

Leverage in Naked Options Trading

Leverage, in the context of naked options, refers to the ability to control a more substantial position in the market with a relatively smaller amount of capital. It magnifies both potential gains and, notably, potential losses. The allure of leverage in naked options trading is the capacity to amplify returns without requiring the investor to invest the full value of the underlying asset.

Consider an investor who sells a naked call option on a stock with a strike price of $50. Instead of purchasing the stock outright, the investor may only need to deposit a fraction of the stock's value as margin. This allows the investor to control the potential gains and losses associated with the full value of the stock while putting up only a fraction of that amount.

While leverage can enhance the profitability of successful trades, it also exposes investors to greater risks. The concept of leverage, often expressed as a ratio (e.g., 2:1, 4:1), indicates how much larger the position is compared to the margin deposited. Higher leverage ratios increase the potential returns but also heighten the risk of significant losses.

Risk and Reward Dynamics

The intricate dance between margin requirements and leverage defines the risk and reward dynamics of naked options trading. Investors must tread carefully, balancing the allure of amplified returns with the sobering reality of potential unlimited losses. The judicious use of leverage requires a keen understanding of the market, risk tolerance, and a robust risk management strategy.

Potential Pitfalls of Leverage in Naked Options

While leverage can be a powerful tool, it comes with its share of potential pitfalls. Investors who miscalculate the market direction or fail to implement effective risk management strategies may find themselves in precarious situations. Margin calls, triggered when the account's equity falls below a certain threshold, can force investors to liquidate positions at unfavorable prices, amplifying losses.

Moreover, the compounding effect of leverage means that losses can accumulate rapidly. A small adverse price movement in the underlying asset can result in a proportionately larger loss for the investor. Understanding the potential pitfalls of leverage is crucial for investors to navigate the challenges of naked options trading successfully.

Risk Management Strategies in Leveraged Trading

Effectively managing risk in leveraged trading involves a combination of prudent decision-making, strategic planning, and ongoing monitoring. Investors engaging in naked options trading should consider implementing the following risk management strategies:

1. Setting Clear Stop-Loss Orders: Establishing predetermined exit points through stop-loss orders can help limit potential losses by automatically triggering a sell order when the option reaches a specified price.

2. Diversification and Position Sizing: Allocating only a portion of the portfolio to naked options and diversifying across different assets and strategies can help mitigate the impact of a significant loss on the overall portfolio.

3. Regularly Monitoring Market Conditions: Vigilant oversight of market conditions and timely adjustments to the trading strategy can help investors respond proactively to changing circumstances, reducing the risk of unexpected losses.

4. Understanding Margin Calls: Investors should be aware of the margin requirements imposed by brokers and understand the implications of margin calls. Adequate funding of the margin account is essential to avoid forced liquidation of positions.

5. Educating Investors on Leverage: Brokerages should provide comprehensive education on the risks and rewards of leverage to ensure that investors fully grasp the implications of using borrowed funds in their trading activities.

Conclusion: Striking a Balance

In the enthralling arena of naked options trading, the delicate balance between margin requirements and leverage is the fulcrum upon which risk and reward pivot. As investors navigate this perilous landscape, they must approach leverage with caution, recognizing its potential for both financial triumph and downfall. Striking the right balance between amplifying returns and safeguarding against unlimited losses is the key to mastering the art of naked options trading.

In the upcoming chapters, we will continue our exploration of high-risk financial ventures, each presenting its unique challenges and rewards. Join us as we unravel the complexities of financial markets and delve deeper into the captivating, yet perilous, world of uncovered options.

Case studies and worst-case outcomes

Embarking on the exploration of naked or uncovered options requires more than theoretical understanding; it demands a practical examination of real-world scenarios. In this chapter, we delve into case studies that exemplify both the potential rewards and, more critically, the worst-case outcomes associated with engaging in the high-risk game of naked options trading.

The Allure of Naked Options: A Brief Recap

Before delving into case studies, it's crucial to revisit the allure that draws investors to naked options. The potential for substantial gains, amplified by leverage and the absence of the need to own the underlying asset, can be tantalizing. However, as we'll see in the following case studies, this allure comes hand-in-hand with a level of risk that, if not carefully managed, can lead to catastrophic consequences.

Case Study 1: The Ascent and Descent of XYZ Corporation

In the early 2000s, an experienced investor named John ventured into the world of naked call options, targeting XYZ Corporation, a high-flying tech stock. With a strike price set at $100 and a bullish outlook, John sold naked call options, enticed by the allure of leveraging his position without having to invest in the actual stock.

Initially, XYZ Corporation's stock price surged, validating John's optimistic expectations. However, unforeseen market dynamics, including a sudden downturn in the tech sector and adverse geopolitical events, triggered a rapid decline in XYZ's stock price.

As the stock plummeted, John found himself facing the harsh reality of unlimited loss potential. With each downward tick in the stock price, his losses mounted exponentially. The absence of a cap on potential losses, combined with the leverage inherent in naked options, led to a financial catastrophe for John. Ultimately, he had to liquidate other assets to cover the losses, resulting in a significant setback to his overall portfolio.

Key Takeaways:

- Naked options, when paired with a bullish outlook, can initially seem promising.

- Adverse market conditions, unforeseen events, and sector-wide downturns can swiftly turn the tide.

- Unlimited loss potential can lead to catastrophic financial consequences for the investor.

Case Study 2: The Pitfalls of Overconfidence

In the mid-2010s, a trader named Sarah, well-versed in the art of technical analysis, engaged in selling naked put options on a volatile biotech stock. Convinced that her analysis could accurately predict the stock's price movements, she leveraged her positions to maximize potential returns.

The stock, however, proved to be more unpredictable than anticipated. Unexpected clinical trial results, regulatory setbacks, and industry-wide shifts led to a sharp decline in the biotech stock's value. Sarah, overconfident in her analytical abilities, had not adequately prepared for the possibility of a significant downturn.

As the stock continued its downward trajectory, the margin requirements escalated. Sarah faced a margin call, requiring her to deposit additional funds to cover potential losses. Strapped for liquidity and unable to meet the call, she faced forced liquidation of her positions at unfavorable prices, exacerbating her losses.

Key Takeaways:

- Overconfidence in analytical abilities can lead to underestimating the risks associated with naked options.

- Failure to adequately prepare for unexpected events and market volatility can result in severe financial setbacks.

- Margin calls, triggered by escalating losses, can force investors into unfavorable positions.

Case Study 3: The Cryptocurrency Rollercoaster

In the volatile world of cryptocurrency trading, a trader named Alex dabbled in selling naked call options on a popular digital asset. Cryptocurrencies, known for their price volatility, presented both opportunities and risks. Alex, enticed by the potential for rapid gains, sold naked calls with a strike price below the current market value.

The cryptocurrency market, notorious for its unpredictability, experienced a sudden surge driven by speculative trading, media hype, and regulatory developments. The price of the digital asset skyrocketed, surpassing the strike price of Alex's naked calls.

Facing significant losses and the potential obligation to sell the cryptocurrency at a price well below its market value, Alex was caught in a precarious situation. The lack of an upper limit on potential losses, coupled with the inherent volatility of cryptocurrencies, resulted in a substantial financial hit.

Key Takeaways:

- Cryptocurrencies, with their inherent volatility, can amplify the risks associated with naked options.

- Speculative trading and external factors can lead to unpredictable and rapid price movements.

- Lack of regulatory oversight in cryptocurrency markets adds an additional layer of risk.

Worst-Case Outcomes: Lessons Learned

These case studies vividly illustrate the worst-case outcomes associated with naked options trading. They underscore the importance of several critical lessons for investors:

1. Risk Mitigation is Essential: Unlimited loss potential demands rigorous risk mitigation strategies. Stop-loss orders, diversification, and an understanding of potential worst-case scenarios are paramount.

2. Market Unpredictability: The market is inherently unpredictable, and even the most sophisticated analyses may fail to anticipate unforeseen events. Investors must be prepared for unexpected downturns and adverse market conditions.

3. Leverage Requires Caution: While leverage can amplify gains, it also magnifies losses. Investors must approach leverage with caution, understanding its potential impact on their portfolios.

4. Continuous Monitoring: Regular monitoring of market conditions, combined with an adaptive approach to the trading strategy, is crucial. Investors should be vigilant and ready to adjust their positions in response to changing circumstances.

5. Educational Imperative: A deep understanding of the risks and dynamics of naked options trading is non-negotiable. Investors must continually educate themselves on market trends, risk management techniques, and the specific characteristics of the assets they trade.

In the subsequent chapters, we will continue our exploration of high-risk financial ventures, each presenting its unique challenges and rewards. Join us as we unravel the complexities of financial markets and delve deeper into the captivating, yet perilous, world of uncovered options..

Risk Management Strategies

In the exhilarating world of naked or uncovered options, where the potential for substantial gains coexists with the specter of unlimited losses, effective risk management strategies are paramount. Investors who dare to navigate this high-risk terrain must employ a sophisticated approach to mitigate potential downsides and safeguard their portfolios. In this chapter, we delve into a comprehensive exploration of risk management strategies tailored for the unique challenges posed by naked options.

1. Diversification and Position Sizing

Diversification, a timeless principle in risk management, remains a stalwart strategy for investors engaging in naked options trading. By spreading investments across a variety of assets and strategies, investors can mitigate the impact of a significant loss on the overall portfolio. This approach is particularly crucial in the context of naked options, where the potential for unlimited losses demands a judicious allocation of resources.

Position sizing, closely linked to diversification, involves determining the amount of capital to allocate to a specific trade or strategy. In the realm of naked options, careful consideration of position sizes ensures that no single trade disproportionately influences the portfolio's performance. By adopting diversified positions and managing position sizes effectively, investors create a buffer against potential catastrophic losses.

2. Setting Clear Stop-Loss Orders

One of the cornerstones of risk management in naked options trading is the implementation of clear stop-loss orders. A stop-loss order specifies a predetermined price at which an option position should be automatically liquidated to limit potential losses. This proactive approach allows investors to establish an exit strategy before emotions come into play during periods of market volatility.

Stop-loss orders act as a safety net, preventing investors from enduring unlimited losses in the event of adverse market movements. The strategic placement of stop-loss orders, coupled with disciplined execution, is instrumental in maintaining risk within predefined limits and avoiding the pitfalls associated with the unchecked progression of losses.

3. Regularly Monitoring Market Conditions

Vigilant monitoring of market conditions is a fundamental component of effective risk management in naked options trading. Market dynamics, economic indicators, and geopolitical events can change rapidly, impacting the risk profile of option positions. Investors must stay informed about relevant developments and be prepared to adjust their strategies in response to evolving market conditions.

Regular monitoring enables investors to identify potential risks and opportunities, facilitating timely adjustments to their positions. By staying attuned to market trends, investors can proactively manage risk, optimize returns, and navigate the complexities of naked options trading with a well-informed perspective.

4. Understanding Margin Requirements

In the realm of naked options, where margin trading is integral to the strategy, understanding and managing margin requirements is a critical aspect of risk management. Brokers impose margin requirements to ensure that investors have adequate funds to cover potential losses, given the heightened risks associated with these high-stakes financial instruments.

Investors should maintain a keen awareness of the margin requirements set by their brokers and ensure that their accounts are adequately funded. Inadequate margin coverage can lead to margin calls, triggering forced liquidation of positions at unfavorable prices and exacerbating losses. Prudent management of margin requirements is essential to avoid unwarranted disruptions to the trading strategy.

5. Utilizing Risk Analysis Tools

In the age of advanced financial technology, investors have access to an array of risk analysis tools that can enhance their decision-making processes. Options pricing models, volatility metrics, and scenario analysis tools empower investors to conduct comprehensive risk assessments before entering into naked options positions.

These tools assist investors in gauging potential outcomes under different market scenarios, quantifying risks, and optimizing their risk-return profiles. By leveraging technology-driven risk analysis, investors can make more informed and strategic decisions in the complex landscape of naked options trading.

6. Incorporating Advanced Options Strategies

Beyond the basic strategies, investors in the realm of naked options can explore advanced options strategies to further tailor their risk management approaches. These strategies may include the use of spreads, collars, and condors, among others, to create more nuanced positions that align with specific market expectations and risk tolerance.

For instance, a vertical spread involves simultaneously buying and selling options of the same type (either calls or puts) but with different strike prices. This strategy can limit both potential gains and losses, offering a more controlled risk-reward profile compared to outright naked options trading.

7. Continuous Education and Adaptation

In the ever-evolving landscape of financial markets, continuous education and adaptation are indispensable elements of effective risk management. Investors engaging in naked options trading must stay abreast of industry trends, regulatory changes, and advancements in financial technology that may impact their strategies.

Ongoing education equips investors with the knowledge needed to adapt their risk management strategies to changing circumstances. It fosters a proactive mindset, enabling investors to navigate the complexities of naked options trading with resilience and agility.

Conclusion: A Holistic Approach to Risk Management

As we conclude our exploration of risk management strategies in the context of naked or uncovered options, it becomes evident that success in this high-risk arena demands a holistic and multifaceted approach. Diversification, stop-loss orders, market monitoring, margin management, risk analysis tools, advanced options strategies, and continuous education collectively form a robust framework for navigating the challenges and opportunities inherent in naked options trading.

In the subsequent chapters, we will delve deeper into the specific characteristics, challenges, and potential rewards of various high-risk financial ventures. Join us as we continue our journey through the intricate and captivating world of uncovered options, where risk management becomes not just a strategy but a guiding philosophy for financial resilience and success.

Chapter 2: Digital or Binary Options Trading
How Binary Options Work

Welcome to the fascinating world of binary options trading, a financial arena that simplifies the complexities of traditional trading into a binary proposition: either a predetermined profit or a total loss. In this chapter, we unravel the mechanics of binary options, exploring how they work and why they have become a popular choice among traders seeking simplicity and speed in their financial ventures.

Understanding the Binary Options Concept

At its core, a binary option is a financial instrument that offers traders a fixed payout if the underlying asset's price meets a specific condition at the option's expiration. The binary nature of these options lies in the outcome: the trader either receives a predetermined profit, often a percentage of the initial investment, or faces a complete loss if the condition is not met.

Unlike traditional options, where the profit and loss potential can be unlimited, binary options simplify the decision-making process by distilling it into a yes-or-no proposition. Traders are not concerned with the magnitude of price movements; they only need to predict whether the asset's price will be above or below a predetermined level at the option's expiration.

Call and Put Options in Binary Trading

In the realm of binary options, the terms "call" and "put" are familiar but take on a simplified meaning. A trader purchasing a binary call option is expressing the belief that the underlying asset's price will be above the predetermined strike price at the option's expiration. Conversely, a trader opting for a binary put option anticipates that the asset's price will be below the strike price at expiration.

These binary options contracts typically have short expiration times, ranging from minutes to hours, enhancing the appeal for traders seeking rapid results. The time-sensitive nature of binary options introduces an element of urgency, with traders making predictions about short-term price movements rather than focusing on long-term market trends.

Strike Price and Expiry Time

Two critical components of a binary option are the strike price and the expiry time. The strike price represents the level at which the trader believes the underlying asset's price will be at or above (for a call option) or at or below (for a put option) at the option's expiration. The expiry time is the point at which the binary option contract concludes, determining whether the trader realizes a profit or incurs a loss.

Traders must carefully consider both the strike price and expiry time when entering into binary options contracts. The selection of these parameters involves a delicate balance, as the strike price needs to be realistic for the anticipated price movement within the chosen timeframe.

Binary Options Brokers and Platforms

To engage in binary options trading, traders typically use specialized online platforms provided by binary options brokers. These platforms serve as the interface for traders to select assets, set strike prices, choose expiry times, and execute trades. The accessibility and user-friendly interfaces of these platforms have contributed to the widespread popularity of binary options trading among both novice and experienced traders.

Binary options brokers offer a diverse range of assets for trading, including currencies, stocks, commodities, and indices.

Traders can select their preferred asset classes based on market knowledge, analysis, and personal preferences.

Binary Options Pricing and Payouts

The pricing of binary options is relatively straightforward, reflecting the binary nature of the outcomes. The price of a binary option, often referred to as the premium, represents the cost of the option contract. Traders pay this premium upfront, and it serves as their maximum risk. If the trader's prediction is correct at expiration, they receive a predetermined payout, which is typically a percentage of the premium paid.

Payout percentages vary among brokers and depend on factors such as the type of option, the asset class, and the specific broker's terms. Some binary options offer fixed payouts, while others may have variable payouts based on the degree to which the asset's price meets or exceeds the strike price.

Market Conditions and Binary Options Trading

The simplicity of binary options trading does not exempt it from the influences of market conditions. Traders must consider factors such as market volatility, economic events, and overall trends when making predictions. While binary options offer a streamlined approach, successful trading still requires a level of market analysis and strategic decision-making.

Market volatility, for instance, can impact the pricing of binary options and the likelihood of the asset's price reaching the specified level by the expiry time. Economic indicators and news events can introduce sudden price movements, creating both opportunities and risks for binary options traders.

Risk and Reward Dynamics

The risk and reward dynamics of binary options are unique compared to traditional trading instruments. With a predetermined payout and maximum loss known in advance, binary options provide traders with a clear understanding of their potential outcomes. This simplicity appeals to those who value defined risk and reward parameters, making binary options an attractive choice for those who prefer a more straightforward approach to trading.

However, the binary nature of the outcomes also means that a single incorrect prediction results in a complete loss of the premium paid. This characteristic underscores the importance of risk management and strategic decision-making in binary options trading.

Binary Options and Market Sentiment

The simplicity of binary options makes them conducive to capturing market sentiment and short-term trends. Traders often use binary options as a tool to express quick views on market movements based on news, events, or technical analysis. The binary nature aligns well with the rapid pace of markets, allowing traders to capitalize on short-term opportunities.

Understanding market sentiment becomes a valuable skill in binary options trading. Traders need to gauge the overall mood of the market, identify potential catalysts for price movements, and anticipate how other market participants are likely to react. This awareness enhances the ability to make informed predictions within the compressed timeframe of binary options contracts.

Conclusion: Navigating the Binary Landscape

As we conclude our exploration of how binary options work, it becomes clear that this form of trading offers a unique blend of simplicity and complexity. The binary proposition simplifies decision-making, making it accessible to a broad range of traders. Yet, beneath this simplicity lies a dynamic landscape where market analysis, strategic thinking, and risk management remain integral to success.

    In the subsequent chapters, we will delve deeper into the intricacies of binary options trading, exploring challenges, strategies, and real-world examples that illuminate the path for those venturing into this captivating financial arena. Join us as we continue our journey through the binary landscape, unraveling the layers that make this form of trading both alluring and nuanced.

Difficulty of Winning Consistently

In the dynamic realm of digital or binary options trading, the allure of simplicity is often counterbalanced by the inherent challenge of winning consistently. Traders are drawn to binary options for their straightforward, all-or-nothing nature, but beneath this simplicity lies a complex landscape where achieving sustained success demands a nuanced understanding of market dynamics, risk management, and strategic decision-making. In this chapter, we delve into the factors that contribute to the difficulty of winning consistently in binary options trading.

Market Randomness and Binary Options

One of the primary challenges faced by binary options traders is the inherent randomness of financial markets. While technical and fundamental analyses provide valuable tools for assessing market conditions, the unpredictable nature of price movements introduces an element of uncertainty that complicates the task of consistently predicting short-term outcomes.

In a market characterized by randomness, even well-informed and well-researched predictions can be subject to unexpected events and sudden shifts in sentiment. Traders navigating binary options must grapple with the reality that, despite their best efforts, market movements can defy conventional expectations, making consistent wins a challenging endeavor.

Short-Term Nature of Binary Options Contracts

Binary options are characterized by their short-term nature, with contracts often expiring in minutes or hours. While this temporal aspect can be advantageous for capturing quick market movements, it also amplifies the difficulty of consistently predicting short-term price fluctuations.

Market dynamics over short timeframes are influenced by a myriad of factors, including news releases, economic indicators, and technical patterns. Traders must contend with the accelerated pace of market reactions, where seemingly minor events can lead to significant price shifts. Successfully navigating this fast-paced environment requires not only accurate analysis but also the ability to make rapid decisions.

Influence of Market Volatility

Volatility is both a friend and a foe in binary options trading. While heightened volatility can create opportunities for substantial gains, it also introduces increased uncertainty and risk. The difficulty arises in accurately gauging the extent and direction of price movements within the short timeframe of a binary options contract.

Traders need to adapt their strategies to different volatility scenarios, understanding that periods of low volatility may offer limited trading opportunities, while excessive volatility can lead to unpredictable market swings. Effectively navigating the impact of market volatility on binary options requires a keen awareness of current market conditions and a flexible approach to strategy.

Limited Risk-Reward Ratio

The binary nature of options—where the outcome is either a fixed profit or a total loss—creates a unique risk-reward dynamic. While this simplicity can be appealing, it also imposes constraints on the potential profits relative to the potential losses. Traders often find themselves in situations where a series of successful trades can be erased by a single incorrect prediction.

The limited risk-reward ratio requires traders to achieve a high percentage of correct predictions to offset potential losses. This places a premium on accuracy and adds to the difficulty of sustaining profitability over the long term. Traders must carefully manage their risk exposure and resist the temptation to overleverage in pursuit of larger profits.

Broker Dynamics and Challenges

The choice of a binary options broker can significantly impact a trader's ability to win consistently. Some brokers may employ practices that tilt the odds in their favor, such as unfair pricing models, delays in trade execution, or restrictions on withdrawals. Traders must navigate the landscape of binary options brokers carefully, selecting reputable platforms with transparent practices.

Broker dynamics also include issues related to slippage, which can impact the actual execution price compared to the expected price. Traders need to be cognizant of these factors and consider the broker's reputation and regulatory compliance when choosing a platform.

Market Manipulation Risks

The relatively unregulated nature of binary options markets exposes traders to the risk of market manipulation. Some unscrupulous actors may engage in practices such as price manipulation, false advertising, or fraudulent schemes that can impact the integrity of the trading environment. Traders must remain vigilant and choose brokers with a commitment to fair and transparent practices.

Psychological Challenges

The psychological aspect of trading plays a significant role in the difficulty of winning consistently in binary options. The pressure to make rapid decisions, the emotional impact of losses, and the psychological toll of consecutive wins or losses can affect a trader's decision-making process.

Maintaining discipline, emotional resilience, and a rational mindset is essential for consistent success. Traders need to cultivate effective coping mechanisms for dealing with stress, anxiety, and the natural inclination to chase losses or become overly confident after wins.

Lack of Comprehensive Education

The learning curve in binary options trading can be steep, and the lack of comprehensive education exacerbates the difficulty of winning consistently. Novice traders may enter the market without a thorough understanding of market analysis, risk management, and strategy development.

Educational resources that cover the nuances of binary options trading are crucial for traders to build a strong foundation. Unfortunately, the availability and quality of educational materials can vary, making it challenging for traders to acquire the knowledge needed to navigate the complexities of binary options effectively.

Market Sentiment and Binary Options

While market sentiment can provide valuable insights for traders, interpreting and gauging sentiment accurately is a nuanced task. The difficulty lies in discerning whether market sentiment is indicative of a genuine trend or is influenced by temporary factors. Traders must navigate the complexities of sentiment analysis to make informed predictions about short-term price movements.

Overcoming the Challenges: Strategies for Consistent Wins

While the challenges of winning consistently in binary options trading are formidable, they are not insurmountable.

Traders can adopt strategies and approaches to enhance their chances of success:

1. Thorough Market Analysis: A robust analysis of market conditions, incorporating both technical and fundamental analysis, provides a solid foundation for decision-making.

2. Effective Risk Management: Prudent risk management strategies, including position sizing, setting stop-loss orders, and diversification, are essential for protecting capital and mitigating losses.

3. Continuous Learning: Commitment to ongoing education and staying abreast of market trends helps traders adapt to changing conditions and refine their strategies.

4. Discipline and Emotional Control: Cultivating discipline and emotional control is crucial for making rational decisions and avoiding impulsive actions driven by fear or greed.

5. Selecting Reputable Brokers: Choosing reputable brokers with transparent practices and a commitment to fair trading environments reduces the risk of broker-related challenges.

6. Adaptability: The ability to adapt strategies to different market conditions and volatility scenarios is key to navigating the ever-changing landscape of binary options trading.

7. Building a Supportive Community: Engaging with a community of traders, sharing experiences, and learning from others can provide valuable insights and emotional support.

In conclusion, the difficulty of winning consistently in binary options trading stems from a combination of market dynamics, risk factors, and psychological challenges. Traders who approach the market with a well-informed and disciplined mindset, coupled with effective risk management strategies, increase their likelihood of navigating the challenges and achieving sustained success in the world of binary options.

Watch Out for Scams

As traders navigate the enticing landscape of digital or binary options trading, they encounter not only legitimate opportunities but also the lurking presence of scams. The promise of quick profits and the simplicity of binary options attract not only earnest participants but also unscrupulous entities seeking to exploit the unwary. In this chapter, we delve into the various scams that traders should be vigilant about, exploring the tactics employed by fraudsters and providing guidance on how to protect oneself in the binary options market.

1. Unregulated Brokers and Phantom Platforms

One of the most common scams in the binary options arena involves unregulated brokers and phantom trading platforms. These entities operate outside the purview of regulatory authorities, allowing them to engage in fraudulent practices without oversight. Traders must exercise caution and thoroughly research the background of any broker or platform before depositing funds.

Characteristics of Unregulated Brokers:
- Lack of regulatory oversight.
- Absence of transparent business practices.
- Unclear ownership and operational details.

Red Flags for Phantom Platforms:
- Limited or no information about the company's history.
- Unrealistic promises of guaranteed profits.
- Lack of customer support or responsiveness.

Protective Measures:
- Verify the regulatory status of the broker through official regulatory websites.

- Conduct thorough research on the broker's reputation and user reviews.

- Avoid platforms that make promises that seem too good to be true.

2. Manipulative Marketing Tactics

Scammers often employ manipulative marketing tactics to lure unsuspecting traders into their schemes. These tactics may involve aggressive sales pitches, false advertising, and misleading information designed to create a sense of urgency and pressure individuals into making hasty decisions.

Common Manipulative Tactics:

- High-pressure sales calls urging immediate deposits.

- False claims of exclusive access to profitable trading strategies.

- Misleading advertising showcasing fabricated success stories.

Protective Measures:

- Exercise skepticism and be wary of high-pressure tactics.

- Verify the legitimacy of claims through independent sources.

- Take time to research and make informed decisions without succumbing to urgency.

3. Account and Fund Manipulation

Fraudulent brokers may engage in account and fund manipulation to deceive traders and siphon funds. This can include unauthorized trades, false reporting of account balances, and refusal to process withdrawals. Traders must remain vigilant about the activities within their accounts and be alert to any signs of irregularities.

Indicators of Account and Fund Manipulation:

- Unexpected and unauthorized trades in the account.
- Inconsistent reporting of account balances.
- Delays or refusals in processing withdrawal requests.

Protective Measures:
- Regularly monitor account activity and statements.
- Report any suspicious transactions or discrepancies to the broker.
- Choose brokers with transparent withdrawal policies and a track record of prompt processing.

4. Signal Service Scams

Signal services claim to provide traders with accurate and profitable trading signals, assisting them in making successful trades. However, some signal services turn out to be scams, providing false or manipulated signals with the intention of inducing traders to make losing trades.

Signs of Signal Service Scams:
- Inconsistent performance and unrealistic success rates.
- Lack of transparency regarding the methodology behind signals.
- Pressure to use a specific broker affiliated with the signal service.

Protective Measures:
- Verify the track record and reputation of the signal service.
- Avoid signal services that make lofty promises without verifiable proof.
- Use signals as a supplementary tool and not the sole basis for trading decisions.

5. Identity Theft and Phishing Attacks

Scammers may resort to identity theft and phishing attacks to gain unauthorized access to personal and financial information. Phishing websites and emails mimic legitimate platforms, tricking traders into providing sensitive details such as usernames, passwords, and credit card information.

Indicators of Identity Theft and Phishing:

- Unsolicited emails requesting personal information.
- Fake websites with URLs similar to legitimate trading platforms.
- Unusual account activity or unauthorized access.

Protective Measures:

- Verify the legitimacy of emails and websites before providing any information.
- Use secure and unique passwords for trading accounts.
- Enable two-factor authentication when available.

6. Fake Investment Schemes and Binary Robots

Fraudulent investment schemes and binary options robots promise automated trading and guaranteed profits without requiring active involvement from traders. These schemes often turn out to be scams, with the intent of collecting deposits or extracting fees without delivering the promised returns.

Characteristics of Fake Investment Schemes:

- Guaranteed profits with minimal or no risk.
- Lack of transparency regarding trading strategies.
- Pressure to deposit funds quickly to access the purported benefits.

Protective Measures:

- Research and verify the legitimacy of any investment scheme.
- Exercise caution with automated trading systems and perform due diligence.

- Avoid schemes that promise unrealistic returns or operate in a secretive manner.

7. Ponzi and Pyramid Schemes

In the realm of binary options, Ponzi and pyramid schemes can manifest in various forms, promising consistent returns through recruitment or investment in purportedly lucrative ventures. These schemes rely on a constant influx of new funds to pay returns to existing participants, ultimately leading to the collapse of the scheme.

Indicators of Ponzi and Pyramid Schemes:

- Emphasis on recruitment rather than actual trading activity.

- Lack of verifiable sources of revenue other than participant contributions.

- Unsustainable and exponential promises of returns.

Protective Measures:

- Be skeptical of schemes that prioritize recruitment over legitimate trading.

- Demand transparency regarding the source of returns and business operations.

- Avoid ventures that rely solely on new investments to sustain returns.

Conclusion: Vigilance and Due Diligence

As traders embark on the journey of digital or binary options trading, the risk of encountering scams underscores the importance of vigilance and due diligence. The binary options market, while offering legitimate opportunities for profit, also attracts nefarious actors seeking to exploit unsuspecting individuals. By staying informed, conducting thorough research, and remaining skeptical of unrealistic promises, traders can safeguard themselves against scams and create a more secure and informed trading environment. In the chapters that follow, we will delve deeper into the nuances of binary options trading, exploring strategies, risk management techniques, and real-world examples that empower traders to navigate this complex landscape with resilience and wisdom.

Technical Analysis Limitations

In the dynamic world of digital or binary options trading, technical analysis stands as a cornerstone for many traders, providing a systematic approach to interpreting market movements and making informed decisions. However, it is essential to recognize that, like any analytical method, technical analysis has its limitations. In this chapter, we explore the constraints and challenges associated with technical analysis, offering insights into the nuanced landscape of binary options trading.

1. Historical Price Data and Assumptions

Challenge: Limited Predictive Power

One of the fundamental premises of technical analysis is the use of historical price data to identify patterns and trends that can inform future price movements. However, this reliance on historical data assumes that past price patterns will repeat themselves in the future. In reality, markets are influenced by an ever-changing combination of factors, making it challenging to predict future outcomes solely based on historical patterns.

Navigating the Challenge:

- Supplement technical analysis with other forms of analysis, such as fundamental analysis, to gain a comprehensive view of market conditions.

- Recognize that historical patterns are probabilistic rather than deterministic, and exercise caution when relying solely on past data for predictions.

2. Market Dynamics and Human Behavior

Challenge: Market Dynamics Evolve

Markets are dynamic and subject to constant changes influenced by a myriad of factors, including economic indicators, geopolitical events, and shifts in investor sentiment.

Technical analysis assumes that historical price patterns reflect the collective actions and emotions of market participants. However, as market dynamics evolve, the effectiveness of certain technical indicators may diminish.

Navigating the Challenge:

- Stay informed about current market conditions and be flexible in adapting technical strategies to changing dynamics.

- Consider combining technical analysis with real-time information to enhance decision-making.

3. Lack of Causation

Challenge: Correlation Does Not Imply Causation

Technical analysis often identifies correlations between certain price patterns and subsequent market movements. However, it is crucial to understand that correlation does not imply causation. Just because a specific pattern historically precedes a certain price movement does not mean that the pattern caused the movement. Correlations identified through technical analysis should be interpreted cautiously to avoid drawing unwarranted conclusions.

Navigating the Challenge:

- Use technical analysis as a tool for probability assessment rather than a definitive predictor of future movements.

- Consider external factors and events that may influence market dynamics, acknowledging the complexity of causation in financial markets.

4. Overreliance on Indicators

Challenge: Indicator Redundancy and Signal Overload

Technical analysis relies on various indicators, each offering unique insights into market conditions. However, an overreliance on multiple indicators can lead to redundancy and signal overload. Traders may face conflicting signals from different indicators, creating confusion and hindering effective decision-making.

Navigating the Challenge:

- Prioritize key indicators that align with your trading strategy and provide meaningful insights.
- Regularly reassess the relevance and effectiveness of chosen indicators, adjusting your approach as needed.

5. Market Noise and False Signals

Challenge: Distortion from Market Noise

Financial markets are prone to periods of volatility and unpredictability, resulting in market noise—random price fluctuations that can distort the effectiveness of technical analysis. False signals may emerge during such noisy periods, leading traders to make misguided decisions based on temporary and erratic market movements.

Navigating the Challenge:

- Implement filters or additional criteria to confirm signals and reduce susceptibility to false indications.
- Exercise caution during periods of heightened market noise, considering a more conservative approach to trading.

6. Lack of Future Predictive Value

Challenge: Limited Ability to Predict Future Events

While technical analysis excels at assessing historical price movements and identifying trends, it has inherent limitations in predicting future events that can impact markets. Economic releases, geopolitical developments, and unexpected news events often introduce unpredictability, challenging the ability of technical analysis to anticipate and adapt to rapidly changing circumstances.

Navigating the Challenge:

- Combine technical analysis with fundamental analysis to incorporate a broader range of market-influencing factors.

- Stay informed about upcoming economic events and major news releases that may impact the markets.

7. Market Efficiency and Pattern Exploitation

Challenge: Efficient Markets and Pattern Exploitation

Efficient market theory suggests that prices already reflect all available information, making it challenging to consistently exploit patterns or anomalies. As technical analysis gains popularity, the effectiveness of certain patterns may diminish as more market participants attempt to capitalize on them, leading to self-fulfilling prophecies that erode their predictive power.

Navigating the Challenge:

- Be aware of the limitations posed by market efficiency and recognize that not all patterns will persist over time.

- Consider combining technical analysis with other forms of analysis to enhance the robustness of your trading strategy.

8. Timeframe Sensitivity

Challenge: Sensitivity to Timeframes

The effectiveness of technical analysis is often influenced by the chosen timeframe for analysis. Different timeframes can yield contrasting signals and patterns, leading to ambiguity in decision-making. Traders must carefully select appropriate timeframes based on their trading goals and preferences.

Navigating the Challenge:

- Align the chosen timeframe with the trading strategy and objectives.

- Consider multiple timeframes to gain a holistic view of market conditions and confirm signals.

9. Lack of Universal Standards

Challenge: Subjectivity and Interpretation Variances

Technical analysis relies on chart patterns, trendlines, and indicators, which can be subject to interpretation. Lack of universal standards for interpreting these elements introduces subjectivity, and different traders may draw different conclusions from the same chart. This variability in interpretation can lead to diverse trading decisions based on individual perspectives.

Navigating the Challenge:

- Develop a clear and consistent set of rules for interpreting chart patterns and indicators.

- Seek validation from multiple indicators or analytical methods to confirm signals and reduce subjectivity.

Conclusion: Holistic Decision-Making

As traders engage with technical analysis in the context of digital or binary options trading, an understanding of its limitations is crucial for informed decision-making. Recognizing that technical analysis is a valuable tool within a broader framework of analysis empowers traders to navigate its challenges effectively. By combining technical analysis with other analytical methods, staying adaptable to changing market dynamics, and acknowledging the inherent uncertainties in financial markets, traders can create a more resilient and nuanced approach to binary options trading. In the subsequent chapters, we will further explore strategies, risk management techniques, and real-world examples that integrate technical analysis into a comprehensive and effective trading toolkit.

Alternatives with Lower Risk

While digital or binary options trading can offer exciting opportunities, it's essential for traders to be aware of alternatives that provide lower risk exposure. This chapter explores various investment avenues and trading strategies that, compared to binary options, come with a more conservative risk profile. Understanding these alternatives equips traders with the knowledge to diversify their portfolios and manage risk effectively.

1. Traditional Stock and Bond Investments

Lower Risk: Stability and Long-Term Growth

Traditional stock and bond investments remain foundational components of a conservative portfolio. Investing in well-established, financially stable companies and government or high-quality corporate bonds provides a balance of potential capital appreciation and income through dividends or interest payments.

Advantages:

- Historical stability and long-term growth.
- Dividend income from stocks.
- Interest income from bonds.

Considerations:

- Diversify across different sectors and industries.
- Assess the creditworthiness of bond issuers.

2. Exchange-Traded Funds (ETFs)

Lower Risk: Diversification and Market Exposure

ETFs offer a diversified approach to investing by tracking a specific index or asset class. These funds provide exposure to a broad range of stocks, bonds, or commodities, reducing the impact of individual asset volatility on the overall portfolio. ETFs can be an effective way to achieve market exposure with lower risk compared to individual stock picking.

Advantages:

- Diversification across multiple assets.
- Lower expense ratios compared to some mutual funds.
- Traded on stock exchanges for easy buying and selling.

Considerations:

- Choose ETFs that align with investment goals and risk tolerance.
- Monitor expense ratios and liquidity.

3. Mutual Funds

Lower Risk: Professional Management and Diversification

Mutual funds pool money from multiple investors to invest in a diversified portfolio of stocks, bonds, or other securities. Professional fund managers make investment decisions, offering investors access to expert management and a level of diversification that can mitigate risk.

Advantages:

- Professional management.
- Diversification across various assets.
- Access to various investment strategies and sectors.

Considerations:

- Evaluate the track record and expertise of fund managers.
- Be aware of fees and expenses.

4. Dividend Stocks

Lower Risk: Income Generation and Stability

Investing in dividend-paying stocks can provide a steady stream of income, making them an attractive option for conservative investors. Companies with a history of paying dividends often demonstrate financial stability and the ability to generate consistent profits, offering a level of security.

Advantages:
- Regular income through dividends.
- Potential for capital appreciation.
- Historically stable performance.

Considerations:
- Research companies with a strong dividend track record.
- Diversify across different sectors.

5. Real Estate Investment Trusts (REITs)

Lower Risk: Income and Asset Diversification

REITs allow investors to participate in real estate ownership without directly owning physical properties. These trusts own and manage income-generating real estate, such as commercial properties, residential developments, or infrastructure projects. REITs often provide a combination of dividend income and potential capital appreciation.

Advantages:
- Income from rental payments or property sales.
- Diversification into the real estate market.
- Professional management of real estate assets.

Considerations:
- Assess the types of properties in the REIT portfolio.
- Understand the tax implications of REIT investments.

6. Certificates of Deposit (CDs) and Treasury Securities

Lower Risk: Capital Preservation and Fixed Returns

For investors prioritizing capital preservation and fixed returns, certificates of deposit (CDs) and Treasury securities are low-risk options. CDs offer a fixed interest rate over a specified term, and Treasury securities, such as Treasury bills, notes, and bonds, are backed by the U.S. government, providing a high level of security.

Advantages:

- Capital preservation.
- Fixed returns with CDs.
- Backing by the U.S. government for Treasury securities.

Considerations:

- Evaluate interest rates and terms for CDs.
- Understand the different maturities of Treasury securities.

7. Conservative Option Strategies

Lower Risk: Hedging and Limited Loss Potential

For traders who wish to remain within the realm of options trading but with lower risk, conservative option strategies can be employed. Covered calls, protective puts, and cash-secured puts are examples of strategies that provide a level of downside protection and reduce risk compared to more aggressive options trading.

Advantages:

- Limited loss potential.
- Income generation through premiums.
- Hedging against potential market downturns.

Considerations:

- Understand the mechanics and risks of each option strategy.
- Align strategies with risk tolerance and market outlook.

8. Dollar-Cost Averaging

Lower Risk: Systematic Investing and Risk Mitigation

Dollar-cost averaging involves consistently investing a fixed amount of money at regular intervals, regardless of market conditions. This strategy reduces the impact of market volatility on investment decisions, as investors buy more shares when prices are low and fewer shares when prices are high.

Advantages:

- Systematic and disciplined approach to investing.
- Mitigates the impact of market fluctuations.
- Reduces the risk of making poorly-timed investment decisions.

Considerations:

- Requires a long-term investment horizon.
- Regularly reassess the investment plan based on financial goals.

9. High-Quality Corporate Bonds

Lower Risk: Income and Capital Preservation

Investing in high-quality corporate bonds provides a reliable income stream through regular interest payments and the return of principal at maturity. Bonds issued by financially stable corporations with strong credit ratings offer a balance of income generation and capital preservation.

Advantages:

- Regular interest payments.
- Preservation of capital at maturity.
- Lower default risk with high-quality corporate bonds.

Considerations:

- Assess the creditworthiness of bond issuers.
- Diversify across different industries.

10. Dollar-Backed Stablecoins in Cryptocurrency

Lower Risk: Stability and Reduced Volatility

For those interested in cryptocurrency exposure with lower risk, dollar-backed stablecoins are pegged to the value of a fiat currency, such as the U.S. dollar. This pegging provides a level of stability, making stablecoins a less volatile option compared to other cryptocurrencies.

Advantages:

- Stability and predictability of value.

- Facilitates quick and low-cost transfers within the cryptocurrency space.

- Reduced exposure to the extreme volatility of other cryptocurrencies.

Considerations:

- Choose reputable stablecoin issuers with transparent backing.

- Understand the mechanisms for maintaining price stability.

Conclusion: Building a Diversified and Resilient Portfolio

While digital or binary options trading may appeal to those seeking high-risk, high-reward opportunities, incorporating lower-risk alternatives into an investment portfolio is crucial for long-term financial health. Diversification across different asset classes, risk profiles, and investment strategies helps manage risk and enhances overall portfolio resilience. By understanding and exploring the range of lower-risk alternatives outlined in this chapter, traders and investors can tailor their approach to align with individual risk tolerance, financial goals, and market outlook. In the subsequent chapters, we will delve deeper into specific investment strategies, risk management techniques, and real-world examples that integrate these alternatives into a comprehensive and well-balanced trading toolkit.

Chapter 3: FOREX Rollover Arbitrage
Understanding Rollover Arbitrage in Forex Trading

In the vast and dynamic landscape of foreign exchange (Forex) trading, various strategies aim to capitalize on market inefficiencies and fluctuations. One such strategy that has gained attention among traders is rollover arbitrage. This chapter explores the intricacies of rollover arbitrage, shedding light on its fundamental concepts, mechanics, and considerations for those navigating the Forex market.

Defining Rollover Arbitrage: A Primer

At its core, rollover arbitrage is a trading strategy that takes advantage of the interest rate differentials between two currencies in a Forex pair. Also known as carry trading, this approach involves profiting from the variance in interest rates by borrowing in a currency with a lower interest rate and investing in a currency with a higher interest rate.

1. The Rollover or Swap in Forex

Before delving into the mechanics of rollover arbitrage, it's essential to understand the concept of rollover or swap in Forex trading. Rollover refers to the interest paid or earned for holding a currency position overnight. In the Forex market, most trades are settled on a spot basis, meaning the transaction is completed "on the spot" or immediately. However, positions held overnight incur an interest rate differential, and this is where rollover comes into play.

2. Interest Rate Differentials

Interest rate differentials form the foundation of rollover arbitrage. Central banks set interest rates to manage monetary policy and control inflation. When a trader engages in rollover arbitrage, they are essentially exploiting the gap between the interest rates of two currencies. The goal is to borrow in the currency with the lower interest rate and lend in the currency with the higher interest rate, profiting from the interest rate spread.

3. Long and Short Positions in Rollover Arbitrage

In rollover arbitrage, traders can take both long and short positions. A long position involves buying a currency with a higher interest rate and selling a currency with a lower interest rate. Conversely, a short position entails selling a currency with a lower interest rate and buying a currency with a higher interest rate. The choice between long and short positions depends on the trader's analysis of interest rate differentials and market conditions.

4. Understanding Currency Pairs for Rollover Arbitrage

Successful execution of rollover arbitrage requires a thorough understanding of currency pairs and their associated interest rates. Traders typically focus on currency pairs where one currency has a significantly higher interest rate than the other. For example, the Australian Dollar (AUD) has historically had higher interest rates than the Japanese Yen (JPY), making the AUD/JPY pair attractive for carry traders.

5. Risks and Challenges in Rollover Arbitrage

While rollover arbitrage presents an opportunity for profit, it is not without its risks and challenges. One of the primary risks is currency exchange rate fluctuations. Even if a trader earns interest differentials, adverse movements in exchange rates can offset those gains. Additionally, geopolitical events, economic data releases, and unexpected central bank actions can introduce volatility, impacting the effectiveness of the strategy.

6. Factors Affecting Rollover Rates

Several factors influence rollover rates in Forex trading. Central bank interest rate decisions play a crucial role, as changes in rates directly affect the interest rate differentials between currencies. Economic indicators, inflation rates, and global economic conditions also contribute to the overall interest rate environment. Traders need to stay informed about these factors to anticipate changes in rollover rates and adjust their positions accordingly.

7. Broker Policies and Rollover Costs

The specific mechanics of rollover arbitrage are influenced by the policies of Forex brokers. Brokers may apply different rollover rates, fees, or commissions, affecting the overall profitability of the strategy. Traders should carefully review the rollover policies of their chosen broker and consider these costs when planning and executing rollover arbitrage trades.

8. Real-World Examples of Rollover Arbitrage

To illustrate the application of rollover arbitrage, examining real-world examples can provide valuable insights. Historical instances where interest rate differentials were exploited successfully, as well as cases where unforeseen market events impacted the strategy, offer practical lessons for aspiring carry traders.

9. Risk Management Strategies for Rollover Arbitrage

Given the inherent risks in rollover arbitrage, effective risk management is paramount. Traders should implement risk mitigation strategies, such as setting stop-loss orders, diversifying positions, and closely monitoring market conditions. Understanding the potential downsides and having a clear risk management plan can help protect traders from significant losses.

10. Regulatory Considerations and Compliance

As with any trading strategy, compliance with regulatory standards is crucial in rollover arbitrage. Traders should be aware of regulatory requirements related to interest rate trading, margin requirements, and any restrictions imposed by financial authorities. Adhering to regulatory guidelines ensures the legality and ethicality of the trading approach.

Conclusion: Navigating the Rollover Arbitrage Landscape

Rollover arbitrage stands as a nuanced and potentially lucrative strategy in the realm of Forex trading. By leveraging interest rate differentials between currencies, traders aim to generate profits from positions held overnight. However, the complexity of global financial markets and the inherent risks in currency trading necessitate a comprehensive understanding of the strategy, meticulous analysis of market conditions, and disciplined risk management. As we proceed through this chapter and the subsequent sections, we will delve deeper into the practical aspects of rollover arbitrage, offering insights, strategies, and considerations to empower traders on their journey through the dynamic world of Forex markets.

Risks of Unexpected Interest Rate Changes

In the intricate world of Forex rollover arbitrage, where traders seek to capitalize on interest rate differentials between currencies, the landscape is not without its perils. One of the significant risks that carry traders face is the specter of unexpected interest rate changes. This section delves into the multifaceted nature of these risks, exploring the potential impact on positions, strategies, and the overall viability of rollover arbitrage in the face of unforeseen shifts in interest rates.

Understanding the Dynamics of Interest Rate Changes

Interest rates serve as the heartbeat of Forex markets, influencing the cost of borrowing and lending currencies. Central banks, as stewards of monetary policy, make decisions to adjust interest rates based on economic conditions, inflation targets, and overall financial stability. For carry traders engaged in rollover arbitrage, these interest rate changes are pivotal, as they directly affect the profitability and risk profile of positions.

1. Adverse Movements in Currency Pairs

One of the immediate consequences of unexpected interest rate changes is the potential for adverse movements in currency pairs. When a central bank decides to raise or lower interest rates unexpectedly, it can trigger substantial volatility in the Forex market. Currency pairs involved in rollover arbitrage are particularly susceptible to sharp price fluctuations, leading to losses if not carefully managed.

Mitigation Strategies:

- Implementing stop-loss orders to limit potential losses.
- Diversifying positions across different currency pairs to spread risk.

- Staying informed about central bank communications and economic indicators.

2. Impact on Interest Rate Differentials

The essence of rollover arbitrage lies in interest rate differentials—the variance in interest rates between the two currencies in a pair. Unexpected changes in interest rates can disrupt these differentials, diminishing the appeal of certain currency pairs for carry traders. A sudden reduction in interest rate differentials may erode expected profits and challenge the viability of existing positions.

Mitigation Strategies:

- Regularly monitoring central bank statements and economic data for signals of potential rate changes.
- Dynamically adjusting positions based on evolving interest rate differentials.
- Diversifying across a range of currency pairs with stable interest rate environments.

3. Unpredictability of Central Bank Actions

Central banks operate with a dual mandate—to foster economic growth and maintain price stability. However, the timing and extent of interest rate changes can be challenging to predict accurately. Central banks may respond to unforeseen economic developments, geopolitical events, or global financial shifts, introducing an element of unpredictability that can catch carry traders off guard.

Mitigation Strategies:

- Staying abreast of economic indicators and global events that may influence central bank decisions.
- Diversifying across currencies with a mix of monetary policy stances.

- Using option strategies to hedge against sudden market moves.

4. Liquidity and Execution Risks

Unexpected interest rate changes can lead to heightened volatility, impacting liquidity in the Forex market. Thin liquidity can result in slippage and challenges in executing trades at desired prices. Carry traders relying on precise execution to optimize profits and manage risks may find their strategies compromised during periods of market turbulence.

Mitigation Strategies:

- Adjusting position sizes to account for potential slippage.
- Utilizing limit orders to specify entry and exit points.
- Being cautious during periods of economic data releases or central bank announcements.

5. Economic and Political Uncertainty

Interest rate changes often accompany periods of economic and political uncertainty. Factors such as elections, geopolitical tensions, or unexpected economic downturns can influence central bank decisions. For carry traders engaged in rollover arbitrage, navigating the uncertainty introduced by these external factors is crucial to mitigating risks associated with sudden interest rate shifts.

Mitigation Strategies:

- Maintaining a keen awareness of geopolitical events and their potential impact on currency markets.
- Hedging against uncertainty through options or other risk management tools.
- Diversifying across currencies with stable political environments.

6. Global Economic Shocks and Systemic Risks

In the interconnected world of finance, global economic shocks or systemic risks can reverberate across currency markets. Unforeseen events such as financial crises, pandemics, or major geopolitical conflicts can trigger central banks to implement emergency measures, including sudden and drastic changes in interest rates. Carry traders must contend with the fallout from these events, which can disrupt established strategies and risk management frameworks.

Mitigation Strategies:

- Maintaining a diversified portfolio to spread risk across different asset classes.
- Monitoring broader economic indicators for signs of systemic risks.
- Having contingency plans and exit strategies in place for extreme market conditions.

7. Inherent Challenges in Predicting Interest Rate Movements

Even with advanced analytics and economic models, accurately predicting the precise timing and magnitude of interest rate changes is a formidable challenge. Central banks employ a data-dependent approach, and market expectations can shift rapidly. The inherent uncertainty in forecasting interest rate movements adds a layer of complexity to the risk landscape for carry traders engaged in rollover arbitrage.

Mitigation Strategies:

- Incorporating a margin of safety in position sizing to account for potential surprises.
- Diversifying strategies to include both directional and non-directional approaches.
- Collaborating with economic analysts or utilizing algorithmic models to enhance forecasting capabilities.

Conclusion: Navigating the Uncharted Waters of Interest Rate Risks

As carry traders venture into the realm of Forex rollover arbitrage, the risks posed by unexpected interest rate changes loom large. Navigating these uncharted waters requires a combination of vigilance, adaptability, and a nuanced understanding of global economic dynamics. While risks are inherent in any trading strategy, carry traders can fortify their positions by integrating robust risk management practices, staying informed about central bank policies, and maintaining a diversified and dynamic approach to their portfolios. In the subsequent sections of this chapter and the following chapters, we will further explore strategies, case studies, and practical insights to empower carry traders in their pursuit of success within the dynamic Forex market.

Central Bank Policy Shifts

In the intricate dance of Forex rollover arbitrage, central bank policy shifts emerge as a pivotal force, capable of sending ripples across currency markets. Understanding the dynamics of central bank policies, the factors influencing their decisions, and the implications for carry traders navigating the interest rate differentials is crucial. This section delves into the nuanced realm of central bank policy shifts, exploring their multifaceted nature and the strategic considerations they impose on those engaged in rollover arbitrage.

Decoding Central Bank Policies

Central banks play a central role in shaping the monetary landscape of a country. Their policies influence interest rates, inflation, and overall economic stability. For carry traders immersed in rollover arbitrage, the policies of key central banks become a guiding force, directing their strategies and influencing the attractiveness of different currency pairs.

Monetary Policy Tools: A Toolkit for Central Banks

Central banks deploy a variety of tools to implement monetary policy. These tools include interest rate adjustments, open market operations, reserve requirements, and forward guidance. Interest rates, however, stand out as a primary lever, and changes in these rates can have profound effects on currency values.

Interest Rate Changes: The Cornerstone of Central Bank Policies

At the heart of central bank policy shifts are changes in interest rates. Central banks raise or lower interest rates to achieve specific objectives, such as controlling inflation, stimulating economic growth, or stabilizing currency values. Understanding the motivations behind interest rate changes is key for carry traders seeking to navigate the terrain of Forex rollover arbitrage.

1. Inflation Targeting and Economic Objectives

Central banks often set inflation targets as part of their monetary policy framework. Inflation targeting involves adjusting interest rates to achieve a specified inflation rate. By raising or lowering rates, central banks aim to keep inflation within a target range, fostering price stability and economic predictability.

2. Economic Growth and Employment Goals

Beyond inflation, central banks are tasked with promoting economic growth and maintaining employment. In periods of economic expansion, central banks may raise interest rates to prevent overheating and excessive inflation. Conversely, during economic downturns, lowering rates can stimulate borrowing, spending, and job creation.

3. Currency Stabilization and Exchange Rate Objectives

Some central banks explicitly target exchange rates as part of their policy objectives. By influencing interest rates, central banks can impact the attractiveness of their currency in the foreign exchange market. This can be particularly relevant for carry traders, as shifts in exchange rates influence the profitability of rollover arbitrage positions.

4. Forward Guidance: Shaping Market Expectations

Central banks employ forward guidance as a communication tool to shape market expectations. Through public statements and press conferences, central bank officials signal their intended course of action regarding interest rates. The effectiveness of forward guidance lies in its ability to influence market perceptions and guide investor behavior.

Factors Influencing Central Bank Decisions

The decision-making processes of central banks are complex and influenced by a myriad of factors. Carry traders engaged in rollover arbitrage must be attuned to these factors, as they can signal potential shifts in interest rates and impact the risk and reward dynamics of currency pairs.

1. Economic Indicators and Data Releases

Central banks closely monitor economic indicators and data releases to assess the health of the economy. Key indicators include GDP growth, employment figures, inflation rates, and consumer spending. Strong or weak economic data can influence central bank decisions on interest rates.

2. Inflation Trends and Expectations

Inflation is a critical consideration for central banks. Consistent deviations from the inflation target, whether above or below, can prompt adjustments to interest rates. Central banks also consider inflation expectations, as these can influence consumer and investor behavior.

3. Global Economic Conditions

The interconnected nature of the global economy means that central banks take into account international developments. Global economic conditions, trade tensions, and geopolitical events can impact a country's economic outlook and influence central bank policy decisions.

4. Financial Market Stability

Central banks are mindful of financial market stability. Sharp declines in stock markets, disruptions in credit markets, or excessive volatility can trigger central bank interventions. Maintaining stability is integral to preserving economic confidence and preventing systemic risks.

5. Currency Valuations and Exchange Rate Trends

The value of a country's currency in the foreign exchange market is a crucial factor for central banks. A currency that is too strong can hurt export competitiveness, while a weak currency may contribute to inflationary pressures. Central banks may intervene to influence currency valuations.

6. Unemployment and Labor Market Dynamics

Central banks assess labor market conditions and unemployment rates when formulating policy. Full employment is often a goal, and central banks may adjust interest rates to support job creation or address concerns about labor market slack.

Impact of Central Bank Policy Shifts on Rollover Arbitrage

Carry traders engaged in rollover arbitrage must navigate the terrain shaped by central bank policy shifts. The consequences of these shifts can reverberate through the Forex market, affecting interest rate differentials, currency valuations, and the overall risk and reward dynamics of carry trade positions.

1. Altered Interest Rate Differentials

Central bank policy shifts, especially changes in interest rates, directly impact interest rate differentials—the lifeblood of rollover arbitrage. As central banks adjust rates, the attractiveness of certain currency pairs for carry traders evolves, influencing position decisions and overall portfolio strategies.

2. Currency Pair Selection Strategies

The selection of currency pairs is a delicate art for carry traders, and central bank policies significantly influence this decision-making process. Savvy traders analyze the policy trajectories of relevant central banks, assessing the potential for stable or widening interest rate differentials that align with their rollover arbitrage goals.

3. Enhanced Volatility and Market Dynamics

Central bank announcements and policy shifts can inject volatility into currency markets. Carry traders must be prepared for heightened market dynamics during these periods. Volatility can present both opportunities and risks, requiring traders to adapt their risk management strategies to evolving market conditions.

4. Strategic Positioning Ahead of Policy Announcements

Anticipating central bank actions and policy announcements becomes a strategic consideration for carry traders. Some traders position themselves ahead of key announcements, seeking to capitalize on expected market reactions. However, this approach carries its own set of risks, as market sentiment can shift unexpectedly.

5. Evaluating Forward Guidance and Communication

Forward guidance from central banks becomes a compass for carry traders navigating the Forex landscape. Clear and transparent communication can guide trading decisions, helping traders align their strategies with the expected direction of interest rates and economic conditions.

Strategies for Navigating Central Bank Policy Shifts

Successfully navigating central bank policy shifts requires a blend of market insight, strategic planning, and adaptability. Carry traders can deploy various strategies to position themselves effectively and manage the risks associated with central bank policy dynamics.

1. Stay Informed and Monitor Central Bank Communications

Vigilance is paramount for carry traders. Staying informed about central bank communications, official statements, and press conferences provides critical insights into the thinking of policymakers. Traders should have a reliable news source and economic calendar to track key events.

2. Utilize Economic Models and Analytics

Sophisticated traders often employ economic models and analytics to assess the potential impact of central bank policy shifts. These models may incorporate economic indicators, interest rate expectations, and historical data to formulate forecasts and guide trading decisions.

3. Diversify Across Currencies and Strategies

Diversification is a foundational principle for managing risks in carry trading. Diversifying across different currencies, regions, and strategies can help mitigate the impact of central bank policy shifts on specific positions. A well-diversified portfolio enhances resilience in the face of unforeseen market developments.

4. Implement Robust Risk Management Practices

Given the inherent uncertainties in the Forex market, robust risk management practices are indispensable. Carry traders should set clear risk parameters, use stop-loss orders judiciously, and regularly reassess their risk tolerance. Adequate risk management becomes a shield against potential adverse effects of central bank policy shifts.

5. Adapt Quickly to Changing Market Conditions

The ability to adapt swiftly to changing market conditions is a hallmark of successful carry traders. Central bank policies can evolve rapidly, and traders need to adjust their strategies in response. This may involve recalibrating position sizes, reassessing currency pair selections, or altering risk management parameters.

Conclusion: Navigating the Central Bank Policy Landscape

Central bank policy shifts introduce both challenges and opportunities for carry traders engaged in Forex rollover arbitrage. As central banks strive to balance economic objectives, traders must decipher the signals, anticipate potential market reactions, and align their strategies accordingly. The dynamic interplay between central bank policies and the Forex market requires a nuanced approach—one that combines a deep understanding of economic fundamentals with strategic agility. In the subsequent sections of this chapter and the chapters that follow, we will delve deeper into case studies, practical insights, and real-world examples to empower carry traders in navigating the complex and ever-evolving landscape of central bank policy shifts within the realm of Forex rollover arbitrage.

Currency Peg Instability

In the intricate tapestry of Forex rollover arbitrage, where traders navigate the terrain of interest rate differentials, currency peg instability emerges as a significant factor shaping the risk and reward dynamics. Understanding the nuances of currency pegs, the reasons behind their establishment, and the potential risks they pose for carry traders is essential. This section delves into the complexities of currency peg instability and its implications for those engaged in the art of rollover arbitrage.

Deciphering Currency Pegs: A Foundation for Stability

Currency pegs represent a commitment by a country's central bank to maintain a fixed exchange rate between its currency and another currency or a basket of currencies. The primary motivation behind pegging a currency is often to promote stability in international trade, attract foreign investment, and control inflation. While currency pegs can provide a sense of predictability, they also introduce unique challenges, particularly when it comes to the strategies employed by carry traders.

1. Types of Currency Pegs

There are various types of currency pegs, each with its own set of implications for the Forex market. Common types include:

- Fixed Peg: The currency is tied to another currency at a specific exchange rate, and central banks intervene to maintain this rate.

- Crawling Peg: The exchange rate is adjusted periodically to reflect changes in economic fundamentals.

- Basket Peg: The currency is pegged to a basket of other currencies, spreading risk and reducing vulnerability to fluctuations in a single currency.

- Currency Board Arrangement: A strict form of peg where the domestic currency is backed by a reserve of foreign currency.

2. Motivations Behind Currency Pegs

Countries adopt currency pegs for various reasons:

- Stability: Pegs provide stability and predictability in international trade, making it easier for businesses to plan and transact.

- Inflation Control: Pegs can help control inflation by anchoring the value of the domestic currency to a more stable external reference.

- Attracting Investment: A peg can make a country more attractive to foreign investors, as it reduces the uncertainty associated with currency fluctuations.

- Trade Balance: Maintaining a stable exchange rate can support a favorable trade balance by making exports and imports more predictable.

3. Risks of Currency Pegs for Carry Traders

While currency pegs offer certain advantages, they also introduce risks, particularly for carry traders engaged in rollover arbitrage. Understanding these risks is crucial for devising effective strategies and risk management approaches.

Currency Peg Instability: Implications for Rollover Arbitrage

1. Limited Flexibility in Interest Rate Adjustments

Countries with currency pegs often face constraints in adjusting their domestic interest rates. The pegged exchange rate limits the freedom to implement independent monetary policies, as interest rate changes may lead to capital flows that challenge the peg. For carry traders, this limited flexibility can impact the attractiveness of certain currency pairs for rollover arbitrage.

2. Vulnerability to External Shocks

Pegged currencies are more vulnerable to external shocks, such as changes in global economic conditions, geopolitical events, or fluctuations in the anchor currency. These external factors can create sudden and unexpected movements in the pegged currency, disrupting the interest rate differentials that carry traders rely on for profits.

3. Speculative Attacks and Peg Breaks

In the world of Forex, speculative attacks on a currency can pose a significant threat to pegged exchange rates. If investors perceive that a currency is overvalued or unsustainable, they may engage in speculative activities to force a devaluation or a break in the peg. Such events can lead to rapid and substantial movements in currency values, impacting carry trade positions.

4. Central Bank Intervention Challenges

Central banks maintaining currency pegs often need to intervene regularly in the foreign exchange market to uphold the pegged rate. Continuous intervention can deplete foreign exchange reserves and pose challenges for central banks in managing monetary policy. For carry traders, the frequency and scale of interventions can introduce uncertainty and affect rollover arbitrage strategies.

5. Impact on Interest Rate Differentials

Currency peg instability can disrupt interest rate differentials—the lifeblood of rollover arbitrage. Sudden changes in exchange rates due to peg-related events can alter the risk and reward dynamics of carry trade positions. Traders must be vigilant and adaptable to navigate the shifting landscape of interest rate differentials influenced by currency pegs.

Navigating Currency Peg Instability: Strategies for Carry Traders

1. Monitor Peg-Related Developments

Vigilance is key for carry traders navigating currency peg instability. Regularly monitoring developments related to the pegged currency, central bank statements, and any indications of potential challenges to the peg can provide valuable insights for adjusting strategies.

2. Diversify Across Currency Pairs and Strategies

Diversification is a fundamental principle for managing risks in rollover arbitrage, and it becomes especially crucial in the context of currency pegs. Diversifying across a range of currency pairs with different peg arrangements and employing multiple strategies can enhance resilience and mitigate the impact of peg-related events.

3. Assess Central Bank Resilience and Intervention Capacity

The resilience and intervention capacity of the central bank maintaining the peg are critical factors for carry traders. Assessing the central bank's ability to withstand external pressures, manage interventions effectively, and uphold the peg provides valuable insights for gauging the stability of the pegged currency.

4. Factor in Potential Peg Adjustments in Risk Models

Incorporating the possibility of peg adjustments into risk models is essential for carry traders. Scenario analysis that considers potential devaluations, breaks in pegs, or changes in central bank policies allows traders to assess the impact on interest rate differentials and adjust their risk management strategies accordingly.

Conclusion: Navigating the Unsteady Waters of Currency Peg Instability

As carry traders embark on the journey of Forex rollover arbitrage, currency peg instability emerges as a dynamic force that shapes the landscape of interest rate differentials. Navigating the unsteady waters of currency pegs requires a keen understanding of the motivations behind pegs, the risks they pose, and the strategic considerations for carry traders. In the subsequent sections of this chapter and the chapters that follow, we will delve deeper into case studies, practical insights, and real-world examples to empower carry traders in navigating the complex and ever-evolving realm of currency peg instability within the context of rollover arbitrage.

Margin Requirements

In the realm of Forex rollover arbitrage, where traders seek to capitalize on interest rate differentials, margin requirements play a pivotal role in shaping risk management strategies and influencing the feasibility of carry trade positions. Understanding the nuances of margin requirements, their impact on leverage, and the implications for carry traders is essential. This section delves into the multifaceted aspects of margin requirements, exploring their significance, considerations, and strategic implications within the context of rollover arbitrage.

Margin requirements refer to the amount of collateral that traders must maintain in their trading accounts to open and sustain positions. In Forex trading, margins are typically expressed as a percentage of the total position size. The use of leverage, which allows traders to control larger positions with a relatively small amount of capital, makes margin requirements a critical element in risk management.

Leverage amplifies both gains and losses in Forex trading, and margin requirements act as a safeguard for brokers and traders alike. While leverage enhances the potential returns of carry trade positions, it also exposes traders to higher risks. Brokers impose margin requirements to ensure that traders have sufficient funds to cover potential losses, minimizing the risk of account liquidation.

The level of leverage available to traders is often expressed as a ratio, such as 50:1 or 100:1. This ratio represents the relationship between the total position size and the margin required to open and maintain that position. For example, a leverage ratio of 50:1 means that for a $100,000 position, a trader would need to maintain $2,000 in margin.

The application of leverage in Forex rollover arbitrage enables traders to control larger positions and potentially amplify profits. However, it also introduces a delicate balance between risk and reward. Excessive leverage can lead to significant losses, especially if market conditions move unfavorably. Traders must carefully consider the margin requirements imposed by brokers and assess their risk tolerance before engaging in carry trade positions.

The calculation of margin requirements involves several factors, including the size of the position, the leverage ratio, and the currency pair being traded. Different brokers may have varying margin requirements based on their risk management policies and regulatory obligations. Traders should be aware of these requirements and factor them into their position sizing and risk management strategies.

In the context of Forex rollover arbitrage, where traders aim to capture interest rate differentials, margin requirements assume particular significance. Carry trades involve holding positions overnight to benefit from rollover interest, and this extended duration can impact margin requirements. Traders need to consider not only the potential profits from interest differentials but also the margin needed to sustain positions during periods of market volatility or adverse price movements.

The dynamics of margin requirements in rollover arbitrage become especially pronounced during events that can trigger increased market volatility. Central bank announcements, economic data releases, or geopolitical developments can lead to rapid and substantial price movements. During such periods, brokers may adjust margin requirements to account for the heightened risk, potentially leading to increased margin calls for traders.

Margin calls occur when a trader's account balance falls below the required margin level. Brokers may issue a margin call to prompt the trader to deposit additional funds or close out positions to meet the margin requirement. Failure to meet a margin call may result in the automatic liquidation of positions to prevent further losses.

For carry traders engaged in rollover arbitrage, the management of margin requirements involves a delicate dance between optimizing leverage for potential profits and ensuring adequate safeguards against account liquidation. Traders need to carefully assess the risk associated with each position, considering not only interest rate differentials but also the impact of leverage and margin on the overall risk profile.

Risk management strategies in the context of margin requirements include setting conservative leverage ratios, diversifying positions across different currency pairs, and establishing stop-loss orders to limit potential losses. Traders should also stay informed about broker policies regarding margin requirements and be aware of any adjustments that may occur during volatile market conditions.

The use of leverage and margin requirements introduces an additional layer of complexity to the already intricate landscape of Forex rollover arbitrage. While leverage can enhance the potential returns of carry trades, it requires a disciplined and strategic approach to mitigate the inherent risks. Traders navigating the world of rollover arbitrage must strike a careful balance between leveraging opportunities and prudent risk management, understanding that margin requirements are a crucial element in the intricate dance of interest rate differentials and potential profits.

Chapter 4: Initial Coin Offerings (ICOs)
ICOs as an Alternative to IPOs

Initial Coin Offerings (ICOs) have emerged as a disruptive force in the financial landscape, presenting a novel alternative to traditional Initial Public Offerings (IPOs). In this paradigm shift, entrepreneurs and blockchain projects are turning to ICOs as a means of fundraising, challenging the established norms of capital markets. Unlike IPOs, which involve the issuance of shares, ICOs center around the creation and sale of digital tokens. This section explores the distinctive features of ICOs, their advantages over IPOs, and the transformative impact they have had on fundraising for innovative ventures.

In the traditional IPO model, companies seeking capital go through a rigorous process of regulatory compliance, due diligence, and underwriting before offering shares to the public. This process is often time-consuming, expensive, and exclusive, limiting access to capital for early-stage companies and innovative projects. ICOs, on the other hand, have democratized fundraising by providing a more accessible and inclusive avenue for entrepreneurs.

ICOs democratize access to capital by allowing a global audience to participate in fundraising activities. Unlike IPOs, which are often restricted to institutional investors and high-net-worth individuals, ICOs open investment opportunities to a broader spectrum of contributors. This inclusivity fosters a decentralized approach to fundraising, aligning with the principles of blockchain technology and decentralization.

In contrast to the regulatory hurdles associated with IPOs, ICOs offer a streamlined and agile fundraising process. The decentralized nature of blockchain technology enables projects to reach a global audience without the need for intermediaries or extensive regulatory approvals. While this has fostered innovation and accelerated fundraising, it has also raised concerns about the lack of regulatory oversight and investor protection.

ICOs leverage blockchain technology to issue digital tokens, often based on standards like ERC-20 on the Ethereum blockchain. These tokens represent various utilities within the project's ecosystem, from access to specific services to governance rights. Unlike traditional IPO shares, these tokens do not equate to ownership in the company but rather grant holders certain privileges or benefits within the project's ecosystem.

One of the key advantages of ICOs over IPOs is the liquidity and tradability of digital tokens. In the traditional IPO model, investors often face lock-up periods, restricting their ability to sell shares for a specified period after the offering. ICO tokens, being digital assets on blockchain platforms, can be traded on various cryptocurrency exchanges shortly after the ICO concludes, providing liquidity and flexibility for investors.

ICOs have unlocked a new frontier for fundraising, enabling projects to tap into global liquidity pools. This has resulted in a paradigm shift in how entrepreneurs approach capital formation, with many choosing ICOs as a primary fundraising method over traditional venture capital or IPOs. The ability to attract funding from a diverse and global pool of contributors has become a compelling value proposition for innovative projects.

Despite the transformative potential of ICOs, they are not without challenges and controversies. The lack of regulatory oversight has led to instances of fraud, scams, and projects with questionable viability raising substantial funds. The absence of investor protections, combined with the speculative nature of the cryptocurrency market, has raised concerns among regulators worldwide.

The surge in ICO activity has prompted regulatory responses in various jurisdictions. Some countries have embraced ICOs as a legitimate fundraising method, providing regulatory frameworks to safeguard investors and promote transparency. Others have taken a more cautious approach, imposing restrictions or outright bans on ICOs to mitigate potential risks.

The evolving regulatory landscape underscores the need for responsible practices within the ICO ecosystem. Projects conducting ICOs must prioritize transparency, disclosure, and investor education to foster trust and credibility. The delicate balance between regulatory compliance and the innovative potential of ICOs remains a central theme in discussions about the future of decentralized fundraising.

As ICOs continue to reshape the fundraising landscape, their impact extends beyond capital formation. They have become a catalyst for innovation, allowing entrepreneurs to experiment with new models of ownership, governance, and incentive structures. The tokenization of assets, the creation of decentralized autonomous organizations (DAOs), and the exploration of novel funding mechanisms are all manifestations of the broader impact of ICOs.

In conclusion, ICOs represent a paradigm shift in fundraising, challenging the traditional norms of capital markets. Their role as an alternative to IPOs has democratized access to capital, enabling a diverse range of projects to reach a global audience. However, this disruptive force comes with challenges, particularly concerning regulatory oversight and investor protection. As the ICO landscape continues to evolve, striking a balance between innovation and responsibility will be crucial for the sustainable growth of this transformative fundraising model.

Lack of Regulation and Oversight

The lack of regulation and oversight has been a defining characteristic of the Initial Coin Offering (ICO) landscape, contributing to both its appeal and its challenges. Unlike traditional financial markets, where regulatory frameworks are well-established, the world of ICOs operates in a relatively uncharted territory. This section explores the implications of the absence of robust regulation and oversight in the ICO space, examining the opportunities it presents for innovation as well as the risks it poses for investors and the broader financial ecosystem.

The absence of a comprehensive regulatory framework has been a double-edged sword for ICOs. On one hand, it has allowed for unparalleled innovation and the rapid evolution of decentralized fundraising models. Entrepreneurs and blockchain projects have been able to bypass the traditional bureaucratic hurdles associated with fundraising, enabling a more agile and inclusive approach. However, this lack of regulation has also created a fertile ground for abuse, fraud, and the proliferation of projects with dubious intentions.

One of the primary challenges stemming from the lack of regulation is the prevalence of fraudulent ICOs. The absence of clear guidelines and oversight mechanisms has made it easier for bad actors to exploit unsuspecting investors. Scams, Ponzi schemes, and projects with no intention of delivering on their promises have tarnished the reputation of the ICO space and eroded trust among potential contributors.

Investor protection is a critical aspect where the lack of regulation poses significant risks. In traditional financial markets, regulatory bodies provide a layer of security through measures such as disclosure requirements, audit standards, and oversight of financial institutions. In the ICO space, investors may lack these safeguards, exposing them to the risk of investing in projects with inadequate transparency, questionable financial practices, or insufficient due diligence.

Market manipulation is another concern exacerbated by the absence of regulation. The relatively low liquidity of many ICO tokens makes them susceptible to price manipulation by a small number of large holders. Pump-and-dump schemes, where the value of a token is artificially inflated and then rapidly sold off, can wreak havoc on unsuspecting investors who enter the market without adequate information or protections.

The lack of regulatory clarity has also hindered institutional participation in the ICO space. Institutional investors, such as pension funds and traditional asset managers, are often bound by strict regulatory requirements. The absence of a clear regulatory framework for ICOs has made it challenging for these institutions to navigate the risks and compliance issues associated with participating in token sales.

The global nature of ICOs adds an additional layer of complexity to the regulatory challenge. With projects and contributors spanning across borders, coordinating a harmonized regulatory approach has proven challenging. Jurisdictional variations in regulatory attitudes and frameworks further complicate efforts to create a unified set of guidelines for the burgeoning ICO ecosystem.

Attempts to address the regulatory vacuum in the ICO space have been varied and jurisdiction-dependent. Some countries have embraced a proactive approach, introducing regulatory frameworks to provide clarity and protection for both investors and projects. Others have opted for a more cautious stance, choosing to observe and assess the landscape before implementing specific regulations. The lack of a universally accepted framework has created a patchwork of regulatory responses worldwide.

The call for regulatory clarity in the ICO space has grown louder as the market matures. Industry participants, including reputable projects and investors, recognize the need for a balanced approach that fosters innovation while safeguarding against abuse. Proposals for self-regulation within the industry, such as the development of best practices and standards by industry associations, have been put forward as a means to address the regulatory gap.

The absence of regulation in the ICO space has implications beyond investor protection and market integrity. It also raises questions about the long-term sustainability and mainstream adoption of blockchain-based fundraising models. Regulatory uncertainty can deter institutional investors and traditional financial institutions from entering the space, potentially limiting the growth and legitimacy of ICOs as a viable fundraising method.

In conclusion, the lack of regulation and oversight in the ICO space is a defining characteristic that has shaped both the opportunities and challenges within this innovative fundraising model. While it has fostered rapid innovation and inclusivity, it has also exposed participants to risks such as fraud, market manipulation, and a lack of investor protections. As the industry continues to evolve, striking the right balance between fostering innovation and implementing responsible regulatory measures will be crucial for the sustainable growth of ICOs and their integration into the broader financial ecosystem.

Evaluating White Papers

Evaluating white papers is a crucial step in the due diligence process for participants in Initial Coin Offerings (ICOs). The white paper serves as the foundational document for a blockchain project, outlining its vision, technology, tokenomics, and overall roadmap. This section explores the significance of white papers in the ICO ecosystem, delving into the key elements that investors, analysts, and contributors should consider when assessing these documents to make informed decisions in the complex and dynamic world of token sales.

A white paper is essentially the project's manifesto, providing a comprehensive overview of its purpose, goals, and technical details. It is the primary source of information for potential investors seeking to understand the value proposition of a project and the potential return on investment. Given the absence of regulatory oversight in the ICO space, the white paper becomes a critical tool for transparency and accountability.

The executive summary of the white paper is often the first section that potential investors encounter. It distills the essence of the project, its objectives, and its unique value proposition. A well-crafted executive summary should provide a clear and concise snapshot of the project, helping readers quickly grasp its key features and potential impact. Investors should pay attention to the clarity of language and the alignment of the executive summary with the broader content of the white paper.

The problem statement is a foundational element of the white paper, articulating the specific issues or challenges that the project aims to address. This section should demonstrate a thorough understanding of the problem domain, presenting relevant data, statistics, or case studies to support the project's assertions. Investors should critically assess the clarity and depth of the problem statement, ensuring that the project is addressing a genuine and significant need within its target market.

The solution proposed by the project is a central component of the white paper. It outlines the technological innovations, protocols, or frameworks that the project introduces to solve the identified problem. Investors should scrutinize this section to evaluate the feasibility and uniqueness of the proposed solution. Key considerations include the technical expertise of the project team, the scalability of the solution, and its alignment with industry best practices.

Tokenomics, or the economics of the project's native token, is a critical aspect that investors must carefully analyze. This section outlines the token distribution model, the purpose of the token within the ecosystem, and any mechanisms for incentivizing or rewarding participants. A well-designed tokenomics model should strike a balance between aligning incentives for all stakeholders and ensuring the sustainability and growth of the project.

The team behind the project plays a pivotal role in its success. The white paper typically includes information about the key team members, their backgrounds, expertise, and previous experiences. Investors should conduct thorough due diligence on the team, verifying their credentials and assessing whether they possess the necessary skills to execute the project's vision. Red flags may include a lack of relevant experience, a history of failed projects, or an absence of key team members in critical roles.

Roadmaps outlined in white papers provide a timeline of the project's development milestones and key deliverables. Investors should carefully evaluate the feasibility and realism of the roadmap, considering whether it aligns with the complexity of the proposed solution and the resources available to the team. A roadmap that is overly ambitious or lacks specific details may raise concerns about the project's execution capabilities.

Community engagement is a qualitative factor that investors should consider when evaluating white papers. A strong and active community can contribute to the project's success by fostering collaboration, providing feedback, and creating a network effect. Investors should assess whether the project has established communication channels, social media presence, and community-building initiatives. An engaged community can be indicative of a project's ability to garner support and adoption.

In conclusion, evaluating white papers is a fundamental step in the due diligence process for participants in Initial Coin Offerings. The white paper serves as the cornerstone of transparency and accountability in the absence of regulatory oversight. By critically assessing the executive summary, problem statement, proposed solution, tokenomics, team, roadmap, and community engagement, investors can make informed decisions and contribute to the overall legitimacy and success of blockchain projects in the dynamic and evolving landscape of ICOs.

High Startup Failure Rate

Navigating the world of Initial Coin Offerings (ICOs) entails grappling with a sobering reality—the high failure rate of blockchain startups that emerge from these token sales. While ICOs have presented a revolutionary fundraising avenue, the landscape is fraught with challenges, and a significant number of projects fail to realize their visions. This section delves into the factors contributing to the high startup failure rate in the ICO space, shedding light on the complexities and pitfalls that entrepreneurs and investors must navigate.

A primary driver of the high startup failure rate in the ICO space is the nascent and rapidly evolving nature of blockchain technology. Many projects embark on ambitious endeavors, aiming to introduce groundbreaking solutions to complex problems. However, the intricacies of blockchain development, coupled with the need for robust and scalable solutions, often lead to technical challenges that some startups struggle to overcome. The fast-paced evolution of blockchain technology itself can render certain solutions obsolete or necessitate constant adaptation, adding a layer of uncertainty to project development.

The lack of regulatory oversight in the ICO space contributes significantly to the high failure rate of startups. While the absence of regulatory burdens is often touted as a benefit, it also means that projects operate in an environment where investor protections are limited. This lack of oversight allows for the proliferation of fraudulent or ill-conceived projects, leading to a loss of investor confidence. Without a regulatory framework to enforce standards and ensure transparency, both genuine projects and investors may fall victim to bad actors within the space.

Tokenomics, the economic model governing the distribution and use of native tokens, plays a crucial role in the success or failure of blockchain startups. Many projects struggle to strike the right balance in designing tokenomics that align incentives for all stakeholders. Poorly structured tokenomics can result in economic inefficiencies, lack of demand for the native token, or a misalignment of interests among participants. Startups must carefully consider the economic dynamics within their ecosystems to ensure sustainability and adoption.

The competitive landscape within the blockchain and cryptocurrency space compounds the challenges faced by startups. With an influx of projects vying for attention and funding, differentiation becomes a key factor in success. Some projects may struggle to articulate a unique value proposition or fail to effectively communicate it to their target audience. The sheer volume of projects also contributes to a dilution of attention and resources, making it challenging for startups to stand out and gain traction.

Market sentiment and the broader economic environment significantly impact the success or failure of ICO-funded startups. The cryptocurrency market is known for its volatility, with token prices subject to rapid and unpredictable fluctuations. External factors, such as regulatory developments, technological breakthroughs, or shifts in investor sentiment, can influence the fate of projects. Startups that fail to adapt to changing market conditions or anticipate external factors may find themselves struggling to survive.

Another factor contributing to the high failure rate is the execution risk associated with project development and delivery. Despite promising white papers and visionary roadmaps, translating concepts into functioning products is a formidable task. Development delays, technical glitches, or unforeseen obstacles can impede progress, erode investor confidence, and contribute to the failure of projects. The inherent challenges of software development, coupled with the complexities of blockchain implementation, make execution risk a pervasive concern.

The role of governance and decision-making structures within blockchain projects cannot be understated. In the absence of centralized authorities, decentralized projects often rely on community governance or token-holder voting mechanisms. Projects that struggle to establish effective governance structures may face challenges in making timely decisions, resolving disputes, or adapting to evolving circumstances. Internal conflicts or governance failures can contribute to the breakdown of projects, further contributing to the high failure rate.

The speculative nature of the cryptocurrency market introduces an additional layer of risk for ICO-funded startups. Investor expectations often run high, driven by the potential for significant returns. However, the disconnect between speculative fervor and the actual progress of projects can lead to disillusionment. Startups that fail to meet inflated expectations or demonstrate tangible progress may experience a loss of investor confidence, negatively impacting their ability to secure continued funding or achieve widespread adoption.

In conclusion, the high startup failure rate in the ICO space is a multifaceted challenge shaped by technical complexities, regulatory uncertainties, economic dynamics, competition, market sentiment, execution risks, governance issues, and the speculative nature of the cryptocurrency market.

Entrepreneurs and investors alike must navigate these challenges with a keen awareness of the unique dynamics within the blockchain space. Acknowledging the factors that contribute to the high failure rate is essential for fostering a more resilient and sustainable ecosystem, where lessons learned from failures contribute to the ongoing evolution and maturation of blockchain technology.

Fraud Risk Warning Signs

In the dynamic and largely unregulated landscape of Initial Coin Offerings (ICOs), the potential for fraud looms as a significant risk for unsuspecting investors. Recognizing the warning signs of fraud is paramount for safeguarding participants in the ICO space. This section explores the red flags and indicators that may signal fraudulent activities within ICO projects, providing a comprehensive guide to help investors navigate the treacherous waters of the cryptocurrency fundraising ecosystem.

One of the most conspicuous warning signs of potential fraud in an ICO is the lack of transparency in the project's white paper. White papers serve as the cornerstone of a project's legitimacy, outlining its vision, technology, and tokenomics. A white paper that lacks specificity, uses vague language, or fails to provide clear details about the project's objectives, technology, and team is a red flag. Investors should scrutinize white papers for substance, ensuring that they convey a credible and well-thought-out plan.

The absence of a verifiable and experienced team is another potent warning sign of potential fraud in ICOs. Legitimate projects typically highlight the expertise of their team members, showcasing their backgrounds and relevant experience. On the contrary, fraudulent projects may either present a team with fictitious credentials or lack transparency altogether. Investors should conduct thorough due diligence on the team, cross-referencing their profiles on professional networks and verifying the accuracy of their claimed qualifications.

Unrealistic promises and guarantees are indicative of potential fraud in the ICO space. Projects that overpromise on returns, use aggressive marketing tactics, or make guarantees of significant profits should be approached with skepticism. The cryptocurrency market is inherently volatile, and genuine projects acknowledge the associated risks rather than making unwarranted assurances. Investors should be wary of projects that create unrealistic expectations to attract funding.

The lack of a clear use case or practical application for the project's native token is a red flag for potential fraud. Legitimate projects design tokens with a specific purpose within their ecosystems, such as enabling access to services or incentivizing user participation. In contrast, fraudulent projects may issue tokens without a clear utility or justification, raising questions about the true value and purpose of the token. Investors should critically assess the functionality and necessity of the native token within the project.

Opaque or non-existent source code is a glaring warning sign of potential fraud in ICOs. Open-source development is a foundational principle in blockchain technology, promoting transparency and collaboration. Legitimate projects typically share their source code on public repositories like GitHub, allowing developers to review, contribute, and validate the code. Projects that withhold or obscure their source code raise suspicions about their commitment to transparency and the verifiability of their technology.

Another red flag for potential fraud lies in the absence of a working prototype or Minimum Viable Product (MVP). Genuine blockchain projects often demonstrate their commitment to development by showcasing a functional prototype or MVP. Fraudulent projects, on the other hand, may rely solely on conceptual presentations without tangible evidence of progress. Investors should exercise caution when evaluating projects that lack a demonstrable track record of development.

A lack of engagement and communication with the community is a notable warning sign of potential fraud in ICOs. Legitimate projects actively engage with their communities through social media, forums, and other communication channels. They respond to inquiries, provide updates on project milestones, and foster a sense of community involvement. Fraudulent projects may remain elusive, offering limited communication and avoiding transparency. Investors should be wary of projects that fail to establish and maintain an open line of communication with their communities.

Unverified or questionable partnerships are additional warning signs of potential fraud in the ICO space. Legitimate projects often form strategic partnerships with established entities, contributing to their credibility and potential for success. Conversely, fraudulent projects may fabricate partnerships or collaborate with entities of dubious reputation to create a façade of legitimacy. Investors should scrutinize the authenticity of claimed partnerships and assess whether they genuinely contribute to the project's goals.

A rushed or overly aggressive fundraising timeline is a potential red flag for fraud in ICOs. Legitimate projects carefully plan and execute their fundraising campaigns, allowing sufficient time for due diligence, community engagement, and strategic development. Fraudulent projects may employ aggressive marketing tactics, create a sense of urgency, or rush through the fundraising process to capitalize on investors' FOMO (Fear of Missing Out). Investors should exercise caution when projects exhibit signs of haste in their fundraising efforts.

In conclusion, recognizing fraud risk warning signs is crucial for investors navigating the complex landscape of Initial Coin Offerings. Vigilance and due diligence are paramount, and investors should approach ICO projects with a discerning eye. By scrutinizing white papers, assessing team credentials, questioning unrealistic promises, evaluating the utility of native tokens, examining source code transparency, demanding a working prototype, seeking community engagement, verifying partnerships, and being cautious of rushed fundraising timelines, investors can better protect themselves from potential fraud and contribute to the establishment of a more trustworthy ICO ecosystem.

Chapter 5: Futures Contracts
Understanding Futures and Leverage

Futures contracts are powerful financial instruments that allow market participants to speculate on the future price movements of underlying assets, ranging from commodities to financial instruments. One key feature that distinguishes futures contracts from other financial instruments is the significant leverage they offer to traders. This section provides a comprehensive exploration of the intricacies surrounding futures contracts, with a specific focus on understanding how leverage operates within the futures market.

At its core, a futures contract is an agreement between two parties to buy or sell an asset at a predetermined price at a specified future date. This contractual arrangement is standardized and traded on organized exchanges, facilitating liquidity and price discovery. Leverage comes into play as traders are not required to pay the full value of the contract upfront but instead only a fraction, known as the margin. This ability to control a large contract with a relatively small amount of capital is the essence of leverage in futures trading.

The concept of leverage in futures trading can be likened to a double-edged sword, amplifying both potential gains and losses. Traders use leverage to enhance their exposure to price movements, allowing them to control larger positions than their initial capital would otherwise permit. While this magnification of trading power opens the door to increased profit potential, it also heightens the risk of substantial losses. Understanding the dynamics of leverage is fundamental for anyone engaging in futures trading.

The leverage in futures contracts is achieved through the margin mechanism. Traders are required to deposit a percentage of the contract's total value as margin with the exchange. This margin serves as a security deposit, ensuring that traders have sufficient funds to cover potential losses. The margin requirement is typically a fraction of the contract's notional value, allowing traders to control a more extensive position with a smaller upfront capital commitment.

The concept of margin is central to understanding how leverage is applied in futures trading. The margin amount acts as a form of collateral, serving as a buffer against adverse price movements. Different futures contracts and exchanges may have varying margin requirements based on factors such as volatility, liquidity, and the overall risk associated with the underlying asset. Traders must carefully manage their margin levels to avoid margin calls, where additional funds must be deposited to maintain open positions.

Leverage in futures trading enables market participants to benefit from price movements in the underlying asset without having to commit the full value of the contract. For example, a trader may enter into a futures contract for a commodity with a notional value of $50,000 but only be required to deposit $5,000 as margin. This 10:1 leverage allows the trader to control a position equivalent to $50,000 with a relatively small capital outlay.

While leverage provides the opportunity for amplified returns, it also exposes traders to the risk of significant losses. The magnification of price movements means that even a small adverse change in the market can result in a substantial loss relative to the initial margin deposit. This heightened risk underscores the importance of risk management strategies for traders engaging in leveraged futures trading.

Risk management in leveraged futures trading involves employing various techniques to mitigate the impact of adverse price movements. Setting stop-loss orders, for instance, allows traders to define the maximum amount they are willing to lose on a particular trade. Diversification, spreading risk across multiple assets or contracts, is another strategy to reduce the impact of a single adverse event on the overall portfolio. Additionally, disciplined position sizing and avoiding excessive leverage can contribute to effective risk management.

Understanding the concept of leverage in futures trading requires a grasp of the notional value and the margin requirement. The notional value represents the total value of the futures contract, while the margin is the amount of capital that traders must deposit to open and maintain the position. Leverage is expressed as a ratio, indicating the multiple by which the trader's capital is leveraged to control the contract. For example, a leverage ratio of 5:1 means that for every $1 of margin, the trader controls a position with a notional value of $5.

The risk-return profile of leveraged futures trading necessitates a thorough understanding of the market, the underlying asset, and the factors influencing price movements. Traders must be adept at technical and fundamental analysis to make informed decisions and navigate the complexities of leveraged positions. Market knowledge, coupled with a disciplined approach to risk management, is key to harnessing the benefits of leverage while mitigating the inherent risks.

In conclusion, understanding futures contracts and leverage is essential for anyone venturing into the dynamic world of futures trading. Leverage amplifies both the potential gains and losses associated with price movements in the underlying asset. Traders must carefully manage their margin, employ effective risk management strategies, and have a comprehensive understanding of the factors influencing the market to navigate the complexities of leveraged futures trading successfully. This knowledge forms the foundation for informed decision-making and prudent risk-taking in the pursuit of financial objectives within the futures market.

Volatility and Margin Calls

Futures trading is inherently tied to the dynamics of price volatility, and understanding how volatility interacts with margin requirements is crucial for market participants. This section explores the intricate relationship between volatility and margin calls in futures contracts, shedding light on the impact of market fluctuations on traders' margin accounts and risk exposure.

Volatility, defined as the degree of variation in the price of an asset, is a fundamental aspect of financial markets. In the context of futures contracts, where the goal is to profit from price movements, volatility represents both opportunity and risk. High volatility can present lucrative trading opportunities, but it also introduces the potential for rapid and sizable price swings that can catch traders off guard.

One of the key implications of volatility in futures trading is its direct influence on margin requirements. Margin is the amount of capital that traders must deposit to initiate and maintain positions in futures contracts. As volatility increases, so does the potential for larger price fluctuations, prompting exchanges to adjust margin requirements to account for the heightened risk. This adjustment is a risk management measure designed to ensure that traders have sufficient funds to cover potential losses in the face of increased market uncertainty.

Margin requirements are typically dynamic, with exchanges regularly reassessing the risk associated with different contracts and adjusting margin levels accordingly. Volatile market conditions may lead to a rise in margin requirements, compelling traders to allocate more capital to maintain their positions. This adjustment aims to mitigate the risk of default by ensuring that traders have an adequate buffer to absorb potential losses.

The relationship between volatility and margin calls becomes particularly evident during periods of extreme market turbulence. Sudden and sharp price movements, often fueled by unforeseen events or market shocks, can trigger margin calls as positions move against traders. A margin call occurs when the equity in a trader's account falls below a predetermined level, prompting the exchange to request additional funds to cover potential losses.

The mechanism of a margin call involves the liquidation of a portion or the entirety of a trader's position to restore the required margin level. This forced liquidation aims to protect both the trader and the integrity of the market by preventing the accumulation of unsustainable losses. However, it also underscores the importance of risk management and capital adequacy in futures trading, especially during periods of heightened volatility.

Volatility-induced margin calls can have cascading effects on market participants and the broader market. As traders face liquidation, the selling pressure can exacerbate price movements, triggering a domino effect of further margin calls and forced liquidations. This phenomenon, known as a "margin spiral" or "cascade," can contribute to extreme price volatility and create challenges for both individual traders and the overall stability of the market.

Risk management strategies play a pivotal role in mitigating the impact of volatility and margin calls in futures trading. Traders can employ various techniques to protect their positions and navigate turbulent market conditions. Setting stop-loss orders, for instance, allows traders to define predetermined exit points to limit potential losses. Diversification, spreading risk across different assets or contracts, can help mitigate the impact of adverse price movements on the overall portfolio.

Effective risk management also involves regularly monitoring and adjusting positions in response to changing market conditions. Traders must stay informed about economic indicators, geopolitical events, and other factors that can influence market volatility. Periodic reassessment of risk exposure, position sizes, and overall portfolio composition is essential for adapting to evolving market dynamics and avoiding excessive risk.

In addition to individual risk management, exchanges and regulatory authorities play a crucial role in maintaining market stability during periods of heightened volatility. Implementing circuit breakers or trading halts, temporarily suspending trading in response to extreme price movements, is one measure used to prevent disorderly markets and provide participants with an opportunity to reassess their positions.

In conclusion, the interaction between volatility and margin calls in futures trading underscores the dynamic and interconnected nature of financial markets. Volatility, while presenting opportunities for profit, introduces the risk of margin calls and forced liquidations, especially during periods of extreme market turbulence. Traders must remain vigilant, employ effective risk management strategies, and adapt to changing market conditions to navigate the challenges posed by volatility in the dynamic world of futures contracts. This awareness and proactive approach are essential for maintaining financial stability and seizing opportunities within the ever-evolving landscape of futures trading.

Contango and Backwardation

Understanding the concepts of contango and backwardation is essential for futures traders navigating the complexities of commodity markets. This section delves into the nuances of these market conditions, exploring how they impact futures prices, trading strategies, and the broader economic landscape.

Contango: The Forward Curve's Upslope

Contango is a term used to describe a situation where the futures price of a commodity is higher than its spot price. In a contango market, the forward curve slopes upward, reflecting an expectation of rising prices over time. This phenomenon is common in commodity markets and is influenced by various factors, including carrying costs, storage expenses, and market participants' expectations.

Carrying costs play a significant role in the contango structure. Commodities, such as oil or agricultural products, often incur expenses for storage, insurance, and financing. In a contango market, buyers are willing to pay a premium for the convenience of deferring their purchase to a future date, accounting for these carrying costs. This creates an upward-sloping forward curve, with deferred delivery contracts priced higher than near-term contracts.

Storage expenses contribute to the contango structure by influencing the cost of holding physical commodities. When storage costs are significant, market participants may opt to store commodities in anticipation of future price increases. This behavior further drives up the prices of deferred delivery contracts, reflecting the expenses associated with holding and storing the physical commodity until the agreed-upon delivery date.

Market expectations also play a crucial role in contango. If traders and investors anticipate future supply increases or demand decreases, they may be more inclined to enter into contracts for deferred delivery, anticipating that prices will rise over time. This collective expectation contributes to the upward-sloping nature of the forward curve in a contango market.

Trading Strategies in Contango Markets

Navigating contango markets requires a nuanced approach, and traders employ various strategies to capitalize on or mitigate the implications of this market condition.

1. Roll Yield Strategies: In a contango market, traders may engage in roll yield strategies. This involves selling near-term contracts and buying deferred contracts as they approach maturity. The goal is to capture the price difference between the contracts, taking advantage of the contango structure. However, it's essential to consider transaction costs and potential adverse price movements.

2. Inventory Financing: Contango markets can incentivize participants to build and store inventories of physical commodities. Traders may finance these inventories at relatively low short-term interest rates, capitalizing on the price differential between spot and futures prices. This strategy, known as inventory financing, leverages the contango structure to generate returns.

3. Options Strategies: Options can be employed in contango markets to manage risk and create income. Writing covered call options on physical commodities or futures contracts allows traders to generate premium income while maintaining exposure to potential price increases. This strategy

is particularly relevant in environments where contango is driven by expectations of moderate future price growth.

Backwardation: The Forward Curve's Downward Slope

In contrast to contango, backwardation occurs when the futures price of a commodity is lower than its spot price. This market condition results in a downward-sloping forward curve and is often associated with supply shortages, increased demand, or expectations of future price declines.

Factors Contributing to Backwardation

1. Supply and Demand Dynamics: Backwardation is frequently driven by immediate supply shortages or heightened demand for a commodity. In situations where current demand outstrips immediate supply, buyers are willing to pay a premium for prompt delivery, leading to lower futures prices relative to the spot price.

2. Storage Costs: In backwardation, storage costs play a role in shaping the market structure. If storage expenses are relatively high, market participants may prefer immediate consumption or delivery, avoiding the costs associated with holding and storing the commodity. This preference contributes to lower futures prices.

3. Interest Rates and Financing Costs: The cost of financing and interest rates can impact backwardation. In a market where interest rates are relatively high, the opportunity cost of tying up capital in deferred delivery contracts increases. Traders may opt for immediate delivery, putting downward pressure on futures prices.

Trading Strategies in Backwardation Markets

Backwardation presents distinct opportunities and challenges for traders, and various strategies can be employed to navigate this market condition.

1. Cash and Carry Arbitrage: In a backwardation market, traders may engage in cash and carry arbitrage. This involves buying the physical commodity at the spot price, simultaneously selling a futures contract for future delivery. The goal is to capture the price difference between the spot and futures prices, taking advantage of the backwardation structure.

2. Rolling Down the Curve: Traders can implement a strategy known as "rolling down the curve" in backwardation markets. This involves continually rolling futures positions from more distant expiration dates to nearer dates as contracts approach maturity. This strategy aims to capture the benefits of declining futures prices in a backwardated market.

3. Enhanced Yield Strategies: In a backwardation environment, investors seeking income may explore enhanced yield strategies. These could involve writing put options or engaging in covered put writing to generate premium income while potentially acquiring the commodity at lower prices.

Economic Implications of Contango and Backwardation

Contango and backwardation are not only essential concepts for futures traders but also have broader economic implications.

1. Inflation Expectations: The presence of contango or backwardation in commodity markets can reflect inflation expectations. Contango may indicate expectations of gradual inflation, prompting investors to seek assets that offer protection against rising prices. Conversely, backwardation may suggest concerns about deflation or economic uncertainty.

2. Investment Flows: The contango and backwardation structures can influence investment flows. Investors may allocate capital to commodities or commodity-linked assets based on their expectations of future price movements.

Understanding these market conditions helps investors make informed decisions about asset allocation and portfolio diversification.

3. Supply Chain Management: Companies involved in the production and distribution of physical commodities may adjust their supply chain management strategies based on market structures. In contango, storing inventory for future use may be more cost-effective, while in backwardation, companies may prioritize immediate consumption or delivery to capitalize on lower futures prices.

In conclusion, contango and backwardation are fundamental concepts that shape the dynamics of futures markets and influence trading strategies, investment decisions, and economic considerations. Traders and investors navigating commodity markets must be attuned to the signals provided by these market structures, recognizing the opportunities and risks they present. A nuanced understanding of contango and backwardation enhances participants' ability to formulate effective strategies and adapt to the ever-changing landscape of commodity futures trading.

Hedging vs Speculation

Futures contracts serve diverse purposes for market participants, with two primary motives—hedging and speculation—guiding their utilization. This section delves into the distinctions between hedging and speculation, exploring the objectives, strategies, and implications associated with each approach in the dynamic world of futures trading.

Hedging: Managing Risk in the Real Economy

Hedging is a risk management strategy employed by businesses and individuals to protect against adverse price movements in the physical or financial assets they own or anticipate owning in the future. It is a fundamental application of futures contracts, allowing market participants to mitigate the impact of market volatility on their operations, production costs, or investment portfolios.

1. Objectives of Hedging:

Hedging aims to achieve specific risk management objectives, including:

- Price Stabilization: Businesses exposed to price fluctuations in commodities or inputs can use futures contracts to stabilize their costs. For example, a wheat farmer may hedge against a potential drop in wheat prices by selling wheat futures contracts, locking in a predetermined price for future delivery.

- Revenue Protection: Companies reliant on the sale of commodities can hedge to protect their revenue streams. An airline, concerned about rising fuel costs, may hedge by buying futures contracts for oil, ensuring a fixed cost for future fuel purchases.

- Interest Rate Risk Mitigation: Financial institutions and borrowers may use interest rate futures to hedge against fluctuations in interest rates. This allows them to manage the impact of changing borrowing costs on their financial positions.

2. Hedging Strategies:

Hedging involves taking an offsetting position in the futures market to balance the risk associated with the underlying asset. Common hedging strategies include:

- Long Hedge: A long hedge involves buying futures contracts to protect against the risk of rising prices. This is often employed by businesses that rely on a commodity as an input for production.

- Short Hedge: A short hedge entails selling futures contracts to guard against the risk of falling prices. Businesses that produce and sell commodities may use short hedges to secure prices for their products.

3. Examples of Hedging:

- Agricultural Hedging: Farmers can hedge against the risk of falling crop prices by selling futures contracts for their agricultural products.

- Currency Hedging: Multinational corporations may hedge against currency risk by using futures contracts to lock in exchange rates for future transactions.

- Interest Rate Hedging: Banks can hedge against changes in interest rates by using interest rate futures to lock in borrowing costs or investment returns.

Speculation: Capitalizing on Market Opportunities

Speculation involves taking positions in the futures market with the primary goal of profiting from anticipated price movements. Unlike hedging, which is driven by a need to manage existing risks, speculation is motivated by the pursuit of financial gain based on expectations about future market conditions.

1. Objectives of Speculation:

Speculators engage in futures trading with various objectives, including:

- Profit Maximization: Speculators aim to capitalize on price fluctuations to generate profits. They may take long (buy) or short (sell) positions based on their predictions about the direction of market movements.

- Portfolio Diversification: Investors may use futures contracts to diversify their portfolios and gain exposure to different asset classes, such as commodities, currencies, or interest rates.

- Risk-Taking: Speculators, by nature, accept a higher level of risk in the pursuit of potential returns. They are willing to assume market risk in exchange for the opportunity for financial gain.

2. Speculative Strategies:

Speculation involves a range of strategies aimed at capitalizing on market trends and price movements. Common speculative strategies include:

- Trend Following: Speculators may adopt a trend-following strategy, taking positions in the direction of prevailing market trends to capitalize on momentum.

- Contrarian Investing: Contrarian speculators go against prevailing market sentiment, taking positions based on the expectation of a reversal in market trends.

- Arbitrage: Speculators may engage in arbitrage, exploiting price differentials between related assets or markets to generate risk-free profits.

3. Examples of Speculation:

- Commodity Speculation: Investors may speculate on the future price movements of commodities, such as gold or oil, based on their assessments of supply and demand dynamics.

- Currency Speculation: Traders may speculate on currency pairs, taking positions based on expectations about exchange rate movements.

- Interest Rate Speculation: Investors may engage in interest rate speculation, anticipating changes in interest rates and taking positions in interest rate futures accordingly.

Hedging vs Speculation: A Comparative Analysis

1. Risk Tolerance:

- Hedging: Hedgers are typically risk-averse and seek to mitigate existing risks in their operations or portfolios.

- Speculation: Speculators, by contrast, are more risk-tolerant and accept the possibility of both gains and losses in pursuit of profits.

2. Time Horizon:

- Hedging: Hedging is often focused on the short to medium term, aligning with the time horizon of the underlying business activities.

- Speculation: Speculators may have varying time horizons, with some focused on short-term market trends and others taking a longer-term investment perspective.

3. Market Impact:

- Hedging: Hedging transactions are generally aimed at reducing market impact and stabilizing prices.

- Speculation: Speculative trading can contribute to market volatility as speculators respond to changing market conditions and price movements.

4. Motivation:

- Hedging: The primary motivation for hedging is risk reduction and protection against adverse market movements.

- Speculation: Speculators are motivated by the potential for profit and may actively seek out opportunities in volatile market conditions.

5. Market Function:

- Hedging: Hedging contributes to market efficiency by allowing businesses to manage and transfer risks associated with their operations.

- Speculation: Speculation adds liquidity to markets and facilitates price discovery by bringing participants with different views and expectations.

Conclusion: Balancing the Roles of Hedging and Speculation

In conclusion, hedging and speculation are two distinct yet interconnected functions within the realm of futures trading. Hedging provides a crucial risk management tool for businesses and investors seeking to protect against adverse price movements, stabilize costs, and manage uncertainties in the real economy. On the other hand, speculation injects dynamism into financial markets, fostering liquidity, price discovery, and opportunities for investors to capitalize on market trends.

Successful market participants often strike a balance between hedging and speculation, recognizing the complementary roles these activities play in maintaining market functionality and achieving financial objectives. Whether managing risks in the production of goods or seeking to profit from market movements, an understanding of the nuanced relationship between hedging and speculation is essential for navigating the intricate landscape of futures contracts and contributing to the overall resilience and efficiency of financial markets.

Limiting Outsized Losses

Futures trading offers ample opportunities for profit, but it also comes with inherent risks. Managing and limiting potential losses is a crucial aspect of a successful trading strategy. This section explores various strategies and techniques employed by traders to mitigate the impact of adverse market movements, emphasizing the importance of risk management in the dynamic world of futures contracts.

Understanding the Nature of Risk in Futures Trading:

Before delving into specific risk management strategies, it's essential to understand the nature of risk in futures trading. Futures markets are characterized by inherent volatility, influenced by factors such as economic indicators, geopolitical events, and supply-demand dynamics. Traders face the potential for rapid and substantial price movements, exposing them to the risk of outsized losses.

1. Volatility and Risk Exposure:

- Inherent Nature: Futures contracts, whether on commodities, currencies, or financial instruments, are sensitive to market volatility. Understanding and quantifying this volatility is fundamental to assessing risk exposure.

- Impact on Positions: High volatility can lead to significant price swings, impacting the value of futures positions. Traders must anticipate and manage these fluctuations to avoid outsized losses.

Risk Management Strategies for Futures Traders:

Effective risk management involves a combination of proactive strategies and disciplined execution. Traders employ various techniques to limit potential losses while maintaining the flexibility to capitalize on market opportunities.

1. Setting Stop-Loss Orders:

- Definition and Purpose: A stop-loss order is a predetermined point at which a trader instructs their broker to sell a position to limit losses. It serves as a risk management tool to automatically exit a trade if the market moves against the trader beyond a specified threshold.

- Determining Stop-Loss Levels: Traders must carefully analyze market conditions, technical indicators, and their risk tolerance to set appropriate stop-loss levels. This involves considering factors such as historical price movements and support/resistance levels.

- Dynamic Adjustments: Stop-loss levels should be dynamic and adjusted based on changing market conditions. Traders may use trailing stops, which automatically adjust as the market moves in their favor, locking in profits while protecting against losses.

2. Diversification of Positions:

- Principles of Diversification: Diversifying a portfolio involves spreading risk across different assets, sectors, or markets. In the context of futures trading, having a diversified set of positions can help mitigate the impact of adverse movements in any single market.

- Reducing Correlation Risk: Traders must consider the correlation between different positions to achieve effective diversification. Correlated assets may move in the same direction during market downturns, limiting the diversification benefits.

3. Position Sizing and Leverage Management:

- Determining Position Size: Calculating the appropriate position size is critical for managing risk. Traders should consider the size of their trading account, risk tolerance, and the volatility of the market they are trading.

- Avoiding Excessive Leverage: While leverage can amplify returns, it also increases the risk of significant losses. Traders must exercise caution with leverage, avoiding excessive positions that could lead to outsized drawdowns.

- Utilizing Risk-Reward Ratios: Establishing risk-reward ratios for each trade helps traders assess the potential return against the amount at risk. This ratio guides position sizing and ensures that potential losses are proportionate to expected gains.

4. Utilizing Options for Risk Hedging:

- Buying Protective Puts: Traders can use options, specifically protective puts, to hedge against potential losses in their futures positions. Buying a put option provides the right to sell an asset at a predetermined price, acting as insurance against downside risk.

- Implementing Collar Strategies: Collar strategies involve simultaneously buying protective puts and selling covered calls. This combination limits both potential losses and potential gains, offering a balanced approach to risk management.

- Assessing the Cost of Hedging: While options provide effective risk hedging, traders must consider the cost of purchasing options. This cost impacts overall profitability and should be weighed against the potential benefits of risk reduction.

5. Continuous Monitoring and Adaptation:

- Real-Time Market Monitoring: Risk management is an ongoing process that requires continuous monitoring of market conditions. Traders must stay informed about economic developments, news events, and changes in market sentiment.

- Adapting to Changing Conditions: The ability to adapt to changing market conditions is a hallmark of successful risk management. Traders should be prepared to adjust their risk management strategies based on evolving factors that may impact their positions.

Case Studies and Lessons Learned:

Examining real-world examples of risk management, including both successes and failures, provides valuable insights for futures traders. Case studies can illustrate the application of risk management principles in different market scenarios and highlight the consequences of inadequate risk mitigation strategies.

1. The Barings Bank Collapse:

- Background: The collapse of Barings Bank in 1995 is a notable example of the consequences of inadequate risk management. A single trader, Nick Leeson, engaged in unauthorized speculative trading in Japanese stock index futures, leading to massive losses that eventually bankrupted the bank.

- Lessons Learned: The Barings Bank collapse underscores the importance of strict risk controls, oversight, and adherence to established trading mandates. It serves as a cautionary tale about the potential impact of unchecked speculation and the need for robust risk management frameworks.

2. Long-Term Capital Management (LTCM) Crisis:

- Background: The LTCM crisis in 1998 involved a hedge fund, Long-Term Capital Management, which experienced substantial losses due to its highly leveraged positions in global markets. The crisis had widespread implications for financial markets and required a coordinated intervention by major financial institutions.

- Lessons Learned: The LTCM crisis highlights the risks associated with excessive leverage and the interconnectedness of financial markets. It emphasizes the importance of understanding the broader economic context and the potential systemic impact of outsized losses.

The Psychological Aspect of Risk Management:

Risk management in futures trading extends beyond technical analysis and strategic decisions; it also encompasses the psychological aspect of trading. Emotions such as fear, greed, and overconfidence can influence decision-making and impact risk management effectiveness.

1. Emotional Discipline:

- Controlling Fear and Greed: Fear of losses and greed for additional profits can lead to impulsive and emotionally driven decisions. Traders must cultivate emotional discipline, sticking to pre-established risk management plans and avoiding decisions based on emotional reactions.

- The Role of Confidence: While confidence is crucial, overconfidence can be detrimental. Traders should remain vigilant and humble, acknowledging the uncertainty of markets and the potential for unforeseen events.

2. Maintaining a Trading Journal:

- Recording Trades and Decisions: Keeping a detailed trading journal helps traders assess the effectiveness of their risk management strategies. Recording trades, decisions, and the rationale behind them provides valuable insights for continuous improvement.

- Analyzing Patterns and Behaviors: Regularly reviewing the trading journal allows traders to identify patterns in their decision-making and behaviors. This self-analysis facilitates adjustments to risk management approaches based on lessons learned from both successful and unsuccessful trades.

Conclusion:

Limiting outsized losses in futures trading is a multifaceted endeavor that requires a comprehensive understanding of market dynamics, disciplined execution of risk management strategies, and an awareness of the psychological aspects of trading. Traders who prioritize risk management as an integral part of their overall strategy are better positioned to navigate the challenges of futures markets, preserve capital, and capitalize on opportunities in a dynamic and often unpredictable financial landscape.

Chapter 6: Options Trading
Basics of Call and Put Options

Options trading is a versatile and dynamic financial strategy that involves the use of contracts, known as options, to speculate on or hedge against future price movements. At the core of options trading are two fundamental types of contracts: call options and put options. This section provides an in-depth exploration of the basics of call and put options, unraveling the key concepts, mechanics, and strategies that form the foundation of options trading.

Defining Call and Put Options:

Options are financial instruments that give the holder the right, but not the obligation, to buy (call option) or sell (put option) an underlying asset at a predetermined price, known as the strike price, within a specified time frame. Understanding the distinctions between call and put options is essential for navigating the intricacies of options trading.

Call Options:

A call option provides the holder with the right to buy an underlying asset at the predetermined strike price before or at the option's expiration date. This bullish contract reflects the expectation that the price of the underlying asset will rise.

Mechanics of Call Options:

When an investor purchases a call option, they pay a premium to the option seller. This premium is the cost of acquiring the right to buy the underlying asset at the agreed-upon strike price. If the market price of the asset exceeds the strike price before the option expires, the call option holder can exercise the option, buying the asset at the lower strike price and potentially realizing a profit.

Covered Call Strategy:

One common strategy involving call options is the covered call strategy. In this approach, an investor who already owns the underlying asset sells a call option against it. This generates income in the form of the premium received for selling the call option but limits the potential upside, as the investor is obligated to sell the asset at the strike price if the option is exercised.

Long Call Strategy:

Conversely, the long call strategy involves buying call options without owning the underlying asset. This strategy is purely speculative, allowing the investor to benefit from potential price increases in the underlying asset without committing to ownership.

Put Options:

In contrast, a put option grants the holder the right to sell an underlying asset at the predetermined strike price before or at the option's expiration date. Put options are considered bearish contracts, as they reflect the expectation that the price of the underlying asset will decrease.

Mechanics of Put Options:

When an investor purchases a put option, they pay a premium to the option seller, similar to call options. If the market price of the underlying asset falls below the strike price before the option expires, the put option holder can exercise the option, selling the asset at the higher strike price and potentially profiting from the price decline.

Put Option Strategies:

Protective Put Strategy:

The protective put strategy involves buying a put option to protect an existing long position in the underlying asset. If the market price declines, the put option serves as insurance, limiting potential losses by allowing the investor to sell the asset at the predetermined strike price.

Long Put Strategy:

The long put strategy is a standalone bearish strategy where an investor buys put options without holding the underlying asset. This strategy profits from a decline in the market price of the underlying asset, offering a speculative approach to capitalizing on downward price movements.

Key Considerations in Options Trading:

1. Option Premiums and Intrinsic Value:

The price of an option is composed of two main components: the intrinsic value and the time value. The intrinsic value is the difference between the market price of the underlying asset and the option's strike price. The time value reflects the potential for the option to gain additional value before expiration.

2. Expiration Dates and Time Decay:

Options have expiration dates, indicating the period during which the option can be exercised. As options approach their expiration dates, time decay accelerates, eroding the time value of the option. Traders must carefully consider the impact of time decay when formulating options trading strategies.

3. Strike Prices and Moneyness:

The relationship between the market price of the underlying asset and the option's strike price determines the option's moneyness. In-the-money (ITM) options have intrinsic value, while out-of-the-money (OTM) options only have time value. At-the-money (ATM) options have a strike price equal to the current market price.

4. Implied Volatility and Options Pricing:

Implied volatility reflects the market's expectations of future price fluctuations. Higher implied volatility generally leads to higher option premiums, as increased uncertainty enhances the potential for significant price movements. Traders often analyze implied volatility when selecting options strategies.

Real-World Application:

Understanding the basics of call and put options is crucial for making informed decisions in real-world options trading scenarios. Consider a scenario where an investor anticipates a bullish trend in a particular stock. They may choose to implement a long call strategy, buying call options to capitalize on potential price increases without committing to ownership of the underlying stock. Conversely, if an investor expects a bearish trend, they may opt for a long put strategy to profit from a decline in the stock's market price.

Conclusion:

In conclusion, call and put options form the cornerstone of options trading, offering investors versatile tools for speculation, hedging, and risk management. Mastery of the basics of call and put options is essential for navigating the complexities of options markets and developing effective trading strategies. Whether engaging in covered call strategies, protective put strategies, or purely speculative approaches, options traders must grasp the mechanics, strategies, and key considerations associated with call and put options to make informed and strategic decisions in the dynamic world of options trading.

Leverage Amplifies Both Gains and Losses

One of the defining characteristics of options trading is the concept of leverage. Leverage provides traders with the ability to control a more substantial position in the market with a relatively smaller amount of capital. While leverage can magnify potential gains, it comes with the inherent risk of amplifying losses. This section delves into the dynamics of leverage in options trading, exploring how it can enhance both profits and risks, and the strategies traders employ to navigate this double-edged sword.

Understanding Leverage in Options Trading:

Leverage Defined:

Leverage in options trading is the use of borrowed funds, typically in the form of options contracts, to increase the potential return on investment. It allows traders to control a larger position in the market than the capital they have invested. Leverage is achieved through the use of options premiums, which represent a fraction of the value of the underlying asset.

Options Premiums and Control:

When an investor purchases options contracts, they pay a premium to the options seller. This premium is a fraction of the cost of purchasing the underlying asset outright. The ability to control a more substantial position with a relatively smaller premium outlay is a key aspect of leverage in options trading.

The Dual Nature of Leverage:

Amplifying Gains:

One of the primary attractions of leverage in options trading is its potential to magnify gains. As the market price of the underlying asset moves in the direction anticipated by the trader, the percentage return on the initial premium investment can be significantly higher than the percentage move in the underlying asset's price. This amplification of gains is particularly appealing to traders seeking enhanced returns in a relatively short timeframe.

Magnifying Losses:

However, the flip side of leverage is its capacity to magnify losses. If the market moves against the trader, the premium paid for the options contracts can be lost in its entirety. The risk of significant losses is inherent in leveraged trading, and traders must be acutely aware of the potential downside when employing leveraged strategies.

Strategies for Managing Leverage:

Risk-Reward Analysis:

Effective management of leverage begins with a thorough risk-reward analysis before entering a trade. Traders must assess the potential gains against the potential losses and determine if the risk profile aligns with their overall risk tolerance and trading objectives. This analysis is particularly crucial when considering leveraged strategies such as buying call or put options.

Position Sizing:

Careful position sizing is a critical component of managing leverage. Traders should determine the appropriate size of their options positions based on factors such as the size of their trading account, risk tolerance, and the volatility of the underlying asset. This disciplined approach helps prevent excessive exposure to the risks associated with leverage.

Diversification:

Diversification is a risk management strategy that involves spreading investments across different assets or positions to reduce overall risk. While options trading inherently involves a degree of concentration due to the focus on specific contracts, traders can still diversify their options portfolio by selecting contracts with different expiration dates, strike prices, or underlying assets.

Real-World Examples of Leverage in Options Trading:

Long Call Options:

Consider a scenario where an investor is bullish on the prospects of a particular stock. Instead of purchasing the stock outright, they decide to buy long call options. The premium paid for the call options is significantly lower than the cost of buying the equivalent number of shares. If the stock's price rises as anticipated, the percentage return on the premium investment is amplified, resulting in a potentially substantial gain.

Long Put Options:

Conversely, an investor anticipating a bearish trend may choose to buy long put options. Similar to the long call example, the premium paid for the put options is a fraction of the cost of selling the equivalent number of shares short. If the market price of the underlying asset declines, the percentage return on the premium investment is magnified, leading to a potentially significant profit.

Risk Mitigation and Hedging with Leverage:

Protective Puts:

Options traders can use leverage not only for speculative purposes but also for risk mitigation. Protective puts, for instance, involve purchasing put options to hedge an existing long position in the underlying asset. While this strategy incurs a premium cost, it provides insurance against potential losses in the value of the underlying asset.

Covered Calls:

In a covered call strategy, an investor who owns the underlying asset sells call options against it. While this strategy generates income in the form of the premium received for selling the call options, it also limits the potential upside, acting as a risk management measure against large price increases in the underlying asset.

The Psychological Aspect of Leverage:

Emotional Discipline:

The use of leverage introduces a psychological component to trading that requires discipline and emotional control. The potential for amplified gains may tempt traders to take on excessive risk, while the prospect of magnified losses can evoke fear and anxiety. Emotional discipline is crucial for adhering to risk management plans and avoiding impulsive decisions based on the emotional reactions to market movements.

Stress Testing Strategies:

Traders employing leverage should stress-test their strategies under various market scenarios. This involves simulating the potential outcomes of trades in different market conditions to assess the resilience of their positions to adverse movements. Stress testing helps traders anticipate the impact of unexpected events and adjust their strategies accordingly.

Conclusion: Navigating the Dual Edge of Leverage in Options Trading

In conclusion, leverage is a powerful tool in options trading that can significantly enhance both gains and losses. Traders must approach leverage with a clear understanding of its dual nature, recognizing its potential for profit magnification and risk amplification. Effective risk management strategies, such as careful position sizing, diversification, and the use of protective options strategies, are essential for mitigating the risks associated with leverage. Moreover, maintaining emotional discipline and stress testing strategies contribute to a comprehensive approach to navigating the double-edged sword of leverage in the dynamic and complex landscape of options trading.

Implied Volatility and Pricing

In the world of options trading, the interplay between implied volatility and pricing is a crucial aspect that significantly influences the value of options contracts. Implied volatility represents the market's expectations of future price fluctuations, and understanding how it impacts options pricing is essential for traders seeking to make informed decisions. This section delves into the intricate relationship between implied volatility and options pricing, exploring the factors at play and the strategies traders employ to navigate this dynamic landscape.

Defining Implied Volatility:

Conceptual Framework:

Implied volatility is a forward-looking measure of the expected volatility or price fluctuations of an underlying asset. Unlike historical volatility, which looks at past price movements, implied volatility is derived from the pricing of options contracts. It reflects the consensus view of market participants regarding the potential magnitude of future price changes in the underlying asset.

Options Pricing Model:

The Black-Scholes options pricing model and other advanced models incorporate implied volatility as a key input. In these models, implied volatility serves as a critical factor influencing the theoretical pricing of options. Traders use implied volatility to assess the relative expensiveness or cheapness of options premiums, guiding their decisions on whether to buy or sell options contracts.

Implied Volatility and Options Pricing Dynamics:

Inverse Relationship:

Implied volatility and options prices generally exhibit an inverse relationship. When implied volatility increases, options premiums tend to rise, and when implied volatility decreases, options premiums often decline. This relationship is rooted in the market's anticipation of greater or lesser price fluctuations in the underlying asset.

Options Premium Components:

Options premiums consist of two main components: intrinsic value and time value. Implied volatility primarily impacts the time value portion of the premium. As market expectations for future volatility change, the time value of options adjusts accordingly, influencing the overall premium.

Factors Influencing Implied Volatility:

Market Sentiment:

Implied volatility is, in part, a reflection of market sentiment. Uncertainty or anticipated events, such as earnings reports, economic indicators, or geopolitical developments, can contribute to shifts in market sentiment and, consequently, changes in implied volatility. Traders often monitor these events to gauge potential impacts on options pricing.

Earnings Announcements:

Earnings announcements are notable events that often lead to heightened implied volatility in options contracts. Traders anticipate significant price movements following earnings releases, and the resulting uncertainty is reflected in increased implied volatility. This phenomenon is particularly pronounced in individual stocks.

Market Events and News:

Unforeseen events or breaking news can trigger rapid shifts in implied volatility. Natural disasters, geopolitical tensions, or sudden economic developments can inject uncertainty into the market, prompting adjustments in options pricing to account for the increased likelihood of significant price swings.

Strategies for Trading Implied Volatility:

Volatility Trading Strategies:

Some traders specialize in volatility trading, employing strategies that capitalize on changes in implied volatility. These strategies include:

- Long Volatility Strategies: Traders anticipate an increase in implied volatility and, consequently, options premiums. They may buy options contracts to benefit from potential price movements.

- Short Volatility Strategies: Conversely, traders anticipating a decrease in implied volatility may employ short volatility strategies. This involves selling options contracts to capitalize on declining premiums.

Volatility Skew:

Volatility skew refers to the uneven distribution of implied volatility across different strike prices and expiration dates. Traders often observe volatility skew to identify potential opportunities. Skew can manifest as a "smile" or "smirk" on a volatility graph, indicating differing implied volatilities for options with different strike prices.

Implied Volatility and Options Strategies:

Iron Condor Strategy:

The Iron Condor is an options trading strategy that benefits from a range-bound market with low volatility. Traders sell both a put spread and a call spread, capitalizing on the premium decay resulting from stable or decreasing implied volatility.

Straddle and Strangle Strategies:

In contrast, the Straddle and Strangle strategies are employed when traders anticipate a significant price movement due to increased volatility. These strategies involve buying both a call and a put (Straddle) or out-of-the-money options on both sides (Strangle) to profit from substantial price swings.

Real-World Application of Implied Volatility:

Evaluating Options Premiums:

Consider a scenario where a trader is assessing options premiums for a stock anticipating an earnings announcement. High implied volatility in options contracts expiring around the earnings date may result in elevated premiums. The trader must decide whether the expected price movement justifies the higher cost of options or if it presents an opportunity for a volatility trading strategy.

Adjusting Positions Ahead of Events:

Experienced traders often adjust their options positions ahead of anticipated events. For instance, if implied volatility is expected to rise significantly before an earnings announcement, a trader might choose to adjust their options strategy to capitalize on the expected increase in premiums.

Risk Management in the Context of Implied Volatility:

Position Sensitivity to Changes in Volatility:

Traders should be aware of how changes in implied volatility can impact their options positions. A sudden spike in volatility may lead to increased options premiums, affecting the profitability of existing positions. Conversely, a decline in volatility may result in reduced premiums.

Monitoring Volatility Changes:

Regularly monitoring changes in implied volatility is a crucial aspect of risk management. Traders can use volatility indices, such as the VIX, to gauge overall market volatility.

Additionally, tracking implied volatility for specific options contracts helps traders stay informed about potential changes in options pricing.

Conclusion: Navigating the Complexities of Implied Volatility and Pricing in Options Trading

In conclusion, implied volatility plays a central role in the pricing dynamics of options contracts, exerting a profound influence on their value. Traders must grasp the nuanced relationship between implied volatility and options pricing to make informed decisions in the dynamic and ever-changing landscape of options trading. Whether employing volatility trading strategies, adjusting positions based on anticipated events, or incorporating volatility considerations into risk management, understanding the intricacies of implied volatility enhances a trader's ability to navigate the complexities of options trading with precision and strategic acumen.

Pick Direction Correctly and Time It Right

Options trading is inherently speculative, requiring traders not only to anticipate the correct direction of price movements in the underlying asset but also to time these movements accurately. Success in options trading hinges on the ability to pick direction correctly and time market entries and exits with precision. This section explores the nuanced strategies and considerations involved in making strategic decisions, delving into the art of selecting the right market direction and executing trades at optimal times.

Anticipating Market Direction:

Technical Analysis:

Technical analysis is a cornerstone of predicting market direction in options trading. Traders analyze historical price charts, patterns, and technical indicators to identify trends and potential reversal points. Chart patterns such as head and shoulders, double tops or bottoms, and trendlines provide visual cues that assist traders in forecasting future price movements.

Fundamental Analysis:

Fundamental analysis involves assessing the underlying factors that influence the value of an asset. Traders examine financial statements, economic indicators, and industry trends to form a comprehensive view of the asset's intrinsic value. By understanding the fundamental drivers, traders can make informed predictions about the likely direction of the underlying asset.

Combining Technical and Fundamental Analysis:

Successful options traders often combine technical and fundamental analysis to enhance their decision-making process. While technical analysis provides insights into short-term price movements, fundamental analysis offers a broader perspective on the asset's long-term value and potential catalysts for price changes.

Timing Entries and Exits:

Considerations for Entry Timing:

Timing entries effectively is a critical aspect of options trading. Traders must consider various factors when deciding when to enter a trade, including:

- Volatility Levels: Low volatility environments may favor certain strategies, while high volatility may benefit others. Traders analyze volatility indices, such as the VIX, to gauge market conditions.

- Options Premiums: The cost of options premiums fluctuates based on factors like implied volatility and time decay. Timing entries when premiums are favorable can enhance the risk-reward profile of a trade.

- Economic Events: Scheduled economic events, such as earnings announcements or economic data releases, can impact options pricing. Traders often time their entries to coincide with or precede these events.

Considerations for Exit Timing:

Exiting a trade at the right time is as crucial as entering it strategically. Key considerations for exit timing include:

- Profit Targets and Loss Limits: Setting clear profit targets and loss limits before entering a trade helps traders make disciplined decisions about when to exit. This approach prevents emotional decision-making during volatile market conditions.

- Expiration Dates: For options with fixed expiration dates, traders need to manage exits based on the remaining time until expiration. Exiting too early may result in missed opportunities, while holding too long may expose traders to increased risk.

- Market Conditions: Adapting exit strategies to prevailing market conditions is essential. Traders assess whether market trends are continuing or reversing and adjust their exit plans accordingly.

Strategies for Picking Direction and Timing Entries:

Bullish Strategies:

- Long Call Options: Traders expecting a price increase may choose to buy long call options. Timing the entry to coincide with anticipated upward momentum is crucial to maximizing potential profits.

- Bull Put Spread: This strategy involves selling a put option while simultaneously buying a put option with a lower strike price. Timing the entry when the market is showing strength can optimize the risk-reward profile of the trade.

Bearish Strategies:

- Long Put Options: Traders anticipating a price decrease may opt for long put options. Timing the entry to align with expected downward momentum enhances the likelihood of capturing significant price declines.

- Bear Call Spread: This strategy entails selling a call option and buying a call option with a higher strike price. Timing the entry during periods of expected weakness in the market can improve the risk-reward ratio.

Considerations for Timing in Different Market Conditions:

Sideways Markets:

In sideways or range-bound markets, where the underlying asset's price remains relatively stable, timing entries becomes crucial. Traders may employ strategies like iron condors or calendar spreads that capitalize on low volatility and aim to profit from minimal price fluctuations.

Trending Markets:

During trending markets, where the underlying asset exhibits a clear upward or downward trajectory, timing entries to coincide with the continuation of the trend is paramount. Trend-following strategies, such as trendline analysis or moving averages, assist traders in aligning their entries with the prevailing market direction.

Risk Management in Directional Trading:

Position Sizing:

Effective risk management in directional trading involves determining the appropriate size of positions based on factors such as risk tolerance, account size, and the volatility of the underlying asset. Traders should avoid overleveraging and ensure that each trade aligns with their overall risk management strategy.

Stop-Loss Orders:

Implementing stop-loss orders is a proactive risk management measure. Traders set predetermined price levels at which they will exit a trade to limit potential losses. Stop-loss orders help maintain discipline and prevent emotional decision-making during adverse market movements.

Real-World Application:

Consider a scenario where a trader is bullish on a stock ahead of its earnings announcement. Using a long call option strategy, the trader times the entry to coincide with expectations of positive earnings results and upward price momentum. They carefully consider the expiration date of the option to capture the anticipated price increase within the desired timeframe.

Psychological Considerations in Directional Trading:

Managing Emotions:

Directional trading involves making predictions about future price movements, introducing an emotional component to decision-making. Traders must manage emotions such as fear, greed, and overconfidence to avoid impulsive actions that may deviate from their strategic plans.

Adapting to Changing Conditions:

Successful directional traders are adaptable. They recognize that market conditions can change, and strategies that were effective in one scenario may need adjustment in different conditions. Flexibility and a willingness to reassess and adapt strategies are essential for sustained success.

Conclusion: Mastering the Art of Directional Trading

In conclusion, mastering the art of picking direction correctly and timing entries and exits is a multifaceted skill that combines technical analysis, fundamental insights, and strategic decision-making. Successful options traders develop a nuanced understanding of market dynamics, employing a range of strategies to align their trades with anticipated price movements. By incorporating effective timing considerations, risk management practices, and psychological discipline, traders can navigate the complexities of directional trading with precision, enhancing their ability to make informed decisions in the ever-evolving landscape of options markets.

Advanced Strategies Briefly

As options trading evolves, sophisticated traders seek strategies that go beyond the basics, delving into advanced techniques that offer nuanced approaches to risk and reward. This section provides a concise exploration of various advanced options trading strategies, offering insights into how these approaches leverage market dynamics for enhanced profitability and risk management.

The Complexity of Advanced Options Strategies:

Advanced options strategies are designed for traders with a solid understanding of basic options concepts. These strategies often involve combinations of multiple options contracts, creating intricate positions that require careful consideration of factors such as volatility, time decay, and market direction. Traders should approach advanced strategies with a comprehensive understanding of the associated risks and a clear strategic rationale.

Key Components of Advanced Options Strategies:

Multi-Leg Structures:

Many advanced options strategies involve the use of multi-leg structures, where traders combine different options contracts to create complex positions. Common multi-leg structures include condors, butterflies, and ratio spreads. These strategies allow traders to fine-tune risk exposure and profit potential based on their market outlook.

Synthetic Positions:

Synthetic positions replicate the risk and reward profile of another financial instrument, such as stocks or futures, using a combination of options contracts. Traders may use synthetic positions for purposes like hedging existing investments or gaining exposure to certain assets without directly buying or selling them.

Iron Condors:

One notable advanced strategy is the Iron Condor, a multi-leg options position designed for markets with low volatility. This strategy involves selling both a put spread and a call spread simultaneously. Traders benefit when the underlying asset's price remains within a defined range, allowing them to collect premiums from both sides of the trade.

Butterfly Spreads:

Butterfly spreads are another class of advanced strategies that involve using three strike prices to create a position with limited risk and limited profit potential. Traders implement butterfly spreads when they anticipate minimal price movement in the underlying asset. The structure aims to capitalize on time decay while mitigating the impact of adverse price movements.

Calendar Spreads:

Calendar spreads, also known as time spreads, involve simultaneously buying and selling options with different expiration dates but the same strike price. This strategy capitalizes on the different rates of time decay between short-term and long-term options. Traders may use calendar spreads to generate income or speculate on changes in volatility.

Ratio Spreads:

Ratio spreads involve an uneven number of options contracts, creating a position that is either bullish or bearish. Traders implement ratio spreads to fine-tune their risk exposure and potentially benefit from significant price movements. However, this strategy requires careful consideration of the potential for unlimited losses in certain scenarios.

Straddle and Strangle Variations:

While the Straddle and Strangle strategies are foundational, advanced traders may explore variations to tailor these approaches to specific market conditions. This could involve adjusting the strike prices, expiration dates, or the ratio of call to put options. These variations allow traders to customize their positions based on their expectations for volatility and directional movement.

The Role of Volatility in Advanced Strategies:

Volatility plays a crucial role in advanced options trading strategies. Traders often select strategies based on their expectations for future volatility levels. For example, the Iron Condor and Butterfly spreads are commonly employed in low-volatility environments, while ratio spreads and certain variations of straddle/strangle strategies may be considered in anticipation of increased volatility.

Dynamic Adjustments in Advanced Strategies:

One hallmark of advanced options trading is the ability to make dynamic adjustments to existing positions. Traders actively manage their portfolios by closing, rolling, or adjusting positions based on changing market conditions. This adaptability is crucial for mitigating risk and capitalizing on evolving opportunities.

Real-World Application of Advanced Strategies:

Consider a scenario where a trader anticipates a period of low volatility in a particular stock. Instead of simply buying or selling options, the trader may construct an Iron Condor, selling both a call spread and a put spread with strike prices based on their volatility expectations. If the stock's price remains within the expected range, the trader profits from the collected premiums.

Risk Management in Advanced Options Trading:

Effective risk management is paramount in advanced options trading. Traders should be mindful of the potential for complex positions to result in unexpected outcomes. This includes understanding the impact of changes in volatility, time decay, and market direction on the overall risk profile of the strategy.

Educational Resources for Advanced Strategies:

Given the complexity of advanced options strategies, traders are encouraged to leverage educational resources. This may include books, courses, webinars, and simulation tools that allow traders to practice implementing advanced strategies in a risk-free environment. Continuous learning and practical experience are essential for mastering these sophisticated techniques.

Conclusion: Navigating the Landscape of Advanced Options Trading

In conclusion, advanced options trading strategies offer experienced traders a toolkit of sophisticated techniques to navigate the complexities of the financial markets. From multi-leg structures like Iron Condors and Butterflies to synthetic positions and dynamic adjustments, these strategies provide a nuanced approach to risk and reward. However, it is crucial for traders to approach advanced strategies with a solid foundation of options knowledge, a clear understanding of risk management principles, and a commitment to ongoing education and adaptation in the ever-evolving landscape of options trading.

Chapter 7: Forex Trading
What is Forex and its Size

Forex, short for foreign exchange, represents the decentralized global marketplace where currencies are traded. This vast financial ecosystem plays a pivotal role in the global economy, serving as the linchpin for international trade and investment. In this section, we delve into the fundamental aspects of what forex entails and explore the sheer size and scope of this dynamic market.

Defining Forex: The Currency Marketplace

At its core, forex trading involves the exchange of one currency for another at an agreed-upon exchange rate. Unlike centralized stock markets, the forex market operates 24 hours a day, five days a week, reflecting the continuous nature of global currency trading. Participants in the forex market include banks, financial institutions, corporations, governments, and individual traders, collectively engaging in buying and selling currencies to meet various financial objectives.

The Size and Scope of the Forex Market: A Global Overview

The forex market stands as the largest financial market globally, dwarfing other financial markets in terms of daily trading volume. The sheer magnitude of the forex market is a testament to its significance in the financial landscape.

Daily Trading Volume:

The daily trading volume in the forex market is staggering, reaching trillions of dollars each day. The exact figure can vary, but it is generally estimated to be over $6 trillion as of the last available data. This immense liquidity is one of the key attractions for traders, offering ample opportunities to enter and exit positions with minimal price slippage.

Market Participants:

A diverse array of participants engages in the forex market, each with distinct objectives and motivations. Central banks play a crucial role, managing currency reserves and implementing monetary policies. Commercial banks facilitate transactions and provide liquidity. Corporations engage in forex to manage international trade and hedge against currency risk. Individual traders, ranging from retail to professional, contribute to the market's vibrancy.

The Role of Major Financial Centers:

The forex market is decentralized, with trading occurring across various financial centers worldwide. Notable hubs include London, New York, Tokyo, and Hong Kong. These centers are strategically positioned to overlap during certain hours, creating periods of heightened trading activity and liquidity. The London-New York overlap, in particular, is renowned for its substantial trading volume and volatility.

Major Currency Pairs: The Cornerstone of Forex Trading

In forex, currencies are traded in pairs, with one currency representing the base and the other the quote. Major currency pairs involve the most traded and widely recognized currencies globally. The U.S. dollar is a key player in these pairs, given its status as the world's primary reserve currency. Major pairs include the EUR/USD, USD/JPY, and GBP/USD, among others.

Cross Currency Pairs and Exotic Pairs: Expanding the Landscape

Beyond major pairs, traders encounter cross currency pairs, which do not involve the U.S. dollar. These pairs, such as

EUR/GBP or AUD/JPY, offer alternative trading opportunities and are influenced by factors specific to the currencies involved. Exotic pairs involve one major currency and one from a smaller or emerging-market economy, introducing additional layers of complexity and risk.

Market Participants and Their Roles:

Central Banks:

Central banks wield significant influence in the forex market. They execute monetary policies, intervene in currency markets to stabilize their currencies, and build or deplete foreign exchange reserves. Central bank decisions, such as interest rate changes or interventions, can trigger substantial market movements.

Commercial Banks:

Commercial banks serve as intermediaries in the forex market, facilitating transactions for their clients and engaging in speculative trading. The interbank market, where major banks trade with each other, is a pivotal component of forex liquidity.

Corporations:

Multinational corporations engage in forex for practical purposes, such as managing currency risk associated with international trade. Hedging strategies involving forward contracts or options help these corporations navigate currency fluctuations.

Institutional Investors:

Institutional investors, including pension funds, hedge funds, and asset managers, participate in forex for investment purposes. They employ various strategies, such as carry trading or macroeconomic analysis, to capitalize on currency movements.

Retail Traders:

The advent of online trading platforms has democratized access to the forex market, enabling retail traders to participate. These individual traders engage in speculative trading, often utilizing leverage to amplify their positions. The retail segment contributes to market liquidity but is also characterized by unique challenges and risks.

The Role of Speculation in Forex Trading:

Speculation is a fundamental aspect of forex trading, where participants seek to profit from anticipated currency price movements. Traders analyze various factors, including economic indicators, geopolitical events, and market sentiment, to form hypotheses about future price trends. The ability to accurately speculate on currency movements is central to success in the forex market.

Leverage in Forex Trading: An Amplifier of Opportunities and Risks

One distinctive feature of forex trading is the availability of leverage, allowing traders to control larger positions with a relatively small amount of capital. While leverage enhances profit potential, it also amplifies the risk of significant losses. Proper risk management is crucial when using leverage to navigate the inherent volatility of the forex market.

Market Hours and Overlaps: A Continuous Cycle of Trading

The forex market operates 24 hours a day, five days a week, aligning with the major financial centers' business hours. This continuous cycle creates distinct trading sessions, each characterized by specific market dynamics. The Tokyo, London, and New York sessions are particularly noteworthy, as they represent key periods of market activity.

Factors Influencing Currency Prices:

Economic Indicators:

A myriad of economic indicators, including GDP growth, employment figures, and inflation rates, shape currency values. Traders closely monitor these indicators to gauge the economic health of a country and anticipate potential shifts in monetary policy.

Interest Rates:

Central banks' decisions regarding interest rates significantly impact currency prices. Higher interest rates may attract foreign capital, boosting a currency's value, while lower rates may have the opposite effect.

Geopolitical Events:

Geopolitical events, such as elections, trade negotiations, or geopolitical tensions, can cause sudden and substantial currency movements. Traders must stay informed about global developments to navigate these potentially volatile situations.

Market Sentiment:

Market sentiment, reflected in trends, patterns, and the positioning of market participants, influences currency prices. Traders often use technical analysis to assess sentiment and make informed trading decisions.

Conclusion: Navigating the Vastness of the Forex Market

In conclusion, understanding what forex is and grasping the size and dynamics of this expansive market is fundamental for anyone venturing into currency trading. The global nature of forex, with its continuous trading cycle and diverse participant base, creates a dynamic environment ripe with opportunities and risks. Whether engaging in speculative trading, managing currency risk for international business, or navigating the complexities of central bank interventions, participants in the forex market must possess a nuanced understanding of its intricacies to navigate successfully through its vast and ever-evolving landscape.

Volatility and Liquidity

In the realm of forex trading, two critical factors that significantly impact market dynamics are volatility and liquidity. These elements are integral to understanding price movements, executing effective trading strategies, and managing risk. In this section, we delve into the nuanced interplay between volatility and liquidity in the forex market.

Understanding Volatility in Forex:

Volatility, in the context of forex trading, refers to the degree of variation in a currency pair's price over time. It is a measure of market uncertainty and can have a profound impact on trading outcomes. Traders and investors actively monitor and analyze volatility to make informed decisions about when to enter or exit positions and to adjust their risk management strategies accordingly.

Market Participants and Volatility:

The behavior of market participants contributes to forex market volatility. Economic events, geopolitical developments, and unexpected news can trigger sudden and substantial price movements. Traders must navigate this environment by anticipating potential volatility spikes and incorporating risk mitigation measures into their trading plans.

Volatility Index (VIX) and Forex:

While the Volatility Index (VIX) is commonly associated with equity markets, forex traders often rely on similar indicators to gauge volatility expectations. These indicators help traders assess the level of risk in the market and adjust their strategies accordingly. A rising volatility index may signal increased market uncertainty and the potential for larger price swings.

Factors Influencing Forex Market Volatility:

Economic Indicators:

Key economic indicators, such as GDP growth, employment data, and inflation rates, can influence market expectations and contribute to volatility. Strong or weak economic data releases may prompt currency movements as traders adjust their positions based on the perceived health of an economy.

Interest Rate Decisions:

Central banks' decisions on interest rates are pivotal events that can significantly impact currency volatility. Rate hikes or cuts, as well as the accompanying guidance provided by central banks, can lead to rapid and substantial price adjustments.

Geopolitical Events:

Geopolitical events, including elections, trade negotiations, and geopolitical tensions, can introduce uncertainty into the forex market. Traders closely monitor these events as they unfold, as they have the potential to trigger sudden and unpredictable currency movements.

Market Sentiment:

Market sentiment, reflected in trends, patterns, and the positioning of traders, plays a crucial role in determining volatility. Positive or negative sentiment can create momentum in the market, leading to extended price trends or abrupt reversals.

Adapting to Volatility:

Volatility-Based Trading Strategies:

Some traders actively seek to capitalize on volatility by employing specific trading strategies. For instance, breakout strategies involve entering positions when prices break through established support or resistance levels, taking advantage of heightened volatility. However, these strategies require careful risk management to navigate the potential for false breakouts.

Risk Management in Volatile Markets:

Effective risk management is paramount in volatile markets. Traders should set appropriate stop-loss orders, adjust position sizes based on volatility levels, and avoid excessive leverage. A disciplined approach to risk management helps traders navigate turbulent market conditions while preserving capital.

Liquidity in Forex:

Liquidity refers to the ease with which an asset can be bought or sold in the market without causing a significant impact on its price. In the context of forex trading, liquidity is a crucial consideration, influencing the efficiency and cost of executing trades. Highly liquid currency pairs generally exhibit tight bid-ask spreads and reduced price slippage.

Major vs. Minor Currency Pairs:

Major currency pairs, involving widely traded currencies such as the U.S. dollar, euro, and Japanese yen, tend to be the most liquid. Traders often prefer major pairs for their lower spreads and higher liquidity, facilitating seamless trade execution. Minor or exotic currency pairs, involving currencies from smaller economies, may experience lower liquidity, leading to wider spreads and potentially higher transaction costs.

Factors Influencing Forex Market Liquidity:

Time of Day:

Forex markets exhibit varying levels of liquidity at different times of the day. The market experiences peak liquidity during overlapping sessions of major financial centers, such as the London-New York overlap. During periods of low liquidity, such as weekends or holidays, trading volumes may decrease, leading to wider spreads and increased price slippage.

Economic Releases:

High-impact economic releases, such as central bank announcements or employment reports, can influence liquidity levels. Around these events, traders may observe heightened volatility and reduced liquidity, creating challenges for timely and cost-effective trade execution.

The Interplay Between Volatility and Liquidity:

Volatility and liquidity are interconnected elements in the forex market. While increased volatility can enhance trading opportunities, it may also lead to reduced liquidity, especially during rapid price movements. Traders must navigate this delicate balance, ensuring that they can execute trades efficiently without incurring excessive transaction costs.

Practical Considerations for Traders:

Choosing Optimal Trading Times:

Understanding the ebb and flow of liquidity throughout the trading day is essential for traders. By aligning trading activities with peak liquidity periods, traders can enhance the efficiency of their trade executions and minimize the risk of unfavorable price movements.

Monitoring Economic Calendars:

Traders should stay informed about scheduled economic releases and major events that may impact volatility and liquidity. This awareness allows traders to adjust their strategies, reduce position sizes, or temporarily refrain from trading during periods of heightened uncertainty.

Conclusion: Balancing Act in Forex Trading

In conclusion, navigating the dynamic landscape of forex trading requires a nuanced understanding of the interplay between volatility and liquidity. Traders must adapt to changing market conditions, leveraging volatility for opportunities while managing the associated risks. By incorporating effective risk management strategies and making informed decisions about trade execution based on liquidity considerations, traders can navigate the challenges and capitalize on the opportunities presented by the ever-evolving forex market.

Technical vs. Fundamental Analysis

Within the realm of forex trading, two distinct yet complementary approaches guide traders in their decision-making processes: technical analysis and fundamental analysis. These methodologies provide unique perspectives on market dynamics, helping traders navigate the complexities of the forex market. In this section, we delve into the nuances of technical and fundamental analysis, exploring their principles, strengths, and limitations.

Understanding Technical Analysis: Unveiling Price Patterns and Indicators

Principles of Technical Analysis:

Technical analysis involves the examination of historical price data, chart patterns, and various technical indicators to forecast future price movements. Traders who employ technical analysis believe that historical price patterns and trends tend to repeat, offering insights into potential future market directions.

Chart Patterns:

Chart patterns are a cornerstone of technical analysis, providing visual representations of price movements. Common chart patterns include head and shoulders, double tops and bottoms, triangles, and flags. Analysts interpret these patterns to make predictions about potential trend reversals or continuations.

Technical Indicators:

A myriad of technical indicators aids traders in assessing market trends and momentum. These indicators include moving averages, relative strength index (RSI), stochastic oscillators, and Bollinger Bands, among others. Traders use these tools to identify potential entry and exit points, gauge overbought or oversold conditions, and confirm trend strength.

Support and Resistance:

Support and resistance levels are crucial concepts in technical analysis. Support represents a price level at which a currency pair historically has difficulty falling below, while resistance is a level where the pair has difficulty rising above. Traders use these levels to identify potential entry or exit points and to set stop-loss orders.

Strengths of Technical Analysis:

Short-Term Trading:

Technical analysis is particularly well-suited for short-term trading strategies. Traders can capitalize on intraday price movements and short-term trends by employing technical tools that provide real-time insights into market dynamics.

Objective Decision-Making:

Technical analysis relies on empirical data and mathematical calculations, fostering a more objective approach to decision-making. Traders can use predefined criteria, such as specific technical indicators or chart patterns, to trigger trades or adjust positions.

Visual Representation:

Charts and graphical representations are integral to technical analysis, offering traders a visual depiction of price movements and trends. This visual approach can simplify the interpretation of market dynamics for traders who prefer a graphical representation of data.

Limitations of Technical Analysis:

Historical Data Reliance:

One key limitation of technical analysis is its reliance on historical price data. While historical patterns may offer insights into potential future movements, they do not guarantee future outcomes, and market conditions can evolve.

Inability to Predict Fundamental Shifts:

Technical analysis may struggle to anticipate or interpret major market shifts driven by fundamental factors. Economic events, geopolitical developments, or policy changes can have profound impacts on currency values, and technical analysis alone may not capture these shifts.

Subjectivity in Interpretation:

The interpretation of chart patterns and technical indicators can be subjective, leading different analysts to reach varying conclusions. Traders may use different timeframes or indicators, resulting in diverse analyses of the same market.

Fundamental Analysis: Peering into Economic Drivers and Market Forces

Principles of Fundamental Analysis:

Fundamental analysis involves the examination of economic, political, and social factors that influence currency values. Traders who employ fundamental analysis aim to understand the broader economic context and identify the underlying drivers shaping currency movements.

Key Economic Indicators:

Fundamental analysts closely monitor a range of economic indicators, including GDP growth, employment figures, inflation rates, and interest rates. These indicators provide insights into the health and performance of an economy, influencing currency values based on perceived economic strength or weakness.

Central Bank Policies:

Central banks play a pivotal role in fundamental analysis. Traders scrutinize central bank decisions on interest rates, monetary policy statements, and intervention strategies.

Changes in interest rates, forward guidance, or unexpected policy shifts can trigger significant market reactions.

Geopolitical Events:

Geopolitical events, such as elections, trade negotiations, and geopolitical tensions, can have profound effects on currency values. Fundamental analysts assess the potential impact of these events on economic stability and investor confidence.

Strengths of Fundamental Analysis:

Long-Term Trends:

Fundamental analysis is well-suited for identifying long-term trends driven by economic shifts. Traders relying on fundamental factors may hold positions for extended periods, aligning with the broader economic cycles.

Understanding Market Context:

Fundamental analysis provides traders with a deeper understanding of the broader market context. By examining economic data, political developments, and central bank actions, traders can contextualize short-term price movements within a broader economic narrative.

Anticipating Fundamental Shifts:

Fundamental analysis can be effective in anticipating major market shifts driven by significant economic or geopolitical events. Traders who are adept at interpreting fundamental factors may position themselves ahead of market-moving events.

Limitations of Fundamental Analysis:

Time Lag:

Fundamental analysis may involve a time lag between the release of economic data and its impact on currency values. Traders relying solely on fundamental factors may miss short-term trading opportunities driven by technical patterns or market sentiment.

Complexity and Subjectivity:

Interpreting fundamental factors involves a level of complexity and subjectivity. Different analysts may interpret economic data or geopolitical events in diverse ways, leading to varied conclusions about the potential impact on currency values.

Unexpected Market Reactions:

Market reactions to fundamental events may not always align with expectations. Traders must be prepared for unexpected reactions or market sentiment shifts that may override fundamental factors in the short term.

Finding Synergy: Integrating Technical and Fundamental Analysis

While technical and fundamental analysis are distinct approaches, many successful traders integrate aspects of both to gain a comprehensive view of the market. By combining the strengths of technical tools for short-term trading with a solid understanding of the fundamental drivers shaping long-term trends, traders can make more informed and well-rounded decisions.

Conclusion: Crafting Informed Trading Strategies

In conclusion, the choice between technical and fundamental analysis often boils down to personal preference, trading style, and time horizon. Successful traders understand the strengths and limitations of each approach and may choose to incorporate elements of both to enhance their analytical toolkit. Whether deciphering price patterns on a chart or analyzing the economic forces shaping currency values, a nuanced and adaptive approach to analysis is key to navigating the multifaceted landscape of forex trading.

Risk Management Essentials

In the dynamic and often unpredictable landscape of forex trading, effective risk management is the cornerstone of a successful and sustainable trading strategy. Traders who prioritize risk management not only protect their capital from significant losses but also position themselves to navigate the inherent uncertainties of the market. In this section, we delve into the essential principles of risk management in the forex market.

Understanding Forex Market Risks:

Inherent Volatility:

The forex market is renowned for its inherent volatility, with currency values subject to rapid and unpredictable price movements. Traders must acknowledge the dynamic nature of the market and recognize that even well-informed decisions may not guarantee success in the face of unforeseen events.

Impact of Leverage:

Leverage is a double-edged sword in forex trading. While it magnifies potential profits, it also amplifies the impact of losses. Traders using leverage must be acutely aware of its implications and implement risk management strategies to mitigate the heightened risk associated with leveraged positions.

External Factors:

External factors, such as economic releases, geopolitical events, and unexpected news, can introduce unforeseen volatility into the forex market. Traders must remain vigilant and adapt their risk management approaches to navigate the impact of external events on currency values.

Principles of Effective Risk Management:

Position Sizing:

Determining the appropriate size of a trading position is a fundamental aspect of risk management. Traders should establish position sizes that align with their risk tolerance and account size. This involves setting stop-loss orders based on the level of risk a trader is willing to accept for each trade.

Setting Stop-Loss Orders:

Stop-loss orders are a crucial tool for limiting potential losses. Traders define a predetermined point at which a losing trade will be automatically closed, preventing further downside. Setting stop-loss orders requires a careful consideration of market conditions, volatility, and individual risk tolerance.

Risk-Reward Ratio:

The risk-reward ratio is a key metric in risk management, representing the relationship between the potential loss and potential gain on a trade. Traders often aim for a favorable risk-reward ratio, where the potential reward outweighs the potential loss. Striking a balance that aligns with individual trading objectives is essential.

Adapting to Changing Market Conditions:

Market Conditions and Risk:

Market conditions can vary, influencing the effectiveness of risk management strategies. During periods of heightened volatility, stop-loss orders may be subject to slippage, and market gaps can impact the execution of trades. Traders must adapt their risk management approach to prevailing market conditions.

Correlation Assessment:

Understanding the correlation between currency pairs is crucial for effective risk management. Highly correlated pairs may move in tandem, increasing the risk of overexposure to a particular currency or market event. Diversifying across uncorrelated pairs can help spread risk more effectively.

Risk Management Tools and Techniques:

Trailing Stop-Loss Orders:

Trailing stop-loss orders adjust automatically as a trade moves in a profitable direction. This allows traders to capture potential gains while maintaining a predefined level of risk. Trailing stops are particularly useful in trending markets.

Risk Mitigation through Hedging:

Hedging involves opening a position to offset the risk of an existing trade. While hedging can be a complex strategy, it provides a way for traders to manage risk, especially in situations where market conditions may be uncertain.

Emotional Discipline and Risk Management:

Emotional Impact on Decision-Making:

Emotions can significantly impact decision-making in forex trading. Fear and greed may lead traders to deviate from established risk management plans, potentially exposing them to higher levels of risk. Maintaining emotional discipline is essential for consistent risk management.

Stress Testing Strategies:

Traders should stress-test their risk management strategies under various scenarios to assess their resilience in different market conditions. This involves simulating potential adverse events and evaluating the impact on account equity and overall risk exposure.

Risk Management in Practice: Real-World Examples:

Case Studies:

Examining real-world examples of risk management in practice provides valuable insights for traders. Case studies can illustrate how effective risk management has protected capital in challenging market conditions and highlight the importance of adapting strategies based on lessons learned.

Continuous Improvement and Evaluation:

Reviewing and Adjusting Strategies:

The forex market is dynamic, and trading strategies must evolve to remain effective. Traders should regularly review and adjust their risk management strategies based on changing market conditions, personal performance metrics, and lessons learned from both successful and unsuccessful trades.

Keeping a Trading Journal:

Maintaining a trading journal is a valuable practice for enhancing risk management. Traders can record details of each trade, including entry and exit points, reasons for the trade, and outcomes. Analyzing the trading journal helps identify patterns, strengths, and areas for improvement.

Educating and Empowering Traders:

Educational Resources:

Educational resources on risk management play a vital role in empowering traders. Access to comprehensive materials on risk management principles, strategies, and tools equips traders with the knowledge needed to make informed decisions and safeguard their capital.

Community and Mentorship:

Engaging with a trading community or seeking mentorship from experienced traders provides opportunities for knowledge exchange and mutual support. Learning from the experiences of others can contribute to a trader's growth and development in risk management.

Conclusion: A Pillar of Successful Trading

In conclusion, risk management stands as a pillar of successful forex trading. Traders who prioritize the protection of their capital through effective risk management strategies are better positioned to navigate the complexities of the market. By embracing principles such as position sizing, setting stop-loss orders, and adapting to changing market conditions, traders can enhance their resilience and longevity in the dynamic world of forex trading.

Watch Out for Scams

As traders venture into the expansive realm of forex trading, an awareness of potential scams is paramount. The allure of profit opportunities can sometimes overshadow the risks posed by unscrupulous entities seeking to exploit unsuspecting traders. In this section, we explore the various scams prevalent in the forex market and provide insights on how traders can protect themselves from falling victim to fraudulent schemes.

Recognizing Forex Scams:

False Promises of Guaranteed Profits:

One common hallmark of forex scams is the promise of guaranteed profits with minimal or no risk. Traders should exercise caution when encountering advertisements or platforms that make lofty claims about consistent, high returns without acknowledging the inherent risks associated with forex trading.

Unregulated Brokers:

Scams often involve unregulated or offshore brokers that operate without proper oversight. Traders should verify the regulatory status of a broker before engaging in any transactions. Reputable regulatory bodies, such as the Financial Conduct Authority (FCA) or the U.S. Commodity Futures Trading Commission (CFTC), provide a layer of protection against fraudulent activities.

Pressure Tactics and Urgency:

Scammers frequently employ pressure tactics, creating a sense of urgency to prompt traders into quick decision-making. Whether through unsolicited phone calls, emails, or pop-up advertisements, scammers may press individuals to deposit funds hastily, capitalizing on the fear of missing out on purported lucrative opportunities.

Common Forex Scams:

Ponzi Schemes and Pyramid Schemes:

Ponzi and pyramid schemes are fraudulent investment structures where returns are paid to earlier investors using the capital from newer investors rather than from profit earned. These schemes eventually collapse, leaving later investors with substantial losses.

Signal Seller Scams:

Signal sellers claim to offer foolproof trading signals that guarantee profitable trades. Traders should be wary of individuals or platforms selling signals that promise consistent success, as these may lack transparency and could be designed to manipulate traders into making uninformed decisions.

Robot Trading (Expert Advisors) Scams:

Scammers often promote automated trading systems, also known as Expert Advisors (EAs), that claim to execute profitable trades without human intervention. Traders should approach such offerings with skepticism, as the effectiveness of automated systems can be exaggerated, and losses may be concealed.

Protecting Yourself from Scams:

Research and Due Diligence:

Thorough research and due diligence are crucial elements of protecting oneself from scams. Traders should investigate brokers, signal providers, and investment opportunities before committing any funds. Checking online reviews, verifying regulatory status, and seeking recommendations from reputable sources can provide valuable insights.

Use Reputable Brokers:

Choosing a reputable and regulated broker is a foundational step in avoiding scams. Regulated brokers adhere to strict standards and are subject to oversight, providing traders with a level of assurance regarding the legitimacy of their operations. Researching broker reviews and ensuring compliance with regulatory requirements are essential steps.

Be Skeptical of Unrealistic Promises:

Traders should approach any opportunity that promises guaranteed, high returns with skepticism. Unrealistic promises often serve as red flags for potential scams. A healthy dose of skepticism and critical thinking can prevent falling prey to enticing yet improbable investment claims.

Red Flags and Warning Signs:

Lack of Transparency:

Scams often lack transparency in disclosing key information, such as trading strategies, fees, and associated risks. Traders should be cautious if a platform or service provider is unwilling or unable to provide clear and comprehensive information about its operations.

Pressure to Deposit Funds Quickly:

Any pressure tactics urging traders to deposit funds hastily should raise concerns. Scammers may create a sense of urgency, emphasizing limited-time opportunities, to exploit impulsive decision-making. Traders should take the time to thoroughly evaluate any investment opportunity.

Unsolicited Communications:

Be cautious of unsolicited communications, whether through emails, phone calls, or social media messages, promoting forex investment opportunities. Legitimate brokers and service providers typically do not engage in aggressive marketing tactics.

Reporting Scams and Seeking Assistance:

Regulatory Authorities:

Traders who encounter scams or suspect fraudulent activities should report them to relevant regulatory authorities. Regulatory bodies, such as the National Futures Association (NFA) in the United States or the Financial Conduct Authority (FCA) in the UK, investigate and take action against entities engaging in illegal or deceptive practices.

Law Enforcement Agencies:

In cases of suspected fraud, traders can report scams to law enforcement agencies. Authorities such as the Federal Bureau of Investigation (FBI) in the United States or the Cyber Crime Unit in other jurisdictions may investigate and take legal action against perpetrators.

Conclusion: Staying Vigilant in the Forex Market

In the ever-evolving landscape of forex trading, staying vigilant and informed is paramount for traders seeking to protect their investments. Recognizing common scams, conducting thorough research, and remaining skeptical of unrealistic promises are essential components of safeguarding oneself against fraudulent activities. By arming themselves with knowledge and adopting a cautious approach, traders can navigate the forex market with confidence and resilience against potential scams.

Chapter 8: Newer Cryptocurrencies
The Appeal of Altcoins

As the cryptocurrency landscape continues to evolve, the emergence of alternative cryptocurrencies, or altcoins, has added a layer of complexity and diversity to the digital asset ecosystem. In this section, we delve into the unique appeal of altcoins, exploring the factors that distinguish them from mainstream cryptocurrencies like Bitcoin and Ethereum and examining the various roles they play within the broader crypto market.

Understanding Altcoins: A Diverse Cryptoverse

Beyond Bitcoin:

While Bitcoin remains the flagship cryptocurrency and a foundational element of the crypto market, altcoins encompass a vast array of digital assets that extend beyond the capabilities and features of Bitcoin. Altcoins represent a dynamic and innovative sector within the crypto space, each offering distinct features, use cases, and technological advancements.

Innovation and Specialization:

The appeal of altcoins lies in their capacity for innovation and specialization. Unlike Bitcoin, which primarily serves as a store of value and medium of exchange, altcoins often focus on specific use cases, introducing unique features such as smart contracts, privacy enhancements, or governance mechanisms. This specialization allows altcoins to cater to a diverse range of needs and preferences within the crypto community.

Factors Contributing to the Appeal of Altcoins:

Technological Advancements:

Many altcoins distinguish themselves through technological advancements that address limitations observed in earlier blockchain networks. Features like faster transaction processing times, improved scalability, and enhanced privacy measures contribute to the appeal of altcoins, attracting users seeking alternative solutions to the challenges faced by more established cryptocurrencies.

Smart Contracts and Decentralized Applications (DApps):

Altcoins often integrate smart contract functionality, enabling the creation of decentralized applications (DApps) on their respective blockchains. This feature extends the utility of altcoins beyond simple transactions, allowing developers to build complex applications, tokenized ecosystems, and decentralized financial services on their platforms.

Diversity of Use Cases:

Altcoins contribute to the diversification of use cases within the cryptocurrency space. While some altcoins aim to improve upon existing financial systems, others target specific industries such as healthcare, supply chain management, or identity verification. This diversity allows users to explore digital assets tailored to their specific interests and needs.

The Appeal of Specialized Altcoins:

Privacy Coins:

Privacy-focused altcoins, such as Monero (XMR) and Zcash (ZEC), appeal to users seeking enhanced anonymity in their transactions. These coins employ advanced cryptographic techniques to obfuscate transaction details, providing users with a level of privacy not achievable with transparent blockchains like Bitcoin's.

Stablecoins:

Stablecoins, pegged to the value of fiat currencies, offer price stability compared to the volatility associated with many cryptocurrencies. Tether (USDT), USD Coin (USDC), and Dai (DAI) are examples of stablecoins that appeal to users looking for a reliable medium of exchange and a store of value within the crypto ecosystem.

Navigating the Altcoin Market: Considerations and Risks

Investment Opportunities:

The appeal of altcoins extends to investors seeking diverse investment opportunities in the crypto market. Altcoins often experience price movements independent of Bitcoin, providing potential for profit through strategic trading and investment decisions. However, this also introduces higher volatility and risk compared to more established cryptocurrencies.

Innovation and Experimentation:

Altcoins serve as platforms for experimentation and innovation within the blockchain space. New consensus mechanisms, governance models, and consensus algorithms are often first introduced through altcoins before potentially influencing broader blockchain development. This aspect attracts developers and researchers interested in pushing the technological boundaries of blockchain technology.

Challenges and Risks in Altcoin Investing:

Volatility and Liquidity:

While the potential for profit is an appeal, the inherent volatility of many altcoins poses risks to investors. Sudden and significant price fluctuations are common, and the liquidity of certain altcoins may be lower than that of major cryptocurrencies, leading to challenges in executing trades at desired prices.

Market Saturation and Competition:

The sheer number of altcoins available in the market contributes to heightened competition. Some altcoins may struggle to gain recognition or maintain relevance in a saturated market, making it essential for investors to conduct thorough research before allocating funds to specific projects.

Navigating Altcoin Investments: Strategies for Success

Thorough Research and Due Diligence:

Successful navigation of the altcoin market begins with thorough research and due diligence. Investors should understand the underlying technology, development team, use case, and market potential of any altcoin before considering an investment. This includes evaluating white papers, roadmaps, and the overall credibility of the project.

Diversification Strategies:

Diversification is a key strategy in managing risks associated with altcoin investments. Rather than concentrating funds in a few projects, spreading investments across a well-researched and diversified portfolio of altcoins can help mitigate the impact of underperforming assets.

Conclusion: The Ever-Evolving Altcoin Landscape

In conclusion, the appeal of altcoins lies in their capacity for innovation, specialization, and the diverse array of use cases they bring to the cryptocurrency landscape. Altcoins contribute to the dynamic evolution of blockchain technology, providing users with choices that align with their specific preferences and requirements. As users navigate the ever-expanding altcoin market, a balanced understanding of the opportunities, risks, and strategic considerations is essential for making informed and successful investment decisions.

Lack of Track Record

In the vast and dynamic landscape of newer cryptocurrencies, investors encounter a unique set of challenges, and one prominent aspect is the lack of a track record. Unlike established cryptocurrencies with years of historical data, these emerging digital assets operate in uncharted territory, presenting both opportunities and risks that investors must carefully navigate.

Understanding the Significance of a Track Record:

Historical Performance as a Benchmark:

A track record serves as a historical benchmark for investors, offering insights into how a cryptocurrency has performed in various market conditions. Established cryptocurrencies like Bitcoin and Ethereum have demonstrated resilience, endured market fluctuations, and established a track record that contributes to investor confidence.

Building Trust and Credibility:

A track record contributes to the trust and credibility of a cryptocurrency project. It provides evidence of a project's ability to deliver on its promises, adhere to development timelines, and navigate challenges effectively. Investors often rely on a track record as a measure of a project's reliability and commitment to its objectives.

Challenges Posed by the Lack of Track Record:

Uncertainty and Risk Perception:

Investing in cryptocurrencies with no track record introduces a level of uncertainty and risk perception. Without historical performance data, investors face challenges in assessing how a new cryptocurrency may behave under various market conditions. This uncertainty can impact risk management strategies and decision-making.

Market Volatility and Price Swings:

The lack of a track record contributes to higher volatility and price swings in newer cryptocurrencies. As investors lack historical data to anticipate potential price movements, the market for these assets can be more susceptible to sudden and unpredictable shifts. This heightened volatility requires investors to exercise caution and adapt to rapidly changing market dynamics.

Factors Contributing to the Lack of Track Record:

Recent Project Launches:

Newer cryptocurrencies often lack a track record simply because they are recently launched projects. The absence of historical data is a natural consequence of being in the early stages of development, and investors must consider the challenges and uncertainties associated with investing in these nascent projects.

Evolution of Technology and Concepts:

Innovations in blockchain technology and the introduction of novel concepts contribute to the lack of track record. Projects exploring groundbreaking ideas or unique use cases may not have precedents, making it challenging for investors to gauge how these innovations will fare over time.

Navigating Investments in Cryptocurrencies with No Track Record:

Conducting Thorough Research:

In the absence of a track record, thorough research becomes paramount for investors considering newer cryptocurrencies. Understanding the project's white paper, the expertise of the development team, the technology behind the cryptocurrency, and its potential use cases are crucial components of informed decision-making.

Evaluating Development Roadmaps:

Investors should closely evaluate the development roadmap of a cryptocurrency project. Clear and realistic milestones, coupled with transparent communication from the development team, can provide insights into the project's trajectory and the likelihood of meeting future goals.

Assessing Market Sentiment:

Market sentiment plays a significant role in the success of newer cryptocurrencies. Monitoring community engagement, online forums, and social media discussions can offer insights into the sentiment surrounding a project. Positive sentiment may indicate growing interest and confidence in the cryptocurrency.

Risk Mitigation Strategies:

Diversification:

Diversification is a fundamental risk mitigation strategy when dealing with cryptocurrencies lacking a track record. Spreading investments across a diverse portfolio of established and newer assets can help offset potential losses from underperforming assets and provide a balanced exposure to different market dynamics.

Investing with Caution:

Investors should approach cryptocurrencies with no track record with a cautious mindset. Allocating smaller portions of their portfolio to these assets and gradually increasing exposure as the project demonstrates progress and viability can help manage risk while maintaining potential for returns.

Case Studies: Learning from Past Successes and Failures:

Examining Successful Projects:

Case studies of successful projects without a track record can offer valuable insights. Understanding how these projects navigated challenges, gained community support, and demonstrated the potential for growth can inform investors about characteristics that contribute to success.

Learning from Failures:

Likewise, examining case studies of projects that faced setbacks or failed to gain traction provides important lessons. Understanding the reasons behind failures, whether related to development issues, lack of community engagement, or other factors, can help investors identify potential red flags in newer projects.

Looking Ahead: The Evolution of Track Records:

The Maturation Process:

As newer cryptocurrencies mature and progress through development milestones, they gradually establish a track record. The maturation process involves overcoming early challenges, building a user base, and proving the viability of the project's underlying technology and use cases.

Investor Adaptation:

Investors must adapt to the evolving nature of track records in the cryptocurrency space. As projects develop, investors can reevaluate their positions based on the emerging track record, adjusting their strategies in response to new information and developments.

Conclusion: Navigating the Uncharted Waters

In conclusion, investing in cryptocurrencies without a track record requires a nuanced approach. While challenges and uncertainties exist, thorough research, risk mitigation strategies, and a focus on the evolving landscape can empower investors to navigate the uncharted waters of newer cryptocurrencies. As these projects mature and establish track records, investors play a crucial role in shaping the future of the cryptocurrency ecosystem.

Understanding White Papers

In the world of newer cryptocurrencies, understanding the white paper is akin to deciphering the blueprint of a project. The white paper serves as a foundational document, outlining the vision, technology, and goals of a cryptocurrency project. In this section, we delve into the significance of white papers, the key elements they encompass, and how investors can navigate these crucial documents to make informed decisions.

The White Paper: A Cryptocurrency Project's Manifesto

Introduction to the White Paper:

A white paper is a comprehensive document that introduces and outlines the core aspects of a cryptocurrency project. Often authored by the project's founders or development team, the white paper serves as a manifesto, presenting the project's purpose, technology, functionality, and the problems it aims to solve within the blockchain and cryptocurrency space.

Importance of the White Paper:

The white paper plays a pivotal role in the lifecycle of a cryptocurrency project. It serves as a communication tool that conveys the project's vision to potential investors, developers, and the broader community. Investors rely on white papers to gain insights into a project's fundamentals before deciding to commit funds.

Key Elements of a Cryptocurrency White Paper:

Project Overview:

The white paper typically begins with an overview of the cryptocurrency project. This section provides a high-level understanding of the project's goals, mission, and the specific challenges it aims to address within the cryptocurrency ecosystem. Investors can gain valuable insights into the purpose and utility of the project from this introductory section.

Technology and Architecture:

One of the central components of a white paper is the detailed explanation of the project's technology and architecture. This includes the consensus mechanism, blockchain structure, and any unique technological features that set the project apart. Investors, particularly those with technical backgrounds, can assess the project's innovation and potential technological contributions to the broader blockchain space.

Tokenomics and Economics:

White papers often include a section on tokenomics and economics, detailing the distribution and use of the native cryptocurrency or tokens associated with the project. This section outlines the token's utility within the ecosystem, mechanisms for token issuance, and the economic incentives designed to encourage user participation and network growth.

Navigating the White Paper for Informed Decision-Making:

Thorough Reading and Analysis:

Investors are advised to thoroughly read and analyze the white paper to gain a deep understanding of the project. This involves scrutinizing the technical details, assessing the feasibility of the proposed solutions, and evaluating whether the project addresses a genuine need or gap in the cryptocurrency market.

Assessing the Development Team:

The white paper often provides information about the development team behind the project. Investors should assess the qualifications, experience, and track record of the team members. A competent and experienced team is crucial for the successful execution of the project's vision and goals.

Potential Red Flags and Warning Signs:

Lack of Technical Details:

A white paper that lacks sufficient technical details about the project's architecture, consensus mechanism, or other core components raises a red flag. Investors should be cautious if the document is vague or does not provide clarity on how the technology works.

Unrealistic Promises:

White papers that make unrealistic promises or guarantees of significant returns without acknowledging potential risks should be approached with skepticism. Projects that focus solely on hyping potential gains rather than addressing challenges may lack substance.

Case Studies: Learning from White Paper Successes and Failures:

Success Stories:

Examining successful projects with well-crafted white papers provides valuable lessons. Understanding how these projects communicated their vision, addressed challenges, and executed their plans can offer insights into the characteristics of effective white papers.

Failures and Pitfalls:

Conversely, analyzing failures attributed to inadequately designed or misleading white papers offers crucial insights. Learning from projects that faced difficulties in execution, failed to deliver on promises, or lacked clarity in their white papers helps investors identify potential pitfalls.

Evolving White Papers and Community Engagement:

Community Feedback and Iterations:

Successful cryptocurrency projects often engage with their communities for feedback on the white paper. Iterative improvements based on community input demonstrate a commitment to transparency and a willingness to adapt based on constructive criticism.

Dynamic Nature of White Papers:

White papers can evolve over time as projects mature. Updates, revisions, and supplementary documents may be released to reflect changes in the project's direction, technology, or economic model. Investors should stay informed about any updates to the white paper to maintain an accurate understanding of the project.

Conclusion: Decoding the Cryptocurrency Blueprint

In conclusion, understanding the white paper is a fundamental step in deciphering the blueprint of newer cryptocurrency projects. Investors who take the time to thoroughly analyze these documents gain valuable insights into a project's vision, technology, and potential for success. By navigating white papers with a discerning eye, investors can make informed decisions, contribute to project success, and play an active role in the ever-evolving landscape of the cryptocurrency ecosystem.

Watch Out for Pump and Dumps

In the dynamic world of newer cryptocurrencies, investors must remain vigilant against the ever-present threat of pump and dump schemes. These deceptive practices, characterized by artificially inflating the price of a cryptocurrency followed by a coordinated sell-off, pose significant risks to unsuspecting investors. This section explores the mechanics of pump and dump schemes, red flags to watch out for, and strategies to safeguard investments in a landscape susceptible to market manipulation.

Understanding Pump and Dump Schemes:

Mechanics of a Pump and Dump:

Pump and dump schemes typically unfold in a cyclical pattern. The orchestrators identify a low-cap or newer cryptocurrency with relatively low liquidity. They then initiate a coordinated buying spree, hyping up the project across social media channels and online forums. This influx of buying activity artificially inflates the price of the cryptocurrency, attracting unsuspecting retail investors who believe they are entering a lucrative investment opportunity.

Coordinated Sell-Off:

Once the price reaches a predetermined peak, the orchestrators execute a coordinated sell-off, often leaving retail investors with substantial losses. The sudden and steep decline in price is a result of the orchestrated selling activity, and those who initiated the scheme capitalize on the price surge, leaving other investors holding depreciated assets.

Red Flags and Warning Signs:

Excessive and Hyped Social Media Activity:

Pump and dump schemes often rely on the hype generated through social media channels. Excessive and hyped-up posts across platforms like Twitter, Reddit, and Telegram can be a red flag. Investors should be cautious when witnessing an overwhelmingly positive sentiment without substantial, objective information supporting the price surge.

Unrealistic Promises and Guarantees:

Pump and dump schemes often involve unrealistic promises and guarantees of significant returns. Investors should exercise caution if a project's marketing materials focus more on potential gains than on the underlying technology, use case, or fundamentals of the cryptocurrency.

Analyzing Trading Volume Patterns:

Unusually High Trading Volume:

Before a pump and dump occurs, there is often an unusual spike in trading volume. This spike is a result of the coordinated buying activity by the orchestrators. Investors should be wary of sudden and unexplained increases in trading volume, especially in low-cap or illiquid cryptocurrencies.

Abnormal Price Movements:

Pump and dump schemes result in abnormal and rapid price movements. Investors should scrutinize price charts for sudden spikes followed by equally rapid declines. The absence of organic growth or genuine market demand may indicate that the price movement is orchestrated rather than driven by fundamental factors.

Strategies to Safeguard Investments:

Diligent Research and Due Diligence:

Diligent research is a crucial aspect of safeguarding investments in the cryptocurrency landscape. Investors should conduct thorough due diligence, examining the project's fundamentals, technology, and community engagement. Scrutinizing the white paper, development team, and roadmaps can help distinguish legitimate projects from those susceptible to pump and dump schemes.

Risk Management and Diversification:

Implementing robust risk management practices, including diversification, is essential. By spreading investments across a diverse portfolio of established and reputable cryptocurrencies, investors can mitigate the impact of losses from potential pump and dump schemes. Diversification serves as a protective measure against the inherent volatility of newer cryptocurrencies.

Community Vigilance and Reporting:

Active Participation in Communities:

Being an active participant in cryptocurrency communities provides investors with valuable insights. Engaging in discussions, staying informed about community sentiment, and participating in forums where users share information about potential pump and dump schemes can enhance an investor's awareness and preparedness.

Reporting Suspected Schemes:

Investors play a vital role in safeguarding the community by reporting suspected pump and dump schemes to relevant authorities and platforms. Reporting fraudulent activities to cryptocurrency exchanges, regulatory bodies, and online platforms helps prevent further victimization and contributes to a safer investment environment.

Educational Initiatives and Awareness:

Promoting Education within the Community:

Educational initiatives within the cryptocurrency community can contribute to increased awareness about the risks associated with pump and dump schemes. Investors, influencers, and platforms should actively promote educational content that empowers individuals to recognize and avoid falling prey to market manipulation.

Regulatory Advocacy:

Advocating for regulatory measures and enforcement against pump and dump schemes is essential for the long-term health of the cryptocurrency ecosystem. Engaging with regulatory bodies to enhance oversight and enforcement mechanisms can create a safer environment for investors.

Case Studies: Learning from Past Incidents:

Analyzing Historical Pump and Dumps:

Examining historical pump and dump incidents provides valuable lessons. Understanding the tactics employed, the vulnerabilities exploited, and the consequences for investors offers insights that can inform risk mitigation strategies and contribute to a more informed and vigilant community.

Conclusion: Building Resilience in the Face of Market Manipulation

In conclusion, safeguarding investments in the volatile landscape of newer cryptocurrencies requires vigilance, education, and community participation. By understanding the mechanics of pump and dump schemes, recognizing red flags, and adopting proactive strategies, investors can build resilience and contribute to a more secure and trustworthy cryptocurrency ecosystem. Staying informed and promoting ethical practices within the community is paramount for fostering a sustainable and resilient investment environment.

Long-Term Adoption Still Uncertain

In the ever-evolving landscape of newer cryptocurrencies, the prospect of long-term adoption remains an enigma. This section delves into the complexities surrounding the mainstream acceptance and sustained adoption of these digital assets. Examining the challenges, opportunities, and factors influencing the trajectory of newer cryptocurrencies offers valuable insights for investors navigating the uncertain road to widespread recognition.

The Allure of Innovation and Uncertainty:

Inherent Appeal of Newer Cryptocurrencies:

Newer cryptocurrencies often emerge with promises of innovation, addressing perceived shortcomings in existing projects, or introducing novel concepts that capture the imagination of the crypto community. This inherent appeal attracts early adopters and enthusiasts who are drawn to the potential for groundbreaking technological advancements and disruptive solutions.

Uncertainties Shaping Long-Term Adoption:

Despite the allure, uncertainties loom over the long-term adoption of newer cryptocurrencies. Factors such as regulatory developments, technological maturation, market dynamics, and community sentiment contribute to the uncertainty surrounding the fate of these digital assets.

Regulatory Hurdles and Shifting Sands:

Impact of Regulatory Developments:

Regulatory scrutiny plays a pivotal role in shaping the destiny of newer cryptocurrencies. The evolving regulatory landscape introduces uncertainties that can either hinder or facilitate adoption. Clarity and consistency in regulatory frameworks are essential for fostering an environment where cryptocurrencies can thrive without the constant threat of legal challenges.

Global Variances in Regulation:

The lack of uniformity in global cryptocurrency regulation adds an additional layer of uncertainty. Cryptocurrencies operate in a borderless digital realm, and variations in regulatory approaches from one jurisdiction to another create challenges for projects seeking widespread adoption. Navigating this patchwork of regulations becomes a complex task for both project developers and potential investors.

Technological Evolution and Scaling Challenges:

Continuous Technological Innovation:

Technological evolution is a double-edged sword for newer cryptocurrencies. While ongoing innovation is vital for staying relevant and competitive, rapid changes can pose challenges for achieving widespread adoption. Projects must strike a delicate balance between introducing new features and maintaining a stable and user-friendly ecosystem.

Scaling Solutions and Network Congestion:

Scalability remains a persistent challenge for many newer cryptocurrencies. As projects gain popularity, the limitations of their underlying technology become apparent, leading to issues such as network congestion and transaction delays. Implementing effective scaling solutions is imperative for overcoming these hurdles and ensuring a seamless user experience.

Market Dynamics and Community Sentiment:

Influence of Market Trends:

The volatile nature of the cryptocurrency market introduces uncertainties into the long-term prospects of newer projects. Market trends, investor sentiment, and external factors can significantly impact the adoption trajectory. Projects that can weather market fluctuations and adapt to changing dynamics stand a better chance of achieving sustained adoption.

Community Sentiment as a Driving Force:

The strength of community sentiment is a determining factor in the success of newer cryptocurrencies. A supportive and engaged community can drive adoption by fostering a positive reputation, encouraging development contributions, and attracting new users. Conversely, negative sentiment or internal conflicts can impede progress and hinder widespread acceptance.

Security Concerns and Trust Building:

Addressing Security Challenges:

Security is paramount in the cryptocurrency space, and newer projects must address vulnerabilities to instill trust among users. High-profile security breaches, smart contract vulnerabilities, and hacking incidents have raised concerns about the safety of digital assets. Projects that prioritize and effectively address security challenges are better positioned for long-term adoption.

Building Trust in the Ecosystem:

Trust is a critical component for the sustained adoption of newer cryptocurrencies. Establishing trust involves transparent communication, reliable technology, and a commitment to the project's mission. Projects that can build and maintain trust within the community and among potential users are more likely to overcome skepticism and gain broader acceptance.

Educational Initiatives and User Awareness:

Educating the Masses:

Educational initiatives play a pivotal role in shaping perceptions and fostering adoption. Many potential users and investors remain unfamiliar with the intricacies of blockchain technology and cryptocurrencies. Projects that invest in educational outreach and user awareness campaigns can demystify the technology, debunk myths, and create a more receptive environment for adoption.

User-Friendly Interfaces and Accessibility:

The user experience is a key factor in driving adoption. Newer cryptocurrencies must prioritize user-friendly interfaces and seamless interactions to attract a wider audience. Improving accessibility, simplifying onboarding processes, and ensuring a positive user experience contribute to the overall adoption journey.

Case Studies: Learning from Successes and Setbacks:

Analyzing Success Stories:

Examining successful projects provides valuable insights into the factors that contribute to sustained adoption. Case studies of projects that have overcome challenges, adapted to market dynamics, and achieved widespread recognition offer lessons for aspiring cryptocurrencies.

Understanding Setbacks and Failures:

Conversely, analyzing projects that faced setbacks and struggled to achieve long-term adoption offers critical insights into potential pitfalls. Understanding the reasons behind failures, whether due to regulatory issues, technological shortcomings, or community discord, provides valuable lessons for mitigating risks.

Looking Ahead: Navigating Uncertainty with Resilience:

In conclusion, navigating the uncertain road to long-term adoption requires resilience, adaptability, and a keen understanding of the challenges and opportunities inherent in the cryptocurrency landscape. As newer projects strive to find their place in the broader ecosystem, stakeholders must collaborate to address regulatory hurdles, enhance technological capabilities, build trust, and foster a community-driven approach. By learning from both successes and setbacks, the cryptocurrency community can collectively contribute to shaping a future where newer cryptocurrencies find sustained adoption and recognition on the global stage.

Chapter 9: Microcap Stocks
What Are Microcaps

Microcap stocks, often referred to as "microcaps" or "penny stocks," represent a distinctive segment of the financial markets that attracts a diverse range of investors. This section explores the characteristics, opportunities, and risks associated with microcap stocks, providing a comprehensive understanding of what makes these small-cap investments unique in the realm of financial markets.

Defining Microcap Stocks:

Microcaps in a Nutshell:

Microcap stocks are companies with a relatively small market capitalization, typically ranging from a few million to a few hundred million dollars. These stocks are situated at the lower end of the capitalization spectrum and often trade at lower prices per share compared to larger companies. Microcaps are distinguished by their small size, making them an intriguing yet challenging investment option.

Market Capitalization Criteria:

While there isn't a universally agreed-upon threshold for what constitutes a microcap, they are generally defined by market capitalization. Commonly, microcaps are companies with a market capitalization below $300 million, but this figure can vary depending on different market participants' classifications and criteria.

Characteristics of Microcap Stocks:

Limited Market Capitalization:

The defining characteristic of microcap stocks is their limited market capitalization. This small size can result in heightened volatility, as these stocks are more susceptible to market fluctuations and can experience significant price swings based on relatively small trading volumes.

Lower Liquidity:

Microcap stocks often exhibit lower liquidity compared to larger counterparts. Limited trading activity can lead to wider bid-ask spreads, making it more challenging to execute trades at desired prices. This lower liquidity also means that large trades can have a disproportionate impact on the stock's price.

Greater Price Volatility:

Due to their smaller size and lower liquidity, microcap stocks are prone to greater price volatility. Investors should be prepared for sudden and substantial price movements, which can be triggered by factors such as news releases, earnings reports, or market sentiment shifts.

Opportunities in Microcap Investing:

Potential for High Returns:

One of the primary attractions of microcap investing is the potential for high returns. The lower stock prices allow investors to accumulate a significant number of shares for a relatively modest investment. If a microcap company experiences substantial growth, the percentage gains on the investment can be significant.

Undiscovered Gems:

Microcap stocks may represent undiscovered or overlooked opportunities in the market. These companies, operating in niche industries or with unique business models, might not receive the same level of attention as larger counterparts. Investors who conduct thorough research may uncover hidden gems with growth potential.

Risks Associated with Microcap Investing:

Limited Analyst Coverage:

Microcap stocks often receive limited attention from financial analysts and institutional investors. The lack of in-depth research and analysis can leave investors with less information to base their decisions on, increasing the importance of independent due diligence.

Higher Risk of Fraud:

The smaller size and lower regulatory scrutiny of microcap companies can create an environment where fraudulent activities are more prevalent. Investors in this space must be vigilant against potential scams, pump-and-dump schemes, and other forms of market manipulation.

Financial Reporting Challenges:

Microcap companies may face challenges in meeting stringent financial reporting standards. This can result in less transparent financial disclosures, making it difficult for investors to assess the true financial health and performance of these companies.

Market Dynamics and Microcap Performance:

Market Sentiment Impact:

Microcap stocks are often influenced by market sentiment and investor perception. Positive or negative sentiment, even unrelated to the company's fundamentals, can significantly impact stock prices. This sensitivity to sentiment underscores the importance of staying attuned to broader market trends.

Macro-Economic Factors:

Microcap stocks can be more susceptible to macro-economic factors, such as economic downturns or industry-specific challenges. Economic events that might have a limited impact on larger companies can disproportionately affect the prospects of microcap stocks.

Investing Strategies for Microcaps:

Thorough Due Diligence:

Investors in microcap stocks must conduct thorough due diligence to mitigate risks. This includes analyzing financial statements, understanding the company's business model, assessing the competitive landscape, and evaluating the management team.

Diversification and Risk Management:

Given the inherent risks of microcap investing, diversification is a key strategy. Spreading investments across multiple microcap stocks can help mitigate the impact of poor performance from any single investment.

Case Studies: Learning from Successes and Failures:

Success Stories in Microcap Investing:

Examining success stories in microcap investing provides insights into the factors that contribute to positive outcomes. Understanding how certain microcap stocks achieved substantial growth and recognition can inform investment strategies.

Learning from Setbacks:

Conversely, learning from setbacks and failures is equally crucial. Analyzing instances where microcap investments faced challenges or failed to deliver expected returns offers valuable lessons for risk mitigation and decision-making.

Conclusion: Navigating the Microcap Landscape with Caution and Insight:

In conclusion, microcap investing presents unique opportunities and challenges. Investors intrigued by the potential for high returns must navigate this segment of the market with caution, conducting thorough research, managing risks, and staying informed about market dynamics. Understanding the distinctive characteristics of microcap stocks is essential for making informed investment decisions in this often-uncharted terrain of small-cap investing.

Risks of Low Liquidity and Regulation

Investing in microcap stocks offers potential rewards but comes with its own set of risks, prominently among them being low liquidity and regulatory challenges. This section delves into the intricacies of these risks, exploring how the combination of limited liquidity and regulatory uncertainties shapes the landscape of microcap investing.

Understanding Low Liquidity:

Characteristics of Low Liquidity:

Low liquidity is a hallmark of microcap stocks, stemming from their relatively small market capitalization and reduced trading activity. These stocks often lack the widespread investor interest that fuels liquidity in larger equities, leading to a scenario where a limited number of shares are traded, and the bid-ask spread can be wider.

Impact on Price Volatility:

Low liquidity contributes significantly to heightened price volatility in microcap stocks. With fewer buyers and sellers in the market, a single large transaction can have a pronounced impact on the stock's price. Investors should be aware that the illiquid nature of these stocks can result in sudden and dramatic price movements.

Challenges in Executing Trades:

For investors in microcap stocks, executing trades can be challenging due to low liquidity. The limited number of shares available for trading may result in difficulties buying or selling shares at desired prices. Investors may need to exercise patience and employ strategies to manage the impact of low liquidity on their trades.

The Regulatory Landscape for Microcap Stocks:

Regulatory Oversight Challenges:

Microcap stocks often operate in a regulatory environment that differs significantly from larger, more established companies. Regulatory oversight tends to be less stringent for microcaps, exposing investors to a higher risk of fraudulent activities, market manipulation, and inadequate financial reporting.

SEC Scrutiny and Enforcement:

While microcap stocks are subject to Securities and Exchange Commission (SEC) regulations, the SEC's focus may be more limited compared to larger companies. This can result in less frequent regulatory scrutiny and enforcement actions, creating an environment where bad actors may attempt to take advantage of regulatory gaps.

The Intersection of Low Liquidity and Regulatory Risks:

Vulnerabilities Amplified:

The intersection of low liquidity and regulatory risks creates a scenario where vulnerabilities are amplified. Illiquid markets may be more susceptible to market manipulation, as large trades can disproportionately impact prices. Inadequate regulatory oversight further exacerbates these vulnerabilities, potentially leaving investors exposed to fraudulent schemes.

Potential for Pump-and-Dump Schemes:

Low liquidity provides an opportune environment for pump-and-dump schemes, where manipulative traders artificially inflate the stock price before selling off their shares. In the absence of robust regulatory scrutiny, these schemes can go undetected for longer periods, posing significant risks to unsuspecting investors.

Challenges in Price Discovery:

Limited Price Information:

The limited number of trades and participants in microcap markets can result in challenges related to price discovery. The lack of continuous and diverse trading activity makes it difficult to establish a consensus market price, leading to potential discrepancies between perceived and actual market value.

Impact on Valuation Models:

For investors relying on valuation models and fundamental analysis, the challenges in price discovery can impact the accuracy of these models. The absence of a liquid and efficient market may result in valuations that do not accurately reflect the underlying fundamentals of microcap stocks.

Navigating Risks for Microcap Investors:

Due Diligence as a Risk Mitigation Strategy:

Given the unique risks associated with microcap stocks, due diligence becomes a critical risk mitigation strategy. Investors should conduct thorough research, scrutinize financial statements, assess management quality, and investigate the company's regulatory compliance to mitigate the impact of low liquidity and regulatory uncertainties.

Diversification to Spread Risks:

Diversification is an essential strategy for mitigating risks associated with low liquidity and regulatory challenges. Spreading investments across multiple microcap stocks can help investors reduce exposure to the specific risks of individual companies, enhancing the overall risk-adjusted return profile.

Case Studies: Learning from Real-World Examples:

Instances of Regulatory Challenges:

Examining real-world examples of regulatory challenges in microcap stocks provides valuable insights. Case studies of companies that faced legal actions, regulatory sanctions, or financial reporting discrepancies shed light on the potential pitfalls investors may encounter in this segment.

Impact of Low Liquidity on Stock Performance:

Analyzing the impact of low liquidity on the performance of microcap stocks offers practical lessons. Case studies where low liquidity contributed to extreme price movements or challenges in executing trades provide tangible examples for investors to consider in their decision-making processes.

Conclusion: Navigating the Dual Challenges with Informed Caution:

In conclusion, navigating the risks of low liquidity and regulatory uncertainties in microcap investing requires a combination of informed caution and proactive risk management. Investors must be aware of the unique characteristics of microcap stocks, conduct thorough due diligence, and consider diversification strategies to mitigate the specific risks associated with limited liquidity and regulatory challenges. By learning from case studies and staying attuned to regulatory developments, microcap investors can enhance their ability to navigate the challenges of this dynamic and potentially rewarding segment of the market.

Susceptibility to Manipulation

Within the realm of microcap stocks, a pervasive and concerning risk is their susceptibility to manipulation. This section explores the various dimensions of manipulation in microcap markets, shedding light on the factors that make these stocks particularly vulnerable to illicit activities and the potential consequences for unsuspecting investors.

Understanding Susceptibility to Manipulation:

Characteristics of Microcap Vulnerability:

The susceptibility of microcap stocks to manipulation is deeply rooted in their inherent characteristics. These stocks, with their limited market capitalization and lower liquidity, create an environment where manipulative actors can exert influence over prices more easily than in larger, more liquid markets.

Limited Investor Awareness:

Microcap stocks often operate under the radar, escaping the attention of mainstream investors and financial media. This lack of widespread awareness can be exploited by manipulators who engage in activities to artificially inflate or deflate stock prices without attracting immediate scrutiny.

Manipulation Techniques in Microcap Stocks:

Pump-and-Dump Schemes:

One of the most prevalent forms of manipulation in microcap stocks is the notorious pump-and-dump scheme. In this scenario, manipulators artificially inflate the stock price—often through false or misleading information—to attract unsuspecting investors. Once the price has reached an artificially high level, the manipulators sell off their shares, causing the price to collapse and leaving other investors with significant losses.

Cherry-Picking Positive News:

Manipulators may selectively release positive news or information about a microcap stock to create a temporary surge in investor interest. By strategically timing the release of favorable information, manipulators can induce buying activity, driving up the stock price before exiting their positions.

Factors Contributing to Vulnerability:

Limited Regulatory Oversight:

The limited regulatory oversight in microcap markets contributes significantly to their vulnerability to manipulation. Regulatory bodies, such as the Securities and Exchange Commission (SEC), may have fewer resources dedicated to monitoring and enforcing regulations in the microcap space, allowing manipulative activities to go undetected for more extended periods.

Opaque Financial Reporting:

Microcap companies, facing fewer regulatory requirements than their larger counterparts, may provide less transparent and comprehensive financial reporting. This opacity can be exploited by manipulators, who might take advantage of the lack of detailed financial information to create false narratives about a company's prospects.

Consequences of Manipulation for Investors:

Financial Losses:

The immediate and tangible consequence of manipulation in microcap stocks is financial losses for investors who fall victim to these schemes. Those who buy into artificially inflated prices during a pump-and-dump, for example, may experience substantial losses when the manipulation unravels.

Erosion of Investor Confidence:

Manipulation not only results in financial losses but also erodes investor confidence in the integrity of the market. When investors perceive that a particular market or segment is prone to manipulation, they may become hesitant to participate, undermining the overall trust in the financial system.

Mitigating Manipulation Risks:

Enhanced Regulatory Scrutiny:

To mitigate the susceptibility of microcap stocks to manipulation, there is a need for enhanced regulatory scrutiny. Strengthening the regulatory framework and dedicating more resources to monitoring microcap markets can act as a deterrent and provide a more robust defense against manipulative activities.

Improved Transparency:

Increasing transparency in microcap markets is crucial for mitigating manipulation risks. This includes encouraging companies to provide more comprehensive and accurate financial information, making it more challenging for manipulators to exploit information gaps.

Educating Investors:

Empowering investors with knowledge about the risks of manipulation in microcap stocks is a proactive strategy. Education initiatives, through both regulatory channels and financial institutions, can help investors recognize potential signs of manipulation and make more informed decisions.

Case Studies: Unraveling Manipulation Scenarios:

Real-World Examples:

Examining real-world examples of manipulation in microcap stocks provides valuable insights into the techniques employed by manipulators and the consequences for investors.

Case studies help investors recognize red flags and better understand the dynamics of manipulation.

Conclusion: Vigilance and Awareness in Microcap Investing:

In conclusion, the susceptibility of microcap stocks to manipulation underscores the importance of vigilance and awareness for investors in this segment. Recognizing the potential risks, understanding manipulation techniques, and advocating for regulatory measures to enhance market integrity are crucial steps toward fostering a more secure and trustworthy environment for microcap investing. By staying informed and actively participating in efforts to combat manipulation, investors can navigate the complex dynamics of microcap vulnerability with greater resilience and confidence.

Financial Reporting Standards Lax

Within the realm of microcap stocks, a critical aspect that heightens the complexity of investing is the laxity in financial reporting standards. This section explores the nuances of lax financial reporting standards in microcap companies, shedding light on the challenges investors face when navigating these less regulated waters.

Understanding Lax Financial Reporting Standards:

Defining Laxity in Standards:

Lax financial reporting standards in microcap stocks refer to a situation where these companies operate under less stringent reporting requirements compared to their larger counterparts. This can manifest in various ways, including less frequent reporting, reduced disclosure obligations, and a generally lower level of scrutiny regarding the accuracy and completeness of financial information.

Regulatory Variances:

One of the contributing factors to lax financial reporting standards in microcap stocks is the variance in regulatory requirements. Microcap companies often fall under different regulatory frameworks, which may not demand the same level of transparency and frequency of reporting as larger, more established companies.

Challenges Posed by Lax Financial Reporting:

Opportunities for Manipulation:

Lax financial reporting standards create opportunities for manipulation and misconduct. With fewer disclosure obligations, manipulative actors may exploit information gaps, selectively disclose positive information, or even engage in fraudulent activities without facing immediate regulatory consequences.

Difficulty in Assessing True Financial Health:

For investors, the laxity in financial reporting standards poses a significant challenge in assessing the true financial health of microcap companies. The absence of comprehensive and regularly updated financial information makes it difficult to gauge the company's performance, potential risks, and overall stability accurately.

Impact on Investor Decision-Making:

Limited Information for Informed Decision-Making:

Investors rely on accurate and timely financial information to make informed decisions. Lax financial reporting standards limit the availability of such information, leaving investors in the dark about crucial aspects of a microcap company's operations, financial position, and future prospects.

Increased Investment Risk:

The lack of robust financial reporting standards increases the overall risk for investors in microcap stocks. Without a clear and transparent view of a company's financial condition, investors may unknowingly expose themselves to heightened risks, including potential financial distress, insolvency, or fraudulent activities.

Regulatory Oversight Challenges:

Resource Constraints:

Regulatory bodies, such as the Securities and Exchange Commission (SEC), may face resource constraints when it comes to overseeing the financial reporting of microcap stocks. The sheer volume of these companies, combined with limited regulatory resources, makes it challenging to ensure comprehensive and effective oversight.

Enforcement Delays:

In instances where lax financial reporting standards lead to misconduct, enforcement actions may be delayed. Investigations into financial irregularities can take time, allowing manipulative actors to continue their activities or exit positions before regulatory actions are initiated.

Investor Education and Due Diligence:

Empowering Investors:

Given the challenges posed by lax financial reporting standards, empowering investors becomes crucial. Education initiatives that highlight the risks associated with limited transparency and encourage investors to conduct thorough due diligence can mitigate the impact of lax reporting on investment decision-making.

Importance of Due Diligence:

Investors in microcap stocks must recognize the importance of conducting comprehensive due diligence. This includes scrutinizing available financial statements, assessing management quality, and seeking alternative sources of information to gain a more holistic understanding of a company's financial position.

Case Studies: Lessons from Real-World Examples:

Instances of Financial Reporting Challenges:

Examining real-world examples of financial reporting challenges in microcap stocks provides practical insights into the consequences of lax standards. Case studies can highlight situations where lax reporting contributed to investor losses or where regulatory interventions were necessary to address reporting deficiencies.

Conclusion: Navigating Lax Financial Reporting in Microcap Investing:

In conclusion, the challenges posed by lax financial reporting standards in microcap stocks emphasize the importance of vigilance and due diligence for investors in this segment. Navigating these less regulated waters requires investors to be aware of the limitations in financial reporting, seek additional sources of information, and advocate for improved transparency within the microcap market. By staying informed and adopting a cautious approach, investors can navigate the complexities of lax financial reporting and make more informed decisions in the dynamic landscape of microcap investing.

Diversification Challenges

Within the intricate domain of microcap stocks, the pursuit of diversification—a fundamental principle in investment strategy—faces unique challenges. This section delves into the complexities and nuances that investors encounter when attempting to diversify their portfolios with microcap stocks, shedding light on the specific challenges that set these investments apart.

Understanding Diversification in Microcap Stocks:

Diversification as a Risk Management Strategy:

Diversification is a time-tested risk management strategy that involves spreading investments across different assets to reduce the impact of poor performance in any single investment. In the realm of microcap stocks, this strategy takes on a distinctive character due to the inherent characteristics of these smaller, less-established companies.

Microcap Characteristics and Portfolio Dynamics:

Microcap stocks are characterized by their small market capitalization, lower liquidity, and higher volatility compared to larger counterparts. These characteristics introduce a set of dynamics that can influence the effectiveness of diversification in a portfolio.

Challenges Posed by Microcap Characteristics:

Limited Sector Representation:

Microcap stocks often hail from specific sectors or industries, limiting the range of sectors available for diversification. This concentration can expose investors to sector-specific risks and reduce the effectiveness of diversification in mitigating overall portfolio volatility.

Impact of Liquidity Constraints:

The lower liquidity of microcap stocks can pose challenges when implementing diversification strategies. Limited liquidity may result in higher trading costs, making it less cost-effective for investors to build well-diversified portfolios within the microcap space.

Risk of Correlation and Market Dynamics:

Correlation Challenges:

Microcap stocks may exhibit higher correlation with each other compared to larger stocks, especially during market downturns or periods of heightened volatility. This higher correlation diminishes the effectiveness of diversification, as the performance of multiple microcap stocks may be influenced by common market factors.

Market Dynamics and Sentiment Swings:

The smaller size and limited analyst coverage of microcap stocks can make them more susceptible to market sentiment swings. Diversifying across microcaps does not necessarily insulate a portfolio from broader market sentiment, as these stocks may collectively respond to macroeconomic trends or shifts in investor sentiment.

Portfolio Management Considerations:

Active Management Challenges:

Successfully diversifying a portfolio with microcap stocks often requires active management. Given the dynamic nature of these smaller companies, staying abreast of developments, conducting ongoing due diligence, and adjusting the portfolio in response to changing market conditions become critical components of effective diversification.

Importance of Research and Analysis:

In the microcap arena, the importance of thorough research and analysis cannot be overstated. Diversification becomes more effective when grounded in a deep understanding of individual microcap companies, their growth potential, and the specific risks associated with their respective industries.

Investor Education and Best Practices:

Educating Investors on Microcap Realities:

To navigate diversification challenges in the microcap space, investor education is paramount. Understanding the unique characteristics, risks, and dynamics of microcap stocks equips investors to make informed decisions and adopt strategies that align with the realities of this asset class.

Best Practices for Microcap Diversification:

Implementing best practices in microcap diversification involves adopting a measured approach, recognizing the limitations inherent in this asset class, and actively managing the portfolio to enhance diversification benefits. This may include periodically rebalancing the portfolio, adjusting sector allocations, and considering macroeconomic factors influencing microcap performance.

Case Studies: Illustrating Diversification Dynamics:

Real-World Scenarios:

Examining case studies that illustrate diversification dynamics in microcap investing provides practical insights into the challenges and successes experienced by investors. These real-world scenarios offer valuable lessons on how diversification strategies can be refined and adapted in response to the complexities of the microcap landscape.

Conclusion: Striking a Balance in Microcap Diversification:

In conclusion, diversifying a portfolio with microcap stocks requires a delicate balance between risk and opportunity. Recognizing the challenges posed by limited sector representation, liquidity constraints, and market dynamics allows investors to approach microcap diversification with a nuanced perspective. By integrating active management, in-depth research, and continuous education, investors can navigate the unique diversification challenges presented by microcap stocks and harness their potential within a well-constructed and resilient investment portfolio.

Chapter 10: Ultra High-Yield Bonds
What Are Junk Bonds

Within the realm of ultra high-yield bonds, commonly known as "junk bonds," lies a financial landscape characterized by high risk and potentially lucrative returns. This section delves into the intricacies of junk bonds, providing a comprehensive understanding of what these high-risk debt instruments entail and the unique dynamics that distinguish them in the fixed-income market.

Defining Junk Bonds: A High-Risk Investment Avenue

Understanding the Terminology:

The term "junk bonds" refers to high-yield, high-risk debt securities issued by companies or entities with lower credit ratings. These bonds are often deemed speculative due to the increased likelihood of default compared to investment-grade bonds. Investors are enticed by the higher interest rates offered by junk bonds, compensating for the elevated risk associated with these fixed-income instruments.

Credit Ratings and Risk Assessment:

The classification of a bond as "junk" is typically associated with credit ratings below investment-grade. Credit rating agencies assign ratings based on an issuer's creditworthiness, considering factors such as financial stability, earnings performance, and overall debt burden. Junk bonds, by virtue of their lower credit ratings, signal to investors a higher likelihood of default compared to their investment-grade counterparts.

The Appeal of High Yields:

Attractive Yields Amidst Elevated Risks:

The primary allure of junk bonds lies in their high yields, which exceed those of investment-grade bonds. Investors seeking income-generating assets are drawn to the prospect of higher returns, understanding that they come with an inherent trade-off—increased exposure to credit risk.

Market Conditions and Yield Dynamics:

Junk bond yields are influenced by prevailing market conditions, economic outlook, and interest rate environments. During periods of economic uncertainty or market distress, yields on junk bonds may rise as investors demand higher compensation for taking on increased credit risk. Understanding the interplay between market dynamics and yields is crucial for investors navigating the world of junk bonds.

Risk Spectrum and Default Probability:

Understanding the Risk Spectrum:

Junk bonds occupy a specific position on the risk spectrum, residing below investment-grade securities. This spectrum is a continuum that ranges from low-risk, low-return government bonds to high-risk, high-return junk bonds. Investors in junk bonds knowingly accept a higher level of risk in exchange for the potential for outsized returns.

Default Probability and Impact on Investors:

The increased risk associated with junk bonds is reflected in their higher default probability compared to investment-grade bonds. Investors in this asset class must carefully assess and manage the risk of default, understanding that the potential for higher returns comes with an elevated likelihood of losses in the event of issuer insolvency.

Market Dynamics and Junk Bond Issuers:

Issuer Profile and Industry Concentrations:

Junk bond issuers span a diverse array of industries, including sectors traditionally associated with higher risk, such as technology, energy, and healthcare. Understanding the profile of junk bond issuers and the concentrations within specific industries is crucial for investors seeking to build a diversified portfolio within this asset class.

Market Perception and Sentiment Swings:

Junk bond prices and yields can be highly sensitive to market sentiment and perceptions of economic health. During periods of economic expansion, investors may be more willing to embrace risk, leading to increased demand for junk bonds and lower yields. Conversely, economic downturns can trigger heightened risk aversion, leading to higher yields as investors demand greater compensation for perceived risks.

Regulatory Considerations and Investor Protections:

Regulatory Framework for Junk Bonds:

Junk bond markets operate within a regulatory framework that sets guidelines for issuer disclosures, trading practices, and investor protections. Understanding the regulatory landscape is crucial for investors seeking to navigate the complexities of junk bonds and ensure compliance with relevant rules and regulations.

Investor Protections and Covenants:

Junk bond issuers may include protective covenants in bond agreements to safeguard the interests of investors. These covenants can cover aspects such as restrictions on additional debt issuance, requirements for maintaining certain financial ratios, and provisions for accelerated repayment in the event of specified triggers. Investors must carefully review these covenants to assess the level of protection afforded to them.

Case Studies: Illustrating Junk Bond Dynamics in Real-World Scenarios

Examining Notable Cases:

Analyzing real-world case studies provides valuable insights into the dynamics of junk bonds, showcasing instances where high yields and elevated risks played a pivotal role in shaping investment outcomes. These case studies offer practical lessons for investors navigating the complexities of the junk bond market.

Conclusion: Navigating the High-Risk, High-Reward Landscape of Junk Bonds

In conclusion, junk bonds represent a high-risk, high-reward segment within the fixed-income market. Investors enticed by the allure of attractive yields must navigate the complexities of credit risk, market dynamics, and regulatory considerations. By understanding the defining characteristics of junk bonds, assessing issuer profiles, and staying attuned to market sentiment, investors can make informed decisions within this distinctive and dynamic corner of the financial landscape.

Appeal of High Yields

The allure of high yields is a magnetic force that attracts investors to the realm of ultra high-yield bonds, commonly known as "junk bonds." This section explores the multifaceted appeal of high yields, examining the factors that make these fixed-income instruments enticing for investors seeking robust returns, and the considerations that accompany the pursuit of lucrative yields in the high-risk landscape of junk bonds.

Understanding Yield Dynamics: The Heart of the Attraction

Yield as a Compensation Mechanism:

The yield on a bond is essentially the return an investor can expect to receive, expressed as a percentage of the bond's face value. In the context of ultra high-yield bonds, the term "yield" takes on added significance, serving as a crucial compensation mechanism for investors willing to bear the heightened risk associated with these debt instruments.

Comparative Yields:

What sets ultra high-yield bonds apart is their offering of significantly higher yields compared to their investment-grade counterparts. Investors enticed by the allure of high yields are drawn to the potential for generating substantial income from their fixed-income investments, often surpassing the returns available in more conservative segments of the bond market.

Factors Contributing to the Appeal:

Income Generation in Low-Interest Environments:

In environments characterized by low interest rates, ultra high-yield bonds stand out as a potential solution for investors hungry for income. With traditional fixed-income instruments offering modest yields, the prospect of earning higher returns from junk bonds becomes particularly appealing, especially for income-oriented investors seeking to augment their cash flow.

Portfolio Diversification and Risk-Return Tradeoff:

The appeal of high yields extends beyond income generation; it plays a pivotal role in portfolio diversification. Investors recognize that including high-yield bonds in a diversified portfolio introduces an element of risk, but it also offers the potential for enhanced returns. The risk-return tradeoff becomes a key consideration as investors balance the allure of high yields with the need to manage portfolio risk effectively.

Market Conditions and Yield Dynamics:

Yield Spreads and Economic Indicators:

Yield spreads, the difference between the yields on high-yield bonds and those on comparable Treasury securities, play a crucial role in assessing the attractiveness of junk bonds. Investors often monitor economic indicators and market conditions to gauge the potential for yield spreads to tighten or widen, influencing the relative appeal of high-yield bonds.

Contrarian Investing and Market Opportunities:

The appeal of high yields is accentuated in contrarian investing strategies. During periods of market distress or economic downturns, high-yield bonds may experience price declines, leading to higher yields. Contrarian investors view these downturns as opportunities to enter the market at more favorable valuations, capitalizing on the potential for capital appreciation alongside attractive yields.

Credit Risk Considerations: Balancing Rewards and Risks

Credit Risk as a Determinant of Yields:

The allure of high yields is intrinsically tied to the credit risk associated with junk bonds. Investors accepting higher levels of credit risk demand commensurately higher yields as compensation for the increased likelihood of default. Understanding the delicate balance between the potential for attractive returns and the inherent credit risk is paramount for investors navigating the ultra high-yield bond market.

Default Probability and Risk Management:

Assessing default probability is a critical aspect of managing the appeal of high yields. Investors must weigh the potential for increased income against the risks of issuer insolvency. Robust risk management strategies, including diversification and thorough credit analysis, become essential tools for investors seeking to capitalize on the allure of high yields while mitigating the associated credit risk.

Case Studies: Illustrating Yield Dynamics in Real-World Scenarios

Realizing Potential Returns:

Examining case studies provides tangible insights into how the appeal of high yields translates into real-world investment outcomes. These scenarios offer lessons on recognizing opportunities, managing risk, and understanding the dynamics that influence yield in different market conditions.

Conclusion: Navigating the Allure with Informed Decision-Making

In conclusion, the appeal of high yields in the world of ultra high-yield bonds is a dynamic force that beckons investors with the promise of lucrative returns. Navigating this allure requires a nuanced understanding of yield dynamics, market conditions, and the interplay between risk and reward. By approaching the pursuit of high yields with informed decision-making, investors can harness the potential for enhanced returns while navigating the challenges inherent in the high-risk landscape of junk bonds.

Credit Risk and Default Likelihood

Delving into the realm of ultra high-yield bonds, often colloquially referred to as "junk bonds," demands a thorough exploration of credit risk and default likelihood. This section unravels the intricate dynamics of credit risk in the context of ultra high-yield bonds, shedding light on the factors that contribute to the heightened risk profile of these debt instruments and the implications for investors navigating the complex terrain of high-risk fixed-income assets.

Understanding Credit Risk: The Core Challenge of Junk Bonds

Defining Credit Risk:

Credit risk, in the context of bonds, encompasses the potential for an issuer to default on its debt obligations, leading to financial losses for bondholders. Ultra high-yield bonds, by virtue of their lower credit ratings, inherently carry a higher level of credit risk compared to investment-grade bonds. Investors venturing into this territory must grapple with the challenge of assessing and managing credit risk effectively.

Credit Ratings and Risk Assessment:

Credit ratings assigned by reputable agencies serve as a critical tool for investors evaluating credit risk. Junk bonds typically receive ratings below investment-grade, reflecting the lower creditworthiness of the issuing entities. Understanding the nuances of credit ratings and the factors influencing risk assessments is paramount for investors seeking to make informed decisions within the high-risk landscape.

Factors Contributing to Credit Risk: Deciphering the Complexity

Financial Stability and Earnings Performance:

Assessing the financial stability and earnings performance of issuers is foundational to gauging credit risk. Ultra high-yield bonds are often associated with companies facing financial challenges, whether due to high debt levels, volatile earnings, or other financial stressors. Investors must delve into the financial health of issuers to gauge their ability to meet debt obligations.

Industry and Sector Influences:

Credit risk is not uniform across sectors and industries. Certain sectors, such as technology or energy, may inherently carry higher risk due to factors like rapid technological change, commodity price volatility, or regulatory uncertainties. Investors must consider the industry dynamics when evaluating credit risk within the ultra high-yield bond market.

The Role of Economic Conditions: Sensitivity to Market Dynamics

Macroeconomic Factors and Default Risk:

Ultra high-yield bonds exhibit sensitivity to macroeconomic conditions. Economic downturns, recessions, or periods of market distress can elevate default risk as companies face challenges in generating sufficient cash flow to service their debt. Investors navigating the high-risk terrain must stay attuned to macroeconomic indicators and their potential impact on credit risk.

Interest Rate Environment and Refinancing Risks:

The interest rate environment plays a crucial role in the credit risk landscape. Rising interest rates can increase the cost of debt servicing for issuers, potentially heightening default risks. Additionally, refinancing risks come to the forefront, particularly for companies with maturing debt that must be refinanced under less favorable market conditions.

Assessing Default Likelihood: Quantifying the Risk

Default Probability Metrics:

Quantifying default likelihood involves the use of various metrics and models. Investors often turn to metrics such as the Altman Z-Score, which assesses a company's financial health based on multiple financial ratios. Additionally, credit default swap (CDS) spreads and market-derived default probabilities provide real-time indicators of market perceptions regarding default risk.

Credit Analysis and Due Diligence:

In-depth credit analysis and due diligence are indispensable tools for investors navigating the high-risk landscape of ultra high-yield bonds. This involves scrutinizing financial statements, understanding business models, and assessing management strategies. The goal is to form a comprehensive view of the issuer's creditworthiness and the potential for default.

Mitigating Credit Risk: Strategies for Risk Management

Diversification as a Risk Mitigation Tool:

Diversification is a fundamental strategy for mitigating credit risk in the ultra high-yield bond market. By spreading investments across a diversified portfolio of bonds, investors can reduce exposure to individual issuer risk. Diversification, however, requires careful consideration to avoid overconcentration in specific industries or sectors.

Protective Covenants and Bondholder Safeguards:

Junk bonds may include protective covenants designed to safeguard bondholders' interests. These covenants can include restrictions on additional debt issuance, requirements for maintaining certain financial ratios, and provisions for accelerated repayment in the event of specified triggers.

Investors must carefully review these protective measures to assess the level of protection afforded.

Case Studies: Real-World Examples of Credit Risk Dynamics

Learning from Historical Cases:

Examining historical case studies provides practical insights into credit risk dynamics within the ultra high-yield bond market. Real-world examples illustrate how credit risk can materialize and impact investors, offering valuable lessons for risk assessment and mitigation strategies.

Conclusion: Navigating Credit Risk in the High-Risk Landscape

In conclusion, credit risk and default likelihood are intrinsic challenges within the ultra high-yield bond market. Navigating this complex terrain requires a nuanced understanding of the factors contributing to credit risk, robust risk assessment tools, and effective risk mitigation strategies. By approaching credit risk with diligence and informed decision-making, investors can navigate the high-risk landscape of junk bonds with a greater degree of confidence.

Bond Covenants Matter

In the intricate landscape of ultra high-yield bonds, commonly known as "junk bonds," the significance of bond covenants cannot be overstated. This section unravels the nuanced world of bond covenants and their pivotal role in safeguarding investor interests. From defining bond covenants to exploring their various types and implications, this exploration provides investors with essential insights into the protective measures embedded in the contractual agreements governing these high-risk fixed-income instruments.

Understanding Bond Covenants: Foundations of Investor Protection

Defining Bond Covenants:

Bond covenants are contractual agreements between the issuer of the bond and its bondholders, outlining certain terms and conditions that both parties must adhere to throughout the life of the bond. These agreements serve as a crucial mechanism for protecting investor interests, particularly in the context of ultra high-yield bonds where default risk is elevated.

Types of Bond Covenants: Varied Protections for Bondholders

Affirmative Covenants:

Affirmative covenants represent commitments made by the issuer to take specific actions or maintain certain conditions. These can include requirements for timely financial reporting, maintaining specified financial ratios, or providing regular updates on the issuer's business operations. Affirmative covenants aim to keep bondholders informed and ensure transparency.

Negative Covenants:

Negative covenants, on the other hand, restrict the actions that the issuer can take without the approval of bondholders. These may include limitations on additional debt issuance, restrictions on asset sales, or prohibitions on certain corporate transactions. Negative covenants act as protective measures to prevent actions that could jeopardize bondholder interests.

The Importance of Bond Covenants: Safeguarding Investor Rights

Protecting Against Excessive Risk-Taking:

Bond covenants play a critical role in protecting against excessive risk-taking by issuers. In the high-risk environment of ultra high-yield bonds, restrictions on actions such as incurring additional debt or engaging in speculative ventures are crucial for preventing undue risk that could compromise bondholder interests.

Preserving Collateral and Asset Protection:

In cases where bonds are secured by specific assets or collateral, bond covenants play a pivotal role in preserving the value of these assets for bondholders. Covenants may include restrictions on selling or encumbering collateral without bondholder consent, ensuring that the assets backing the bonds remain intact and available to satisfy bondholder claims.

Negotiating and Drafting Bond Covenants: A Balancing Act

Issuer-Bondholder Dynamics:

The negotiation and drafting of bond covenants involve a delicate balancing act between the interests of issuers and bondholders. Issuers seek flexibility to operate their businesses effectively, while bondholders aim to secure robust protections. The dynamics of this negotiation impact the strength and scope of bond covenants, influencing the level of investor protection afforded.

Legal Counsel and Due Diligence:

The involvement of legal counsel is instrumental in the negotiation and drafting of bond covenants. Legal professionals specializing in securities law and debt instruments guide both issuers and bondholders in crafting covenants that align with their respective interests. Due diligence is paramount to ensure that the covenants effectively address potential risks and contingencies.

Case Studies: Illustrating the Impact of Bond Covenants

Real-World Examples:

Examining case studies provides tangible examples of how bond covenants can impact investor outcomes. Instances where bond covenants were either robust or lacking offer valuable insights into the practical implications of these protective measures in real-world scenarios.

Evolution of Bond Covenants: Responding to Market Dynamics

Adaptation to Changing Conditions:

The landscape of bond covenants evolves in response to changing market conditions, regulatory environments, and investor expectations. The dynamics of the ultra high-yield bond market influence the ongoing adaptation and refinement of bond covenants to address emerging risks and challenges.

Conclusion: Empowering Investors through Informed Covenant Analysis

In conclusion, bond covenants are instrumental in empowering investors within the high-risk realm of ultra high-yield bonds. Understanding the types and importance of covenants, participating in their negotiation, and analyzing their impact through case studies provide investors with the tools needed to navigate the complexities of the bond market effectively. As bond covenants continue to play a central role in investor protection, a proactive and informed approach becomes paramount for those engaging in the world of ultra high-yield bonds.

Recession Impacts

In the dynamic landscape of ultra high-yield bonds, the specter of economic recessions looms as a critical factor shaping the risk profile of these high-yield debt instruments. This section delves into the nuanced impacts of recessions on ultra high-yield bonds, exploring how economic contractions can amplify existing risks and introduce new challenges for investors navigating the complexities of the high-risk fixed-income market.

Understanding Recessions and Their Ramifications

Defining Recessions:

Before delving into the specific impacts on ultra high-yield bonds, it is essential to understand the nature of recessions. Recessions are characterized by a significant decline in economic activity, typically measured by a contraction in gross domestic product (GDP), increased unemployment, and a downturn in various economic indicators. These periods of economic decline can be triggered by various factors, such as financial crises, external shocks, or systemic imbalances.

Heightened Default Risks: The Domino Effect

Default Dynamics during Recessions:

One of the most pronounced impacts of recessions on ultra high-yield bonds is the heightened risk of defaults. Economic contractions place increased strain on companies, particularly those already operating with a high level of debt. As revenue streams dwindle and access to financing becomes more challenging, the likelihood of issuers defaulting on their debt obligations escalates, exposing bondholders to increased default risks.

Sector-Specific Vulnerabilities: Varied Responses to Economic Stress

Sector Sensitivities:

The impact of recessions on ultra high-yield bonds is not uniform across sectors. Certain industries may be more sensitive to economic downturns due to factors such as cyclical demand, exposure to commodities, or susceptibility to changes in consumer spending. Understanding sector-specific vulnerabilities is crucial for investors seeking to navigate the high-risk landscape during recessions.

The Role of Interest Rates: Navigating Monetary Policy Challenges

Interest Rate Dynamics:

During recessions, central banks often implement accommodative monetary policies, including interest rate reductions, to stimulate economic activity. While lower interest rates can be beneficial for companies refinancing debt, they also pose challenges for bond investors seeking attractive yields. The search for yield in a low-interest-rate environment can lead investors to take on additional risks in pursuit of higher returns.

Credit Spreads Widening: Assessing Market Sentiment

Credit Spreads and Investor Sentiment:

Recessions often coincide with widening credit spreads, reflecting increased investor aversion to risk. As market sentiment sours, investors demand higher yields to compensate for the perceived increase in default risk. The widening of credit spreads can impact the pricing and performance of ultra high-yield bonds, influencing investor decisions and portfolio strategies.

Liquidity Challenges: The Unraveling of Market Dynamics

Liquidity Strains during Economic Contractions:

Recessions can trigger liquidity challenges in financial markets, and ultra high-yield bonds are not immune to these dynamics. Reduced market liquidity can exacerbate price volatility, making it more challenging for investors to execute trades and exit positions. Liquidity strains may result in wider bid-ask spreads and increased transaction costs for investors in the high-risk fixed-income space.

Mitigation Strategies: Navigating Recessions with Resilience

Diversification as a Risk Mitigation Tool:

In the face of recession-related challenges, diversification emerges as a key strategy for mitigating risks associated with ultra high-yield bonds. A well-diversified portfolio spanning different sectors and industries can help spread risk and reduce the impact of defaults in any single sector.

Active Portfolio Management: Adapting to Changing Conditions

Dynamic Allocation Strategies:

Active portfolio management becomes crucial during economic downturns. Portfolio managers need to adapt their strategies based on changing market conditions, reassessing risk exposures, and identifying opportunities that may arise amid market dislocations. Proactive decision-making is essential to navigate the challenges and capitalize on potential value in distressed markets.

Case Studies: Real-World Lessons from Recessionary Environments

Learning from Historical Recessions:

Examining case studies from historical recessions provides valuable insights into how ultra high-yield bonds have performed under different economic conditions. Real-world examples offer practical lessons for investors, illustrating the diverse range of outcomes and the importance of adaptive strategies during recessionary periods.

Conclusion: Navigating the Recessionary Landscape of High-Risk Bonds

In conclusion, the impact of recessions on ultra high-yield bonds is a multifaceted challenge that demands a nuanced and adaptive approach from investors. Understanding the dynamics of default risks, sector-specific vulnerabilities, interest rate impacts, and liquidity challenges is essential for navigating the recessionary landscape of high-risk fixed-income instruments. By incorporating resilience and flexibility into investment strategies, investors can better position themselves to weather the challenges and seize opportunities within the complex world of ultra high-yield bonds during economic downturns.

Chapter 11: Penny Stocks
Definition of Penny Stocks

In the vast landscape of financial markets, penny stocks stand as enigmatic entities, often capturing the imagination of investors seeking high-risk, high-reward opportunities. This section aims to demystify penny stocks by delving into their definition, characteristics, and the unique dynamics that distinguish them from more conventional investments. Understanding the essence of penny stocks is the foundational step for investors navigating the treacherous terrain of low-priced securities.

Penny Stocks in a Nutshell: The Basics

Defining Penny Stocks:

At its core, a penny stock refers to a low-priced equity security, typically trading at a price per share well below conventional market thresholds. While there isn't a strict, universally agreed-upon definition based solely on price, penny stocks are generally considered those trading at a value of $5 or less per share. This low price is a defining feature that sets them apart from higher-priced stocks and positions them as accessible to a broad range of investors.

Market Capitalization and Penny Stocks: A Different Scale

Market Capitalization Dynamics:

Beyond the per-share price, another critical factor distinguishing penny stocks is their market capitalization. Market capitalization, calculated by multiplying the stock's price per share by its total outstanding shares, is a key metric reflecting the company's overall value in the market. Penny stocks, often associated with smaller companies, tend to have lower market capitalizations compared to their higher-priced counterparts.

Characteristics of Penny Stocks: The High-Risk Landscape

Volatility and Liquidity Challenges:

Penny stocks are notorious for their heightened volatility, a characteristic stemming from their lower price levels and smaller market capitalizations. This volatility can create opportunities for rapid gains but also exposes investors to significant risks. Additionally, liquidity challenges are prevalent in the penny stock arena, with lower trading volumes making it more difficult to buy or sell shares without impacting the stock's price.

Regulatory Considerations: The OTC Markets and Pink Sheets

Listing on OTC Markets:

Many penny stocks are not listed on major stock exchanges but instead trade on over-the-counter (OTC) markets. The OTC Markets, including the OTCQX, OTCQB, and Pink Sheets, provide a platform for the trading of stocks that do not meet the listing requirements of larger exchanges. Understanding the regulatory landscape of OTC trading is crucial for investors venturing into penny stocks.

Investor Perception and Penny Stocks: Risk and Reward Paradigm

Risk-Return Dynamics:

The allure of penny stocks lies in their potential for substantial returns, often driven by significant price movements within short periods. However, this high-reward potential is inherently tied to elevated risks. Investors must carefully weigh the risk-return dynamics, acknowledging that the same volatility that can lead to rapid gains may also result in substantial losses.

Market Sentiment and Speculation: Shaping Penny Stock Dynamics

Speculative Nature:

Penny stocks are frequently characterized by a speculative nature, with investor sentiment playing a significant role in their price movements. Positive news or rumors can trigger sharp price increases, while negative sentiment or adverse developments can lead to steep declines. The speculative element adds an additional layer of complexity for investors navigating the penny stock landscape.

Market Manipulation and Risks: The Dark Side of Penny Stocks

Manipulation Challenges:

Due to their lower liquidity and market capitalization, penny stocks are susceptible to market manipulation. Pump-and-dump schemes, where the stock's price is artificially inflated (pumped) and then rapidly sold off (dumped), are a common risk. Investors must be vigilant and aware of the potential for manipulation, exercising caution and thorough due diligence.

Investor Caution and Due Diligence: Navigating the Penny Stock Minefield

Due Diligence Imperative:

Given the unique risks associated with penny stocks, thorough due diligence is imperative for investors. Researching the company's financials, understanding its business model, evaluating management, and scrutinizing regulatory filings are essential steps. Investors should approach penny stocks with a cautious mindset, recognizing the potential rewards but also acknowledging the elevated risks inherent in these low-priced securities.

Conclusion: Decoding the Enigma of Penny Stocks

In conclusion, penny stocks represent a distinct and often perplexing segment of the financial markets. Defined by their low price, smaller market capitalization, and elevated volatility, these securities offer a unique set of opportunities and challenges. As investors navigate the enigma of penny stocks, a careful balance of risk and reward, coupled with diligent research and a cautious approach, becomes paramount in unlocking the potential within this high-risk, high-reward corner of the investment landscape.

Risks of Newly Public Companies

The world of penny stocks is often intertwined with the realm of newly public companies, where stocks with low prices find their way to the market for the first time. This section explores the specific risks associated with investing in penny stocks of companies that have recently gone public. From the challenges of untested business models to the uncertainties surrounding financial disclosures, understanding the unique risks posed by newly public companies is essential for investors seeking to navigate the complex landscape of penny stocks.

The Allure of IPOs: A Magnet for Risk-Taking Investors
The Initial Public Offering (IPO) Appeal:

Newly public companies often enter the market with an Initial Public Offering (IPO), marking their transition from private to public ownership. The allure of IPOs lies in the potential for early investors to capitalize on the company's growth, but this transition also introduces a host of risks, particularly when dealing with low-priced stocks characteristic of the penny stock universe.

Untested Business Models: Navigating the Unknown
Challenges of Unproven Models:

One of the inherent risks associated with newly public penny stocks is the untested nature of their business models. Many of these companies operate in sectors that are innovative but unproven, introducing uncertainties about their ability to generate consistent revenue and achieve profitability. Investors must carefully assess the viability of the business model and the company's competitive positioning in the market.

Limited Track Record: The Absence of Historical Performance
The Absence of Historical Performance:

Unlike established companies with a track record of financial performance, newly public companies often lack a comprehensive history of operational and financial success. This absence of historical data makes it challenging for investors to gauge the company's ability to weather economic downturns, adapt to market changes, and sustain growth over the long term.

Financial Reporting Reliability: A Critical Evaluation

Challenges in Financial Reporting:

The reliability of financial reporting becomes a critical consideration when dealing with penny stocks of newly public companies. The process of transitioning from private to public status can introduce complexities in financial reporting, and investors must scrutinize the accuracy and transparency of the company's financial disclosures. Instances of inadequate reporting can obscure the true financial health of the company, posing a significant risk to investors.

Volatility and Liquidity Challenges: The Aftermath of IPOs

Post-IPO Volatility:

The period following an IPO often witnesses heightened volatility in the stock's price. Newly public penny stocks can experience dramatic price swings driven by factors such as investor sentiment, market speculation, and the company's performance. This volatility introduces risks for investors, as rapid price movements may not always be grounded in fundamental factors.

Market Sentiment Fluctuations: The Impact on Penny Stock Dynamics

Sentiment-Driven Fluctuations:

Newly public companies are particularly susceptible to fluctuations in market sentiment. Positive news or negative developments can have outsized impacts on the stock's price, influencing investor perceptions and driving short-term price movements. Investors in newly public penny stocks must be prepared for sudden shifts in market sentiment and the associated impacts on stock performance.

Market Manipulation Risks: Vulnerability to Schemes

Manipulation Vulnerabilities:

The vulnerability of newly public penny stocks to market manipulation adds an additional layer of risk. Pump-and-dump schemes, where the stock's price is artificially inflated and then rapidly sold off, are more prevalent in the early stages of a company's public presence. Investors must exercise caution, recognizing the potential for manipulation and taking steps to mitigate associated risks.

The Importance of Due Diligence: Navigating Risk Through Research

Due Diligence Imperative:

Given the unique risks posed by newly public penny stocks, conducting thorough due diligence is paramount for investors. Scrutinizing the company's financial statements, understanding the competitive landscape, and assessing the management team's track record are essential steps. Investors should be vigilant in their research efforts to identify any red flags or uncertainties associated with the company's recent transition to public trading.

Conclusion: Navigating the Turbulence of Newly Public Penny Stocks

In conclusion, investing in penny stocks of newly public companies is a venture fraught with uncertainties and unique challenges. From untested business models to limited track records and the potential for market manipulation, navigating the risks requires a combination of caution, research, and a thorough understanding of the dynamics at play. While the allure of early-stage growth can be enticing, investors must approach newly public penny stocks with a discerning eye, recognizing the complexities and uncertainties inherent in these high-risk, high-reward opportunities.

Financial Reporting Reliability

Delving into the world of penny stocks requires investors to navigate through a myriad of challenges, and chief among them is the reliability of financial reporting. This section sheds light on the critical aspect of financial reporting reliability, examining the unique dynamics that surround the disclosure practices of penny stocks. From the challenges posed by limited resources to the potential for manipulation, understanding the intricacies of financial reporting reliability is essential for investors seeking to make informed decisions in the unpredictable landscape of low-priced securities.

The Landscape of Financial Reporting: A Penny Stock Paradox

The Dual Nature of Financial Reporting:

Financial reporting serves as the backbone of investor decision-making, offering insights into a company's performance, profitability, and overall financial health. However, in the realm of penny stocks, this essential aspect takes on a dual nature, presenting both opportunities and challenges. While accurate and transparent reporting can instill confidence, the inherent limitations of penny stock companies, such as resource constraints and regulatory disparities, contribute to an environment where reliability becomes a central concern.

Resource Constraints and Reporting Challenges

Penny Stock Companies and Limited Resources:

Many penny stocks operate within the realm of small and micro-cap companies, characterized by limited resources compared to their larger counterparts. This resource constraint extends to financial reporting practices, where these companies may face challenges in maintaining robust accounting and reporting systems. The lack of dedicated financial teams and sophisticated reporting mechanisms introduces an element of vulnerability to the reliability of financial disclosures.

Regulatory Disparities and Reporting Standards

Navigating Regulatory Disparities:

Penny stocks often find themselves subject to different regulatory frameworks than larger, more established companies. The reporting standards for smaller companies may not align with the stringent requirements imposed on their larger counterparts. While these regulatory disparities offer certain flexibilities for penny stocks, they also create an environment where the uniformity and comparability of financial disclosures may be compromised. Investors must be cognizant of these regulatory nuances when assessing the reliability of reported financial information.

The Potential for Manipulation: A Persistent Risk

Manipulation Risks and the Penny Stock Challenge:

Financial reporting in the penny stock arena is not immune to the persistent risk of manipulation. The limited analyst coverage and lower levels of institutional scrutiny create an environment where unscrupulous actors may exploit vulnerabilities. Pump-and-dump schemes, where stock prices are artificially inflated through misleading information, are a recurring threat. Investors must exercise caution, recognizing the potential for manipulation, and undertake comprehensive due diligence to distinguish between genuine performance and deceptive practices.

The Role of Auditing and Independent Reviews

Auditing in the Penny Stock Sphere:

While the absence of comprehensive resources may pose challenges, the role of auditing becomes paramount in enhancing financial reporting reliability. Companies that engage reputable auditing firms demonstrate a commitment to transparency and accountability. Independent reviews conducted by qualified professionals can provide investors with an additional layer of assurance regarding the accuracy and completeness of financial disclosures. Investors should carefully examine the presence and outcomes of audits as part of their due diligence process.

Transparency and Investor Communication

Open Communication Channels:

Financial reporting reliability extends beyond the mere presentation of numbers; it encompasses a company's commitment to transparent communication with investors. Penny stock companies that actively engage with their investor base, provide timely updates, and address inquiries contribute to a more transparent environment. Investors should assess the clarity and completeness of communications from the company's management as a complementary aspect of evaluating financial reporting reliability.

The Importance of Due Diligence: Mitigating Risks Through Research

Due Diligence Imperative:

Given the complexities surrounding financial reporting in the penny stock realm, due diligence becomes a non-negotiable aspect of the investment process. Investors should delve into the company's financial statements, scrutinize the notes and disclosures, and assess the consistency of reporting over time. Thorough due diligence helps discern between companies committed to transparent reporting and those that may raise red flags related to financial reporting reliability.

Conclusion: Navigating the Fog of Financial Reporting in Penny Stocks

In conclusion, the reliability of financial reporting stands as a crucial but intricate aspect of investing in penny stocks. As investors navigate the fog of uncertainty surrounding limited resources, regulatory disparities, and the potential for manipulation, a meticulous approach to due diligence becomes paramount. By understanding the challenges, recognizing the importance of auditing, and actively seeking transparent communication from penny stock companies, investors can better position themselves to make informed decisions in the ever-evolving landscape of low-priced securities.

Volatility and Liquidity Challenges

Venturing into the realm of penny stocks requires investors to confront the inherent dynamics of volatility and liquidity, two intertwined elements that significantly shape the landscape of low-priced securities. In this section, we delve into the unique challenges posed by the volatile nature of penny stocks and the often elusive liquidity that characterizes their trading environment. From rapid price fluctuations to the impact on execution and risk management, understanding these challenges is essential for investors seeking to navigate the turbulent seas of penny stock investments.

The Volatility Conundrum: An Inherent Characteristic of Penny Stocks

Penny Stocks and Inherent Volatility:

Volatility is a defining feature of penny stocks, reflecting the rapid and sometimes unpredictable price movements that characterize these securities. The low market capitalization and limited trading activity of many penny stocks contribute to an environment where even small trades can have outsized impacts on stock prices. Investors in penny stocks must be prepared for a higher degree of price variability compared to more established stocks, acknowledging that volatility can present both opportunities and risks.

Market Sentiment and Penny Stock Volatility

Sentiment-Driven Swings:

Penny stocks, often driven more by sentiment than fundamental factors, are susceptible to dramatic price swings influenced by market perceptions, news releases, or even social media activity. Positive news can trigger rapid upward movements, while negative sentiment can lead to sharp declines. Investors must be attuned to the sentiment-driven nature of penny stocks, recognizing that these securities are particularly responsive to shifts in market perception.

Limited Analyst Coverage and Information Asymmetry

Information Gaps and Limited Analysis:

Penny stocks typically receive limited coverage from financial analysts and mainstream media. This information gap creates an environment where investors may not have access to comprehensive and reliable analyses, leading to a higher degree of uncertainty. The lack of available information can amplify volatility, as investors may react more strongly to new developments or news, lacking the mitigating influence of a broader analyst consensus.

Liquidity Challenges: Navigating the Waters of Sparse Trading

Understanding Liquidity in Penny Stocks:

Liquidity, or the ease with which an asset can be bought or sold without affecting its price, is a critical factor in any investment. In the realm of penny stocks, achieving liquidity can be challenging due to the lower trading volumes and fewer market participants. Investors may find it difficult to execute trades at desired prices, and the bid-ask spread—the difference between the buying and selling prices—can be wider, impacting overall transaction costs.

The Impact on Execution: Slippage and Price Variability

Execution Risks and Slippage:

Liquidity challenges in penny stocks contribute to execution risks, with slippage being a common concern. Slippage occurs when the actual trade execution price differs from the expected price at the time the order was placed. In low-liquidity environments, larger order sizes may lead to more significant price variations, increasing the likelihood of slippage. Investors must consider the potential impact on overall portfolio performance when navigating the waters of penny stock trading.

Risk Management in a Low-Liquidity Environment

Risk Management Strategies:

The limited liquidity of penny stocks necessitates a tailored approach to risk management. Investors should carefully consider position sizes, recognizing that larger positions may be challenging to exit without impacting prices. Stop-loss orders, while a standard risk management tool, require careful calibration in low-liquidity environments to avoid triggering excessive slippage. Diversification becomes a crucial aspect of risk management, spreading exposure across multiple penny stocks to mitigate the impact of volatility in any single security.

The Role of Market Makers and OTC Markets

Market Makers and Over-the-Counter (OTC) Markets:

Market makers play a significant role in providing liquidity to penny stocks, facilitating buying and selling by quoting bid and ask prices. Understanding the role of market makers and the dynamics of Over-the-Counter (OTC) markets, where many penny stocks trade, is essential for investors. OTC markets can lack the centralized exchange structure, further influencing liquidity dynamics and the execution of trades.

Conclusion: Navigating the Seas of Penny Stock Volatility and Liquidity Challenges

In conclusion, the world of penny stocks is marked by its inherent volatility and liquidity challenges, creating an environment that demands careful navigation. Investors must embrace volatility as a characteristic of penny stocks, recognizing its potential for both gains and losses.

Simultaneously, an astute understanding of liquidity dynamics, risk management strategies, and the role of market makers is crucial for those navigating the seas of penny stock investments. By approaching these challenges with diligence and awareness, investors can position themselves to weather the storms and uncover opportunities in the unpredictable world of low-priced securities.

Avoiding Pump and Dumps

In the unpredictable landscape of penny stocks, the specter of market manipulation looms large, and one of the most notorious schemes is the "pump and dump." This section explores the dynamics of pump and dump schemes, offering investors insights into how these manipulative practices unfold and, more importantly, providing strategies to avoid falling victim to such orchestrated market activities.

Understanding Pump and Dump Schemes: The Anatomy of Manipulation

Pump and Dump Defined:

A pump and dump scheme is a form of market manipulation where the price of a stock is artificially inflated, or "pumped up," through the dissemination of misleading information. Once the price reaches an artificially high level, the orchestrators, often the ones spreading the false information, sell off their holdings, causing the price to plummet—the "dump" phase. Unwitting investors who bought into the inflated hype are left with substantial losses.

Identifying the Warning Signs: Red Flags of Manipulation

Aggressive Hype and Unsubstantiated Claims:

Pump and dump schemes often start with aggressive promotion and hype, typically disseminated through social media, email newsletters, or online forums. Investors should be wary of penny stock promotions that make grandiose claims without substantial evidence or credible sources. Unsubstantiated promises of astronomical returns and guaranteed profits should raise red flags, prompting investors to scrutinize the legitimacy of the information.

Low Liquidity and Thin Trading Volumes

Liquidity as a Manipulation Indicator:

Pump and dump schemes thrive in low-liquidity environments, taking advantage of thin trading volumes to artificially inflate prices. Investors should be cautious when trading penny stocks with exceptionally low average daily volumes, as these may be susceptible to manipulation. Illiquid stocks can experience exaggerated price movements, making it easier for manipulators to create artificial spikes and subsequent dumps.

Sudden and Unexplained Price Spikes

Suspicious Price Movements:

Pump and dump schemes often involve rapid and unexplained price spikes in a short period. Investors should be alert to sudden, abnormal increases in a stock's price without corresponding fundamental developments. Analyzing the trading patterns and identifying instances where price movements deviate from typical market behavior can serve as an early warning system for potential manipulation.

Promoter Track Record and Credibility

Vetting Promoters and Information Sources:

Penny stock promotions are frequently orchestrated by third-party promoters who may have a history of involvement in dubious schemes. Investors should conduct due diligence on the promoters behind the stock recommendations, assessing their track record and credibility. Reputable promoters prioritize transparency, while those with a history of pump and dump involvement may exhibit a pattern of frequent stock promotions with questionable results.

Strategies to Avoid Falling Victim: Protecting Your Investments

Thorough Due Diligence:

One of the most effective strategies to avoid falling victim to pump and dumps is thorough due diligence. Investors should scrutinize the company's fundamentals, financial health, and business model before considering any investment. Verifying the accuracy of the information provided and cross-referencing data from multiple sources can help discern between legitimate opportunities and orchestrated pump and dump schemes.

Risk Management and Diversification

Risk Mitigation Through Diversification:

Diversification is a fundamental principle of risk management that holds particular importance in the volatile world of penny stocks. By spreading investments across multiple securities, investors can mitigate the impact of losses from a single stock that may fall victim to manipulation. Diversification should be approached strategically, considering the risk profiles of individual stocks and industries.

Setting Realistic Expectations and Goals

Tempering Expectations:

Investors should set realistic expectations and goals when engaging with penny stocks. Recognizing that the potential for manipulation exists, it is crucial to approach these investments with a level-headed mindset. Unrealistic expectations of rapid and astronomical returns may make investors more susceptible to falling for pump and dump schemes. A disciplined approach to investing, grounded in realistic expectations, can serve as a protective barrier against manipulation.

Monitoring and Exit Strategies

Vigilance and Exit Plans:

Active monitoring of investments is essential in the penny stock arena. Investors should stay vigilant for any signs of manipulation and be prepared to exit positions promptly if red flags emerge. Establishing clear exit strategies, such as setting stop-loss orders or profit-taking targets, can help investors respond decisively to changing market conditions and protect their capital from the potential fallout of pump and dump schemes.

Reporting Suspected Manipulation: Contributing to Market Integrity

Taking a Proactive Stance:

Investors play a crucial role in maintaining market integrity by reporting suspected cases of manipulation. Regulatory bodies rely on the vigilance of market participants to identify and investigate potential pump and dump schemes. By taking a proactive stance and reporting suspicious activities to relevant authorities, investors contribute to a safer and more transparent investment environment for themselves and others.

Conclusion: Safeguarding Investments in the Face of Manipulative Threats

In conclusion, the threat of pump and dump schemes underscores the importance of diligence, awareness, and strategic decision-making in the world of penny stocks. By understanding the dynamics of manipulation, identifying warning signs, and implementing protective strategies, investors can safeguard their investments and navigate the market with greater resilience. In an environment where opportunistic schemes may lurk, knowledge and prudence become powerful shields against the manipulative forces that seek to exploit unsuspecting investors.

Chapter 12: NFTs
What Are NFTs

In the ever-evolving landscape of digital assets, Non-Fungible Tokens (NFTs) have emerged as a revolutionary force, reshaping the way we perceive and exchange value in the digital realm. At their core, NFTs represent a form of unique, indivisible ownership of digital or physical assets, leveraging blockchain technology to provide authenticity, provenance, and scarcity in a decentralized ecosystem.

Defining Non-Fungibility in the Digital Realm

Beyond Fungibility:

The term "non-fungible" refers to the distinctive nature of each token, in stark contrast to fungible assets like cryptocurrencies that are interchangeable on a one-to-one basis. NFTs, built on blockchain standards like Ethereum's ERC-721 and ERC-1155, introduce a new dimension to digital ownership by encapsulating the uniqueness and scarcity of digital assets, ranging from digital art and music to virtual real estate and in-game items.

Blockchain Foundations: The Technology Behind NFTs

Immutable Ledgers and Smart Contracts:

NFTs rely on the secure and transparent foundation of blockchain technology. Each NFT is recorded on an immutable ledger, providing an unalterable record of ownership and transaction history. Smart contracts, self-executing pieces of code embedded in the blockchain, govern the creation, transfer, and ownership rules of NFTs, ensuring trustless and automated transactions without the need for intermediaries.

Tokenizing the Intangible: Understanding Digital Ownership

From Art to Virtual Real Estate:

NFTs have transcended traditional notions of ownership by tokenizing intangible assets. Digital art, once confined to the digital realm, can now be owned and traded as a unique NFT, with ownership information permanently recorded on the blockchain. Beyond art, virtual real estate in online worlds, music, tweets, and even moments captured in the form of GIFs can be tokenized, transforming them into scarce and tradable digital assets.

Scarcity and Rarity: The Cornerstones of NFT Value

Digital Scarcity in an Infinite World:

Scarcity is a fundamental economic principle that NFTs leverage to confer value. Through limited issuance and provable rarity, NFTs create a sense of exclusivity in the digital realm. Artists and creators can imbue their digital creations with scarcity, much like limited edition physical artworks, fostering a sense of rarity and uniqueness that resonates with collectors and enthusiasts alike.

Provenance and Authenticity: Immutable Records of Digital Creation

Immutable Records on the Blockchain:

One of the most compelling aspects of NFTs is their ability to establish and maintain provenance and authenticity. The blockchain serves as an immutable ledger, tracing the entire lifecycle of an NFT from its creation to every subsequent transfer. This unbroken chain of custody ensures that the true origin and authenticity of a digital asset can be verified with unparalleled certainty.

The Role of Interoperability in the NFT Ecosystem

Cross-Platform Compatibility:

Interoperability is a key feature shaping the NFT landscape. With various blockchain networks and standards,

NFTs can exist and be traded across different platforms, expanding their reach and utility. This interoperability fosters a more interconnected ecosystem where digital assets can seamlessly move between platforms, unlocking new possibilities for creators and collectors.

Challenges and Criticisms: Addressing the Darker Side of NFTs

Environmental Concerns and Digital Plagiarism:

While NFTs present exciting opportunities, they are not without challenges and criticisms. Environmental concerns related to the energy consumption of blockchain networks, particularly in the case of proof-of-work systems, have sparked debates about the sustainability of NFTs. Additionally, issues like digital plagiarism and unauthorized tokenization of existing works raise questions about intellectual property rights and ethical considerations in the NFT space.

Future Horizons: The Evolving Landscape of NFTs

Beyond Digital Art:

The future of NFTs extends beyond the realm of digital art, with ongoing exploration into diverse applications. Virtual reality, augmented reality, and the gamification of NFT experiences are poised to redefine how we interact with and value digital assets. As technological advancements continue, NFTs are likely to play a central role in shaping the future of ownership, creativity, and commerce in the digital age.

Conclusion: NFTs as a Paradigm Shift in Digital Ownership

Transforming the Notion of Ownership:

In conclusion, NFTs represent a paradigm shift in our understanding of digital ownership. By introducing scarcity, provenance, and authenticity to the digital realm, NFTs empower creators, collectors, and enthusiasts with new possibilities. As the NFT ecosystem continues to evolve, it remains a dynamic space where the fusion of technology, creativity, and ownership redefines the boundaries of the digital frontier. Whether in the form of digital art, virtual real estate, or novel applications yet to be imagined, NFTs stand as a testament to the transformative power of blockchain technology in reshaping the landscape of digital assets and ownership.

Digital Scarcity Model

In the expansive world of Non-Fungible Tokens (NFTs), the concept of digital scarcity stands as a cornerstone, reshaping the traditional understanding of value in the digital age. This subtopic delves into the intricacies of the digital scarcity model, exploring how scarcity is embedded within NFTs and how it transforms the perception of value in the realm of digital assets.

Defying Infinite Replication: The Essence of Digital Scarcity

Breaking the Replication Myth:

At its core, the digital scarcity model challenges the notion that digital assets are infinitely replicable. Unlike traditional digital files that can be copied without limit, NFTs introduce scarcity by leveraging blockchain technology. Each NFT is a unique token with distinct characteristics, provably scarce due to the limited number issued, introducing rarity in the otherwise boundless digital landscape.

Blockchain as the Arbiter of Scarcity

Immutable Ledgers as Guardians of Rarity:

Blockchain technology serves as the guardian of digital scarcity within the NFT ecosystem. The decentralized and immutable nature of the blockchain ensures that the scarcity assigned to each NFT is transparent, verifiable, and indisputable. The blockchain ledger becomes a testament to the scarcity of a digital asset, creating a reliable and tamper-proof record of its uniqueness.

Limited Issuance: Crafting Rarity in the Digital Realm

The Power of Limited Issuance:

The scarcity of NFTs is often intentionally crafted through limited issuance. Artists, creators, and developers can choose to issue only a specific number of tokens, mirroring the limited editions found in traditional art and collectibles. This intentional limitation establishes a sense of exclusivity and rarity, driving the perceived value of the digital asset.

Provoking Desire: The Psychology of Digital Scarcity

Psychological Impact on Perception:

The digital scarcity model taps into the psychology of human desire and exclusivity. The inherent scarcity of NFTs triggers a sense of urgency and value appreciation among collectors. As humans are wired to appreciate rarity, the limited availability of digital assets fosters a heightened emotional connection, influencing how individuals perceive and assign value to these unique tokens.

Collectibles and Limited Editions: Analogous Concepts in the Digital Sphere

Bridging the Analog-Digital Gap:

Analogous to the world of physical collectibles and limited editions, NFTs bring these concepts into the digital sphere with a technological twist. While a traditional collector may treasure a limited edition print, a digital collector values a scarce NFT, both rooted in the allure of exclusivity. This parallel enhances the acceptance of digital scarcity, bridging the gap between traditional and digital forms of ownership.

The Ripple Effect: How Digital Scarcity Transforms Markets

Impact on Markets and Valuation:

The introduction of digital scarcity has profound implications for markets and valuation within the NFT ecosystem. As scarcity becomes a driving force, secondary markets witness fluctuations in prices based on the principles of supply and demand. The rarer an NFT, the higher its perceived value, leading to a dynamic market where scarcity is a key determinant of pricing.

Challenges and Criticisms: Addressing Concerns Around Scarcity

Balancing Scarcity and Accessibility:

While digital scarcity is a powerful tool in enhancing the value of NFTs, it also raises concerns about accessibility. Striking a balance between scarcity and inclusivity is a challenge, as creators navigate the fine line between crafting exclusive, valuable assets and ensuring a broader audience can participate in the NFT space without feeling excluded.

Future Trends: Digital Scarcity's Role in Shaping the NFT Landscape

Beyond the Present:

Looking ahead, the role of digital scarcity is expected to evolve further, influencing the trajectory of the NFT landscape. Innovations in blockchain technology, creative approaches to scarcity, and the integration of NFTs into various industries may redefine how digital scarcity contributes to the ongoing narrative of value and ownership in the digital age.

Conclusion: Digital Scarcity as a Catalyst for NFT Evolution

An Evolutionary Force:

In conclusion, the digital scarcity model serves as a catalyst for the evolution of NFTs, injecting a sense of rarity, exclusivity, and value into the digital realm. As creators, collectors, and technology converge, the concept of scarcity reshapes the landscape of digital assets, pushing the boundaries of what is possible in the ever-expanding world of Non-Fungible Tokens.

Very Speculative Pricing

The realm of Non-Fungible Tokens (NFTs) introduces a paradigm shift in the valuation of digital assets, ushering in an era of very speculative pricing. This subtopic explores the factors contributing to the highly speculative nature of NFT pricing, delving into the complexities that make determining the value of these unique tokens a nuanced and often unpredictable endeavor.

Digital Rarity and Subjective Value: The Core of Speculative Pricing

Defining Digital Rarity:

At the heart of the speculative pricing phenomenon in the NFT space lies the concept of digital rarity. Unlike traditional assets with tangible attributes, the scarcity of NFTs is often intangible, stemming from the subjective value assigned by creators, collectors, and the broader market. This subjectivity amplifies the speculative nature of pricing, as it becomes intertwined with individual perceptions and preferences.

Celebrity Endorsements and Influencer Impact on Valuation

The Celebrity Factor:

One significant driver of very speculative pricing in the NFT market is the involvement of celebrities and influencers. When high-profile individuals endorse or create NFTs, the perceived value often skyrockets based on their existing fanbase and influence. This phenomenon amplifies speculation, as the market responds not only to the inherent scarcity of the digital asset but also to the celebrity association attached to it.

Exclusivity and Limited Editions: Fueling FOMO and Price Surge

Fear of Missing Out (FOMO):

The scarcity created through limited editions and exclusivity fuels a sense of urgency and Fear of Missing Out (FOMO) within the NFT market. As collectors compete for a limited number of tokens, bidding wars can erupt, driving prices to levels that may seem disproportionate to traditional valuation metrics. The fear of being excluded from owning a unique digital asset contributes to the speculative frenzy.

Algorithmic Trading and Market Dynamics

Algorithmic Triggers:

The integration of algorithmic trading in the NFT market introduces an additional layer of complexity to pricing dynamics. Algorithmic traders leverage data, market trends, and predefined algorithms to execute trades swiftly. This speed and automation can contribute to rapid price fluctuations, creating an environment where speculation is heightened, and valuations can be influenced by algorithmic triggers.

NFT Marketplaces and Price Discovery Challenges

Decentralized Markets:

The decentralized nature of NFT marketplaces adds a layer of unpredictability to price discovery. Unlike traditional markets with centralized oversight, NFTs are often traded across various decentralized platforms, each with its own dynamics. This decentralized landscape can lead to variations in pricing strategies, making it challenging for participants to ascertain a fair market value for a given NFT.

Artistic Subjectivity and Valuation Challenges

The Artistic Element:

Artistic subjectivity introduces a unique challenge to NFT valuation. Unlike traditional financial assets with measurable performance metrics, the value of NFTs tied to artistic endeavors is inherently subjective. Factors such as the reputation of the artist, the cultural significance of the work, and the emotional impact on the audience contribute to a speculative pricing environment where traditional valuation models may fall short.

Speculative Bubbles and Corrections: Riding the Waves of Market Sentiment

Bubble Dynamics:

The NFT market is not immune to speculative bubbles, where prices surge rapidly based on market sentiment and hype. These bubbles can lead to inflated valuations, with participants entering the market driven more by the expectation of quick profits than a measured understanding of the intrinsic value of the digital assets. Recognizing and navigating these speculative bubbles is crucial for participants to avoid potential market corrections.

Regulatory Uncertainty and Its Impact on Speculative Pricing

Navigating Regulatory Gray Areas:

The regulatory landscape surrounding NFTs is still evolving, contributing to an environment of uncertainty. The lack of clear guidelines and oversight can lead to speculative pricing as market participants navigate gray areas. Regulatory developments, or the lack thereof, have the potential to influence market sentiment and, consequently, the speculative pricing of NFTs.

Conclusion: Navigating the Waters of NFT Speculation

Balancing Act:

In conclusion, the very speculative pricing of NFTs reflects the delicate balance between digital rarity, market dynamics, and individual perceptions. As participants navigate these uncharted waters, understanding the factors that contribute to speculative pricing becomes essential for informed decision-making. The future of NFT valuation will likely continue to be shaped by a combination of technological advancements, market maturation, and regulatory clarity in the evolving landscape of digital assets.

High Volatility

In the vibrant world of Non-Fungible Tokens (NFTs), the aspect of high volatility stands as a defining characteristic of market dynamics. This subtopic explores the various dimensions and drivers behind the remarkable volatility witnessed in NFT markets, shedding light on the factors that contribute to price fluctuations, market sentiment shifts, and the challenges and opportunities presented by this volatility.

Market Sentiment Swings and Emotional Trading

Emotional Rollercoaster:

One primary contributor to the high volatility in NFT markets is the emotional nature of trading within this space. Unlike traditional financial markets driven by fundamentals and economic indicators, NFT markets often witness rapid sentiment swings. Emotional reactions to news, social media trends, and celebrity endorsements can create an emotional rollercoaster, with prices experiencing sharp and unpredictable movements.

Hype Cycles and Speculative Frenzies

Riding the Hype:

The NFT space is no stranger to hype cycles, where certain trends or projects capture the collective imagination of the market. During these cycles, a surge in demand driven by hype can propel prices to astronomical levels. However, as hype subsides, the market often experiences corrections, leading to significant volatility. Understanding the dynamics of hype cycles is crucial for participants navigating the highs and lows of the NFT market.

Influence of Celebrity Endorsements on Market Swings

Celebrities as Market Movers:

The involvement of celebrities in the NFT space can have a profound impact on market volatility. Celebrity endorsements, announcements, or even disassociations can trigger substantial price movements. The influence of celebrities as market movers adds an extra layer of unpredictability to NFT markets, with their actions often causing rapid and sometimes exaggerated market reactions.

Rarity and Scarcity: Amplifiers of Price Swings

Scarcity-Driven Peaks and Valleys:

The inherent scarcity of NFTs, often tied to limited editions or unique digital assets, contributes significantly to market volatility. As collectors vie for a limited number of tokens, the interplay between supply and demand can lead to extreme price swings. Understanding how rarity amplifies volatility is essential for market participants seeking to navigate these peaks and valleys.

Algorithmic Trading and Rapid Market Reactions

Algorithmic Triggers:

The integration of algorithmic trading in NFT markets introduces an element of rapid and automated decision-making. Algorithms, reacting to predefined triggers, can execute trades at lightning speed. While this speed can enhance liquidity, it also contributes to rapid market reactions and increased volatility. Participants need to be aware of algorithmic triggers and their potential impact on price movements.

Regulatory Developments and Market Uncertainty

Regulatory Whiplash:

The evolving regulatory landscape surrounding NFTs introduces an additional layer of uncertainty and volatility. Market participants often react swiftly to regulatory developments or even speculations, leading to sudden and intense price movements. As regulatory frameworks continue to take shape, market participants must stay informed and prepared for potential regulatory whiplash.

Liquidity Challenges and Flash Crashes

Flash Crash Dynamics:

The liquidity challenges inherent in certain NFT markets can contribute to flash crashes, characterized by sudden and severe price declines followed by rapid recoveries. These flash crashes, while potentially creating opportunities for savvy traders, also highlight the fragility of liquidity in specific NFT markets. Navigating the aftermath of flash crashes requires a nuanced understanding of market dynamics.

Marketplace Dynamics and Decentralization

Decentralized Volatility:

The decentralized nature of NFT marketplaces adds an extra layer of complexity to market dynamics. Different marketplaces may operate with varying rules and liquidity levels, contributing to decentralized volatility. Participants need to consider the impact of marketplace dynamics on the overall volatility of NFTs, as the absence of centralized oversight can lead to diverse and sometimes divergent market behaviors.

Conclusion: Navigating the Volatility Landscape

Strategies for Volatility Navigation:

In conclusion, the high volatility in NFT markets is a characteristic that both defines and challenges participants in this space. Navigating the volatility landscape requires a combination of strategic awareness, risk management, and a thorough understanding of the drivers behind market movements. As the NFT ecosystem continues to evolve, market participants must remain adaptable and prepared to embrace the opportunities and challenges presented by the inherent volatility of these unique digital assets.

Long-term Value Uncertain

In the ever-evolving landscape of Non-Fungible Tokens (NFTs), the notion of long-term value remains a subject of significant debate and uncertainty. This subtopic delves into the complexities surrounding the assessment of long-term value in the NFT space, examining the factors that contribute to the uncertainty and the challenges faced by investors seeking to navigate the ambiguous terrain of NFT investments.

Dynamic Nature of Digital Collectibles

Transient Trends and Shifting Tastes:

One of the key challenges in ascertaining the long-term value of NFTs is the dynamic nature of digital collectibles. Trends in the NFT space can be transient, influenced by rapidly shifting tastes and preferences. What captures the attention and demand today may not necessarily hold the same allure in the future. Investors must grapple with the challenge of predicting the trajectory of digital collectibles in a market known for its rapid evolution.

Technological Advancements and Obsolescence Risks

Technological Prowess and Obsolescence Concerns:

The rapid pace of technological advancements introduces an additional layer of uncertainty regarding the long-term value of NFTs. As new technologies emerge, there's a risk that older NFT formats or platforms could become obsolete. Investors must carefully assess the technological underpinnings of the NFTs they hold and consider how evolving technologies might impact the relevance and value of their digital assets over time.

Evolving Cultural and Artistic Significance

Shifting Cultural Narratives:

The cultural and artistic significance of NFTs is subject to evolving narratives. What may be considered groundbreaking and culturally relevant today might undergo reinterpretation or reassessment in the future. Investors in NFT art and cultural assets must grapple with the challenge of anticipating how societal perspectives and values will evolve, influencing the long-term perception and value of their NFT holdings.

Market Saturation and Digital Abundance

Abundance versus Rarity:

The concept of scarcity, a traditional driver of value in various asset classes, faces unique challenges in the digital realm. The ease of creating digital content and the potential for market saturation pose questions about the long-term value of individual NFTs. As the market becomes flooded with digital assets, discerning the truly scarce and valuable from the abundant and commonplace becomes a formidable task for investors.

Regulatory Developments and Legal Uncertainties

Regulatory Clouds on the Horizon:

The uncertain regulatory landscape surrounding NFTs adds an additional layer of complexity to assessing long-term value. Regulatory developments, whether clarifying or ambiguous, can significantly impact the value and viability of NFT investments. Investors must remain vigilant in monitoring regulatory shifts and anticipate how legal uncertainties may influence the long-term prospects of their NFT holdings.

Cultural Shifts and NFT Adoption

Mainstream Integration or Subculture Status:

The trajectory of NFT adoption within broader culture remains uncertain. Will NFTs become fully integrated into mainstream society, or will they maintain a more niche status within certain subcultures? The cultural acceptance and integration of NFTs into daily life will inevitably shape their long-term value. Investors must consider the potential scenarios of cultural acceptance and factor these into their long-term investment strategies.

Sustainability Concerns and Environmental Impact

Sustainable Practices and Ethical Considerations:

The growing awareness of environmental concerns related to NFTs introduces an ethical dimension to their long-term value. As the NFT community grapples with the environmental impact of blockchain technology, investors must navigate the evolving landscape of sustainable practices and consider how these considerations may influence the perception and value of NFTs in the long run.

Conclusion: Navigating Uncertainty with Informed Strategies

Strategies for Long-term NFT Investments:

In conclusion, the uncertainty surrounding the long-term value of NFTs requires investors to approach their strategies with a blend of vigilance and adaptability. Navigating the ambiguous terrain of NFT investments involves staying informed about technological, cultural, and regulatory developments while maintaining a nuanced understanding of the dynamic nature of digital collectibles. As the NFT ecosystem continues to mature, investors must develop informed strategies that acknowledge and address the uncertainties inherent in the long-term value assessment of these unique digital assets.

Chapter 13: Offshore Private Placements
Risks of Limited Information

Offshore private placements offer investors an avenue to explore opportunities beyond traditional markets, but with this exploration comes the challenge of navigating the shadows cast by limited information. This subtopic delves into the inherent risks associated with the scarcity of information in offshore private placements, shedding light on the complexities investors face when operating in environments characterized by limited transparency.

Opaque Financial Landscapes

Navigating in the Dark:

One of the primary challenges in offshore private placements lies in the opacity of financial landscapes. Limited disclosure requirements and lax reporting standards in certain jurisdictions contribute to an environment where investors must operate with reduced visibility. The lack of comprehensive financial information poses challenges in evaluating the true health and performance of investment opportunities, requiring investors to develop strategies to navigate these opaque financial terrains.

Information Asymmetry and Insider Advantage

The Power of the Privileged Few:

Limited information often results in information asymmetry, where a privileged few possess insights that are not readily available to the broader investor community. This insider advantage introduces a layer of complexity, as those with access to crucial information may gain an upper hand in decision-making. Investors must be cognizant of the potential for information imbalances and consider how this dynamic may impact their investment strategies in offshore private placements.

Due Diligence Challenges

Piecing Together the Puzzle:

The scarcity of information complicates the due diligence process for investors in offshore private placements. Conducting thorough investigations into the financial health, governance structures, and operational practices of potential investments becomes a meticulous task. Investors must develop robust due diligence frameworks that leverage the available information while acknowledging the gaps that may exist in their understanding of offshore opportunities.

Regulatory Ambiguities and Compliance Risks

Navigating Regulatory Fog:

Offshore jurisdictions often present regulatory ambiguities, adding a layer of uncertainty to the compliance landscape. Limited information about regulatory frameworks and oversight mechanisms requires investors to tread carefully. Failure to navigate these regulatory nuances can expose investors to compliance risks, underscoring the importance of a nuanced understanding of the legal and regulatory environments in offshore private placements.

Market Manipulation and Fraud Risks

Shadows of Deception:

The limited information environment in offshore investing can create fertile ground for market manipulation and fraudulent activities. Investors must be vigilant against the shadows of deception, employing strategies to identify red flags and warning signs that may indicate potential fraud. Heightened awareness and a proactive approach to risk mitigation are essential elements of safeguarding investments in offshore private placements.

Geopolitical and Economic Instabilities

Navigating Uncharted Waters:

Offshore private placements often involve exposure to geopolitical and economic landscapes that may be prone to instability. Limited information about the political climate, economic policies, and geopolitical tensions in certain jurisdictions requires investors to navigate uncharted waters. Strategies for risk management must incorporate geopolitical and economic analysis, allowing investors to anticipate and mitigate potential challenges arising from instability.

Communication Challenges and Language Barriers

Breaking Through Barriers:

Language barriers and communication challenges further compound the risks associated with limited information. Offshore investments may involve dealings in languages unfamiliar to investors, making effective communication challenging. Investors must develop strategies to bridge these communication gaps, recognizing the importance of clear and transparent communication in mitigating risks associated with limited information.

Conclusion: Illuminating the Shadows with Informed Strategies

Strategies for Mitigating Risks:

In conclusion, the risks posed by limited information in offshore private placements necessitate a strategic and informed approach. Investors must acknowledge the challenges presented by opaque financial landscapes, information asymmetry, and regulatory ambiguities. Developing robust due diligence processes, staying vigilant against fraud, and understanding the geopolitical and economic contexts are integral components of navigating the shadows of offshore investing. By illuminating these challenges with informed strategies, investors can better position themselves to make sound decisions in the complex world of offshore private placements.

Lack of Regulatory Oversight

The allure of offshore private placements is often accompanied by a lack of regulatory oversight, creating an environment where investors must navigate uncharted terrain. This subtopic explores the multifaceted challenges arising from the absence or inadequacy of regulatory scrutiny in offshore investing, shedding light on the risks associated with unregulated financial landscapes.

Regulatory Void in Offshore Jurisdictions

Regulatory Lacunas:

One of the defining features of offshore private placements is the presence of regulatory voids in certain jurisdictions. Offshore financial centers may lack robust regulatory frameworks, leaving investors in a position where traditional safeguards are notably absent. Understanding the nature and extent of regulatory lacunas is crucial for investors seeking to engage in offshore private placements.

Implications for Investor Protections

Protecting Investor Interests:

The absence of comprehensive regulatory oversight has direct implications for investor protections. In conventional financial markets, regulatory bodies play a pivotal role in safeguarding investor interests through mechanisms such as investor compensation schemes and dispute resolution mechanisms. The lack of such structures in offshore jurisdictions heightens the importance of thorough due diligence and risk mitigation strategies for investors.

Market Integrity and Fair Practices

Guarding Against Malpractices:

Regulatory oversight serves as a bulwark against market malpractices and ensures fair and transparent market operations. In the absence of robust regulatory scrutiny, offshore private placements may be more susceptible to market manipulation, insider trading, and other unfair practices. Investors must be cognizant of these risks and employ vigilant strategies to guard against potential malfeasance.

Challenges in Enforcement and Legal Recourse

Navigating Legal Ambiguities:

Enforcing legal rights and seeking recourse in offshore jurisdictions can pose significant challenges due to the lack of regulatory infrastructure. Legal ambiguities, differing judicial systems, and potential jurisdictional hurdles may impede investors' ability to pursue legal remedies effectively. This underscores the importance of proactive risk management and the consideration of legal factors when engaging in offshore private placements.

Opacity in Ownership and Structures

Unmasking Ownership Structures:

Regulatory oversight typically requires transparency in ownership structures, ensuring that beneficial ownership information is accessible. In the absence of robust oversight, offshore investments may be characterized by opaque ownership structures, making it challenging to ascertain the true ownership and control of entities. Investors must contend with this lack of transparency when evaluating the legitimacy and stability of offshore opportunities.

Risk of Financial Crime and Money Laundering

Money Trails and Financial Crime:

The lack of regulatory oversight heightens the risk of financial crime, including money laundering, within offshore jurisdictions. The absence of stringent monitoring and reporting requirements makes it easier for illicit funds to flow through offshore financial systems. Investors need to be acutely aware of these risks, implementing enhanced due diligence processes to detect and mitigate potential involvement in illicit financial activities.

Strategies for Mitigating Regulatory Risks

Proactive Risk Mitigation:

Given the challenges posed by the lack of regulatory oversight, investors must adopt proactive risk mitigation strategies. This includes thorough due diligence, engagement with reputable legal counsel, and a deep understanding of the regulatory environments in specific offshore jurisdictions. By incorporating these strategies into their approach, investors can better navigate the complexities of offshore private placements and mitigate the inherent risks associated with the lack of regulatory oversight.

Conclusion: Navigating the Regulatory Void with Informed Strategies

Striking a Balance:

In conclusion, the lack of regulatory oversight in offshore private placements presents both challenges and opportunities for investors. While the absence of regulatory constraints may offer flexibility, it also exposes investors to heightened risks. Striking a balance between seizing opportunities and implementing informed risk management strategies is paramount. By navigating the regulatory void with foresight and diligence, investors can position themselves to make sound decisions in the dynamic landscape of offshore private placements.

Difficulty Evaluating Opportunities

The landscape of offshore private placements is characterized by its opacity, making the evaluation of opportunities a formidable task. This subtopic delves into the multifaceted challenges investors face when attempting to assess the viability and legitimacy of offshore opportunities, shedding light on the intricacies that contribute to the difficulty of evaluating these ventures.

Limited Access to Information

Information Asymmetry:

One of the primary obstacles in evaluating offshore opportunities lies in the limited access to information. Unlike in more regulated environments where comprehensive financial disclosures are mandatory, offshore jurisdictions may lack stringent reporting requirements, leading to information asymmetry. Investors grapple with the challenge of making informed decisions when critical financial data may be unavailable or difficult to obtain.

Complex Ownership Structures

Deciphering Ownership:

Offshore entities often employ complex ownership structures, adding a layer of complexity to the evaluation process. Deciphering the true ownership of a venture becomes challenging when entities are nested within intricate legal frameworks designed to obfuscate ownership details. Investors must navigate through these convoluted structures to determine who holds control and whether their interests align with the success of the investment.

Unreliable Financial Reporting Standards

Navigating Reporting Inconsistencies:

The absence of consistent and standardized financial reporting standards in offshore jurisdictions introduces another layer of difficulty. Investors accustomed to transparent financial reporting may find it challenging to assess the financial health and performance of offshore opportunities when reporting standards vary widely. Navigating through reporting inconsistencies becomes crucial for accurate financial evaluation.

Evaluating Economic and Political Stability

Assessing Stability Factors:

Evaluating the economic and political stability of offshore jurisdictions adds an additional layer of complexity to the investment decision-making process. Factors such as geopolitical risks, economic volatility, and the potential for sudden policy shifts contribute to the difficulty of predicting the long-term viability of investments. Investors must factor in these stability considerations to assess the resilience of offshore opportunities.

Navigating Legal and Regulatory Ambiguities

Legal Ambiguities:

The legal and regulatory landscape in offshore jurisdictions is often characterized by ambiguities and variations. Investors face challenges in navigating these complexities, including understanding the legal frameworks governing their investments and anticipating potential regulatory changes. The difficulty in obtaining clear legal guidance further complicates the evaluation of opportunities, requiring a nuanced approach to legal due diligence.

Risk of Fraud and Scams

Guarding Against Deception:

Offshore jurisdictions, while offering legitimate opportunities, can also be breeding grounds for fraudulent schemes. Investors must contend with the risk of encountering scams, deceptive practices, and entities designed to exploit information asymmetry. Distinguishing between genuine opportunities and fraudulent schemes becomes a critical aspect of the evaluation process.

Cultural and Language Barriers

Cross-Cultural Challenges:

Investors engaging in offshore opportunities often encounter cultural and language barriers that add a layer of complexity to the evaluation process. Understanding the local business culture, legal practices, and nuances in communication becomes essential for accurate assessment. Overcoming these barriers is crucial for building trust and fostering successful partnerships in offshore investments.

Strategies for Overcoming Evaluation Challenges

Proactive Evaluation Strategies:

Despite the challenges, investors can implement proactive strategies to overcome the difficulty of evaluating offshore opportunities. This includes engaging local experts, conducting thorough due diligence, and leveraging technology to bridge information gaps. By adopting a comprehensive and adaptive approach, investors can enhance their ability to assess the viability and risks associated with offshore private placements.

Conclusion: Navigating Complexity with Informed Decision-Making

Balancing Risks and Rewards:

In conclusion, the difficulty of evaluating opportunities in offshore private placements is an inherent aspect of navigating these complex investment landscapes. Investors must balance the potential rewards with the challenges posed by limited information, complex structures, and regulatory uncertainties. By acknowledging and addressing these difficulties through strategic evaluation processes, investors can position themselves to make informed decisions in the dynamic realm of offshore private placements.

Scams and Fraud Risk

The allure of offshore private placements is often accompanied by the looming threat of scams and fraud. This subtopic delves into the intricacies of scams and the associated risks that investors face when engaging in offshore opportunities. Understanding the strategies employed by fraudulent entities is crucial for investors to safeguard their capital and make informed decisions in this complex investment landscape.

Deceptive Schemes and Tactics

Crafting Illusions:

Scammers operating in the realm of offshore private placements are adept at crafting elaborate illusions to deceive investors. They may present seemingly lucrative opportunities through sophisticated marketing materials, glossy websites, and impressive testimonials. Investors must remain vigilant in discerning between genuine ventures and deceptive schemes designed to lure them into financial traps.

Information Asymmetry Exploitation

Exploiting Knowledge Gaps:

Scammers thrive on information asymmetry, capitalizing on the lack of transparency inherent in offshore investments. By exploiting knowledge gaps and presenting selectively curated information, fraudulent entities can create a facade of legitimacy. Investors, unaware of critical details, may fall victim to these tactics, emphasizing the importance of due diligence in mitigating the risk of scams.

Complex Ownership Structures as a Smokescreen

Obfuscating Ownership:

Fraudulent offshore entities often employ complex ownership structures to obfuscate their true nature. The opacity created by intricate legal frameworks and nested entities serves as a smokescreen for illicit activities. Investors must navigate through these complexities to unveil the actual ownership and control, recognizing that fraudulent schemes often hide behind layers of legal intricacy.

False Promises and Unrealistic Returns

Promises of Extravagance:

One hallmark of offshore scams is the promise of extravagant returns that seem too good to be true. Fraudulent entities entice investors with the allure of quick and substantial profits, playing on the desire for high-yield investments. However, these promises often crumble under scrutiny, and investors must exercise caution when confronted with opportunities that deviate significantly from market norms.

Pump and Dump Strategies

Inflating Value, Deflating Investments:

Pump and dump strategies are a common tactic employed by scammers in offshore private placements. This scheme involves artificially inflating the value of an investment through misleading information, only to sell off shares at the peak, leaving unsuspecting investors with devalued holdings. Recognizing the signs of pump and dump schemes is essential for investors to avoid falling victim to orchestrated market manipulation.

Phantom Investments and Fictitious Assets

Creating Illusory Wealth:

Some scams involve the creation of phantom investments and fictitious assets that exist only on paper. Fraudulent entities may fabricate the existence of lucrative projects, properties, or holdings to attract investor funds. Unraveling these illusions requires meticulous investigation, highlighting the need for due diligence and scrutiny of the purported assets backing offshore opportunities.

Regulatory Arbitrage and Lack of Oversight

Exploiting Regulatory Gaps:

Scammers operating in offshore jurisdictions often capitalize on regulatory arbitrage and the lack of stringent oversight. The absence of robust regulatory frameworks allows fraudulent entities to operate with relative impunity. Investors should be wary of jurisdictions with lax regulatory environments, as these may provide fertile ground for fraudulent activities to flourish.

Strategies for Fraud Prevention and Risk Mitigation

Empowering Investors:

Mitigating the risk of scams and fraud in offshore private placements requires a proactive and vigilant approach. Investors can adopt strategies such as conducting thorough due diligence, seeking independent verification, and engaging with reputable legal and financial experts. By empowering themselves with knowledge and leveraging external expertise, investors can fortify their defenses against the ever-present threat of scams in offshore investments.

Conclusion: Navigating Safely in Uncharted Waters

Safeguarding Capital in Offshore Investments:

In conclusion, the risk of scams and fraud adds a layer of complexity to the already intricate landscape of offshore private placements. Investors must navigate these uncharted waters with caution, recognizing the red flags and deploying robust strategies for fraud prevention. By staying informed, exercising due diligence, and leveraging external expertise, investors can safeguard their capital and make more informed decisions in the dynamic world of offshore investments.

Accessing Investments

Accessing investments in offshore private placements requires a nuanced understanding of the channels through which investors can engage with these opportunities. This subtopic explores the various avenues available for investors to participate in offshore ventures, highlighting the complexities and considerations involved in navigating the pathways to these unique and often exclusive investment opportunities.

Private Equity Firms and Fund Managers

Entrusting Professionals:

One common avenue for accessing offshore private placements is through private equity firms and fund managers specializing in international investments. These entities pool funds from multiple investors to create diversified portfolios, offering exposure to a range of offshore assets. Investors can tap into the expertise of fund managers who navigate the complexities of offshore markets, providing a more hands-off approach for those seeking professional management.

Offshore Investment Platforms and Brokerages

Direct Access to Markets:

The rise of digital platforms has democratized access to offshore investments. Specialized offshore investment platforms and brokerages facilitate direct access to international markets, allowing investors to build their portfolios without the need for a middleman. These platforms provide a user-friendly interface, comprehensive research tools, and often offer a diverse array of investment options, enabling investors to tailor their offshore portfolios to their preferences.

Offshore Mutual Funds and Exchange-Traded Funds (ETFs)

Diversification through Funds:

Investors seeking instant diversification in offshore markets may opt for offshore mutual funds and ETFs. These investment vehicles pool funds from multiple investors to invest in a diversified portfolio of assets. Offshore mutual funds offer actively managed portfolios, while ETFs provide a passive investment approach, tracking specific indices. Both options offer investors exposure to a broad spectrum of offshore opportunities without the need for direct management.

Direct Investment in Offshore Companies

Ownership and Control:

For those inclined toward a more hands-on approach, direct investment in offshore companies is a viable option. This involves acquiring ownership stakes in specific businesses or projects. While this approach provides a higher level of control and customization, it also demands a deeper understanding of the target company, its operating environment, and compliance with international regulations. Direct investment requires thorough due diligence to navigate the intricacies of offshore business landscapes.

Offshore Real Estate Investment

Bricks and Mortar Abroad:

Investing in offshore real estate is a tangible way for investors to diversify their portfolios. Whether through direct property acquisition or investment in real estate funds, offshore real estate provides an avenue for capital appreciation and potential rental income. However, navigating foreign real estate markets requires an understanding of local regulations, market dynamics, and potential currency risks.

Offshore Bond Markets

Fixed-Income Options:

Participating in offshore bond markets is an avenue for investors seeking fixed-income opportunities. Offshore bonds issued by governments, corporations, or international organizations can offer attractive yields. However, investors must carefully assess credit risks, currency exposure, and market conditions when venturing into offshore bond investments. Diversifying across different issuers and regions can mitigate risks associated with individual bonds.

Navigating Regulatory Hurdles and Compliance Requirements

Understanding Regulatory Environments:

Accessing offshore investments also entails navigating regulatory hurdles and compliance requirements. Each jurisdiction has its own set of rules governing the participation of foreign investors. Investors must stay abreast of regulatory changes, tax implications, and compliance obligations to ensure a seamless and legally sound investment experience. Engaging legal and financial professionals with expertise in international regulations is crucial for navigating these complexities.

Conclusion: Crafting a Personalized Approach

Tailoring Strategies to Individual Goals:

In conclusion, the landscape of accessing offshore private placements is diverse, offering investors a spectrum of options to align with their goals and risk appetites. Whether opting for the expertise of private equity firms, the convenience of offshore platforms, or the direct ownership of offshore assets, investors can craft personalized strategies. Navigating the channels of offshore opportunities demands a blend of diligence, understanding, and, in some cases, professional guidance to unlock the potential benefits of international investments.

Chapter 14: Unregulated Online Lending
How P2P Lending Platforms Work

Peer-to-peer (P2P) lending platforms have emerged as a disruptive force in the financial landscape, connecting borrowers directly with individual lenders. This subtopic delves into the intricate workings of P2P lending, shedding light on the mechanisms that underpin this alternative form of online financing. From loan origination to repayment, understanding the journey of funds in P2P lending is crucial for both borrowers and lenders navigating the uncharted waters of unregulated online lending.

Origination and Listing of Loans

Creating the Marketplace:

P2P lending platforms operate as digital marketplaces where borrowers can present their loan requests and potential lenders can browse through available opportunities. The process begins with a borrower submitting a loan application detailing the purpose, amount, and desired terms. The platform assesses the borrower's creditworthiness, often utilizing algorithms and traditional credit scoring methods to evaluate risk. Once approved, the loan is listed on the platform for potential lenders to review.

Investor Participation and Funding

Empowering Individual Investors:

Individual investors play a pivotal role in the P2P lending ecosystem. Interested lenders can browse through a variety of loan listings, each presenting unique risk and return profiles. Lenders have the flexibility to diversify their investments across multiple loans or concentrate on specific borrowers based on their risk preferences. The lending platform facilitates the flow of funds from investors to borrowers, creating a direct and decentralized lending process.

Interest Rates and Loan Terms

Negotiating Terms in a Decentralized Arena:

The interest rates and terms of P2P loans are often determined through a competitive process. Borrowers may propose the interest rate they are willing to pay, and lenders can choose to fund the loan at the offered rate or negotiate for more favorable terms. The decentralized nature of P2P lending empowers both parties to engage in a transparent and open negotiation process, fostering a dynamic marketplace where interest rates reflect the equilibrium between borrower risk and lender return expectations.

Risk Assessment and Credit Scoring

Algorithmic Evaluation:

P2P lending platforms employ advanced algorithms and data analytics to assess the creditworthiness of borrowers. While traditional financial institutions may rely heavily on credit scores, P2P platforms leverage a broader range of data points, including income, employment history, and even social media activity. This multifaceted approach enhances the accuracy of risk assessments, allowing for a more inclusive evaluation of borrowers who may not have an extensive credit history.

Loan Agreements and Documentation

Smart Contracts and Digital Agreements:

Once a loan is funded, P2P lending platforms facilitate the creation of legally binding loan agreements between the borrower and individual lenders. Many platforms utilize smart contracts, self-executing contracts with the terms of the agreement directly written into code. These digital agreements automate various aspects of the lending process, including disbursements, repayments, and the distribution of returns to lenders.

Repayment and Collection Mechanisms

Ensuring Timely Repayments:

Repayment mechanisms in P2P lending are designed to ensure timely and efficient collection of loan payments. Automated systems often deduct monthly installments from borrowers' bank accounts and distribute the funds to individual lenders. In the event of a missed payment, P2P platforms may employ collection agencies or alternative mechanisms to recover funds. The transparency of these processes is a crucial aspect, providing both borrowers and lenders with visibility into the status of loan repayments.

Secondary Market Trading

Creating Liquidity in P2P Investments:

Some P2P lending platforms offer a secondary market where lenders can sell their loan investments to other investors. This feature introduces liquidity to P2P investments, allowing lenders to exit positions before the maturity of the loans. The secondary market also enables investors to adjust their portfolios based on changing financial goals or risk tolerance, creating a dynamic and flexible investment environment.

Regulatory Considerations and Investor Protection

Navigating Uncharted Regulatory Waters:

The regulatory landscape for P2P lending varies globally, with some regions implementing comprehensive frameworks, while others navigate a more ambiguous terrain. Investors and borrowers engaging in P2P lending must be cognizant of the regulatory considerations that impact the industry. In the absence of robust regulations, platforms may implement their own risk mitigation measures and investor protection protocols to enhance the overall integrity of the P2P lending ecosystem.

Conclusion: The Evolution of Peer-to-Peer Lending

From Concept to Reality:

In conclusion, understanding how P2P lending platforms operate unveils the transformation of traditional lending into a decentralized, technology-driven ecosystem. The journey of funds from origination to repayment highlights the efficiency, transparency, and flexibility that P2P lending brings to the financial landscape. As the industry continues to evolve, both borrowers and lenders can navigate this unregulated frontier armed with a deeper comprehension of the mechanics that drive peer-to-peer financing.

Underwriting Standards Vary Widely

In the universe of unregulated online lending, the diversity of underwriting standards stands out as a defining characteristic. Unlike traditional financial institutions bound by stringent regulatory frameworks, unregulated lenders have the latitude to set their own criteria for evaluating borrower eligibility. This subtopic delves into the intricacies of underwriting in this dynamic landscape, exploring the factors that influence loan approval, interest rates, and overall risk assessment.

1. Platform-Specific Criteria: The Uniqueness of Each Lending Platform

Defining Parameters:

Unregulated lending platforms often establish their own set of underwriting criteria, creating a bespoke framework that reflects their risk tolerance and business model. These criteria can encompass a range of factors, from credit history and income verification to more unconventional metrics such as social media activity. As a result, borrowers encounter a mosaic of underwriting standards, each tailored to the specific goals and risk appetite of the lending platform.

2. Embracing Alternative Data: Beyond Traditional Credit Scores

Expanding the Lens:

One notable feature of underwriting in unregulated online lending is the incorporation of alternative data sources beyond traditional credit scores. While conventional lenders heavily rely on credit history, unregulated platforms often tap into a broader spectrum of information. This may include analyzing digital footprints, online behavior, and even psychometric data to assess a borrower's creditworthiness.

Embracing alternative data allows unregulated lenders to reach a more diverse pool of borrowers who may lack a robust credit history.

3. Flexibility and Speed: The Trade-Off Between Rigor and Efficiency

Balancing Act:

Unregulated online lenders, unencumbered by the bureaucratic processes of traditional institutions, boast unparalleled speed in their underwriting processes. However, this efficiency often comes at the cost of a more relaxed scrutiny of borrower financials. The trade-off between rigor and speed is a defining characteristic of unregulated lending, where borrowers can access funds swiftly but face a varied landscape of underwriting standards that may prioritize expediency over exhaustive risk assessment.

4. Collateral and Asset-Backed Loans: A Shift in Risk Dynamics

Securing the Transaction:

Some unregulated lenders opt for collateral or asset-backed loans as a risk mitigation strategy. In such cases, the underwriting process involves assessing the value and liquidity of the collateral rather than solely relying on the borrower's creditworthiness. While this approach provides an additional layer of security for lenders, it also introduces complexities in the evaluation of the collateral's true worth and the potential challenges in the event of default.

5. Risk-Based Pricing Models: Tailoring Interest Rates to Borrower Risk

Customizing Costs:

Unregulated lending platforms often employ risk-based pricing models, tailoring interest rates to match the perceived risk associated with each borrower. This personalized approach to pricing acknowledges the diverse financial profiles of borrowers and allows lenders to adjust interest rates based on the specific risk factors present in each loan application. While providing a nuanced approach to risk management, it also adds to the overall variability in underwriting standards across the unregulated lending landscape.

6. Lack of Uniform Regulatory Oversight: Navigating the Regulatory Void

Regulatory Ambiguity:

One of the key challenges in the realm of unregulated online lending is the absence of uniform regulatory oversight. With no standardized guidelines dictating underwriting standards, each platform operates within its interpretation of risk and responsibility. This lack of regulatory homogeneity contributes to the wide spectrum of underwriting criteria, making it imperative for borrowers to carefully scrutinize the terms and conditions of each lending platform.

Conclusion: Navigating the Diverse Tapestry of Unregulated Underwriting

Inherent Complexity:

In conclusion, the variability in underwriting standards within unregulated online lending adds a layer of complexity to the borrowing landscape. Borrowers must navigate a diverse tapestry of criteria, from alternative data assessments to collateral requirements. As the industry continues to evolve, understanding and adapting to these diverse underwriting standards become crucial for both lenders seeking profitable opportunities and borrowers searching for accessible and transparent financial solutions in this unregulated terrain.

Default and Collection Challenges

The aftermath of borrower distress poses significant challenges for unregulated online lending platforms. Unlike traditional financial institutions with established frameworks for collections, unregulated lenders navigate a complex landscape when borrowers default on their loans. This subtopic explores the intricacies of defaults and the subsequent challenges in collections, shedding light on the strategies employed by unregulated lenders in the absence of standardized regulatory guidance.

1. Understanding Default Dynamics: Unraveling the Causes

Roots of Default:

Defaults in unregulated online lending can stem from various factors, ranging from unexpected financial hardships to broader economic downturns. Understanding the multifaceted causes of default is essential for both lenders and borrowers. Common contributors include job loss, medical emergencies, or simply the inability to manage debt, underscoring the importance of a nuanced approach to collections that considers the individual circumstances of each borrower.

2. Lack of Regulatory Safeguards: The Void in Default Management

Regulatory Blank Spaces:

One distinctive challenge in the realm of unregulated online lending is the absence of standardized regulatory safeguards for handling defaults. Unlike traditional lenders subject to regulatory oversight, unregulated platforms must craft their own strategies for managing default situations. This regulatory void demands a proactive and adaptive approach from lenders, who must balance the need for effective collections with ethical considerations and a commitment to fair treatment of borrowers.

3. Collections Strategies: Tailoring Approaches to Individual Cases

Customized Solutions:

Unregulated lenders often adopt a case-by-case approach to collections, tailoring their strategies based on the circumstances of each defaulted loan. Rather than relying on one-size-fits-all solutions, these platforms may engage in personalized communication, negotiation, and alternative payment arrangements. This flexibility allows lenders to address the unique challenges faced by borrowers in default while working towards a resolution that is fair to both parties.

4. Communication Challenges: Navigating Delicate Dialogues

Sensitivity in Communication:

Engaging with borrowers in default requires a delicate balance between assertiveness and empathy. Unregulated lenders face communication challenges in ensuring that their messages convey the urgency of resolving the default while acknowledging the financial difficulties faced by borrowers. Striking this balance is crucial for maintaining a positive borrower-lender relationship and increasing the likelihood of successful collections.

5. Legal Landscape: Evolving Dynamics in Unregulated Default Cases

Legal Considerations:

The absence of strict regulatory guidelines does not mean that unregulated lenders operate in a legal vacuum. Navigating the legal landscape of defaults involves an understanding of contract law, consumer protection laws, and potential legal challenges that may arise. Unregulated lenders must stay abreast of evolving legal dynamics and be prepared to adapt their collections strategies in response to changes in the legal environment.

6. Debt Settlement and Forgiveness: Balancing Risk and Compassion

Ethical Considerations:

Unregulated lenders may explore debt settlement or forgiveness as options in the face of borrower distress. Balancing the financial risk associated with such decisions against a compassionate approach to borrowers facing genuine hardships requires a nuanced understanding of ethical considerations. Striving for a fair and ethical resolution that recognizes the challenges faced by borrowers contributes to the long-term reputation and sustainability of unregulated lending platforms.

Conclusion: Navigating the Complex Aftermath of Borrower Distress

Adapting to the Uncharted:

In conclusion, the challenges of defaults and collections in unregulated online lending necessitate adaptive strategies and a commitment to ethical practices. As the industry evolves, unregulated lenders must continually refine their approaches to default management, acknowledging the absence of regulatory safeguards and embracing a responsibility to navigate the complexities of borrower distress with sensitivity, fairness, and a long-term perspective.

Lack of FDIC Insurance

In the realm of unregulated online lending, a prominent distinction from traditional banking is the absence of Federal Deposit Insurance Corporation (FDIC) insurance. This subtopic delves into the implications of lacking FDIC insurance, exploring the risks faced by both lenders and borrowers in an environment where the safety net of federal insurance is notably absent.

1. The FDIC and Traditional Banking: A Safety Net for Depositors

Foundations of FDIC Insurance:

The FDIC, established in the aftermath of the Great Depression, has long been a cornerstone of depositor confidence in the traditional banking system. The insurance provided by the FDIC assures depositors that, even in the event of a bank failure, their funds are protected up to a certain limit. This safety net has played a crucial role in maintaining stability and trust within the banking sector.

2. Unregulated Online Lending: A Different Risk Landscape

Distinct Nature of Unregulated Lending:

Unlike traditional banks that fall under the purview of FDIC regulations, unregulated online lending platforms operate in a different risk landscape. These platforms facilitate transactions and loans without the safety net of FDIC insurance, exposing both lenders and borrowers to a level of risk that contrasts starkly with the protected environment of traditional banking.

3. Risks for Lenders: Operating Without a Safety Net

Lack of Guarantees:

For lenders in the unregulated online lending space, the absence of FDIC insurance means a lack of federal guarantees for their financial stability. Unlike traditional banks, which benefit from the confidence instilled by FDIC insurance, unregulated lenders must establish their credibility through other means, relying on transparent practices, risk management strategies, and effective communication to foster trust among investors and stakeholders.

4. Risks for Borrowers: Limited Protections in Financial Transactions

Vulnerabilities of Borrowers:

The absence of FDIC insurance in unregulated online lending poses inherent risks for borrowers. Without the safety net that FDIC insurance provides to depositors in traditional banks, borrowers may face increased vulnerabilities in their financial transactions. Understanding and mitigating these risks become crucial components of responsible borrowing within the unregulated lending landscape.

5. Regulatory Safeguards vs. Industry Practices: Balancing Risk Management

Industry Self-Regulation:

In the absence of FDIC insurance, unregulated online lending platforms must rely on industry practices and self-regulation to manage risks effectively. This includes implementing robust risk assessment frameworks, transparent disclosure practices, and proactive measures to protect the interests of both lenders and borrowers. Striking a balance between fostering innovation and safeguarding participants requires a concerted effort from the industry.

6. Building Trust Through Transparency: Communicating Risk to Stakeholders

Transparent Communication:

Building trust in an environment without FDIC insurance demands heightened transparency from unregulated lenders. Communicating the risks inherent in the lending process, outlining risk management strategies, and providing clear and comprehensive information to stakeholders contribute to establishing a foundation of trust. Transparency becomes a linchpin in cultivating a positive reputation and fostering responsible practices within the unregulated lending space.

Conclusion: Navigating Uncharted Waters Without FDIC Insurance

Forging Ahead Responsibly:

In conclusion, the lack of FDIC insurance in unregulated online lending necessitates a conscientious approach from both lenders and borrowers. While the absence of this federal safety net introduces unique challenges, it also opens avenues for innovative risk management strategies and industry best practices. As the landscape continues to evolve, stakeholders in unregulated lending must prioritize transparency, responsible practices, and effective communication to navigate the risks associated with operating in uncharted financial waters.

Secondary Market Opacity

In the realm of unregulated online lending, the dynamics of secondary markets introduce a layer of complexity to an already intricate financial landscape. This subtopic explores the concept of secondary market opacity, shedding light on the challenges and risks faced by participants in unregulated lending when navigating transactions beyond the primary lending platform.

1. Understanding Secondary Markets: A Critical Component of Unregulated Lending

Defining Secondary Markets:

Secondary markets in unregulated online lending refer to the platforms or channels where existing loans are bought and sold among investors. Unlike traditional financial markets, the secondary markets in unregulated lending often lack the transparency and oversight seen in more regulated environments, leading to increased opacity and potential challenges for participants.

2. Lack of Regulatory Oversight: The Veil Over Secondary Market Transactions

Regulatory Ambiguity:

One of the primary contributors to secondary market opacity is the lack of comprehensive regulatory oversight. Unlike traditional securities markets, where regulatory bodies impose strict guidelines, unregulated lending's secondary markets operate in a regulatory gray area. This lack of clear regulatory frameworks can lead to challenges related to information disclosure, market manipulation, and investor protection.

3. Information Asymmetry: Navigating Unequal Access to Information

Challenges for Participants:

Secondary market opacity often stems from information asymmetry among participants. While some investors may have access to detailed information about the loans being transacted, others may face challenges in obtaining comprehensive data. This unequal access to information creates an environment where certain participants may be at a disadvantage, impacting the overall fairness and efficiency of the secondary market.

4. Risks for Investors: Navigating Uncertainty in Loan Purchases

Investor Challenges:

Investors engaging in secondary market transactions within unregulated lending face heightened risks due to the lack of transparency. Assessing the quality of loans, understanding the risk profile of borrowers, and evaluating the overall health of the market become more challenging. This opacity may deter risk-averse investors and contribute to increased market volatility.

5. Market Liquidity Concerns: Balancing Supply and Demand

Market Dynamics:

Opacities in the secondary market can lead to liquidity concerns. The lack of standardized practices and transparency makes it challenging to match supply and demand effectively. Participants may encounter difficulties in buying or selling loans at desired prices, contributing to market inefficiencies and potentially impacting the overall stability of the unregulated lending ecosystem.

6. Industry Initiatives for Transparency: Striving for Improved Practices

Industry Responses:

Acknowledging the challenges posed by secondary market opacity, industry participants are increasingly recognizing the need for improved transparency. Some unregulated lending platforms are taking proactive measures to enhance information disclosure, standardize reporting practices, and establish guidelines that promote fair and transparent secondary market transactions.

7. Balancing Innovation and Investor Protection: The Path Forward

Navigating Regulatory Considerations:

As the unregulated online lending sector evolves, striking a balance between fostering innovation and ensuring investor protection in secondary markets becomes paramount. Regulatory bodies, industry stakeholders, and market participants must collaboratively explore frameworks that enhance transparency, mitigate risks, and foster the responsible growth of unregulated lending's secondary markets.

Conclusion: Toward a Transparent Future in Secondary Markets

Path to Transparency:

In conclusion, addressing the challenges associated with secondary market opacity in unregulated online lending requires a multifaceted approach. Industry-wide initiatives, regulatory clarity, and a commitment to transparency can collectively contribute to a more navigable and secure environment for participants in secondary markets. As the sector matures, stakeholders must actively engage in shaping practices that promote transparency and uphold the integrity of unregulated lending's secondary markets.

Chapter 15: High Risk ETFs
Understanding Leveraged ETFs

Leveraged Exchange-Traded Funds (ETFs) represent a unique and complex investment instrument that amplifies returns by using financial derivatives. This subtopic delves into the intricacies of leveraged ETFs, exploring how these funds operate, the mechanisms behind their performance, and the inherent risks that investors must grapple with when engaging with these high-risk financial instruments.

1. The Basics of Leveraged ETFs: A Primer

Defining Leveraged ETFs:

Leveraged ETFs are a subset of exchange-traded funds designed to provide amplified returns corresponding to a multiple of the daily or monthly performance of an underlying index. Unlike traditional ETFs, which aim to mirror the performance of an index, leveraged ETFs utilize financial derivatives and debt to magnify gains or losses.

2. Leveraged ETF Mechanisms: Unraveling the Operational Dynamics

Financial Derivatives Usage:

Central to the operation of leveraged ETFs is the use of financial derivatives, such as futures contracts and swaps. These instruments enable fund managers to achieve leverage, allowing investors to potentially earn returns that exceed the performance of the underlying index. However, this amplified exposure comes with heightened volatility and risk.

3. Daily Compounding: The Impact on Long-Term Performance

Compounding Dynamics:

Leveraged ETFs employ daily compounding, a mechanism that can lead to a deviation in performance from the multiple of the index's return over longer periods. This compounding effect, while intended to provide daily magnification, can result in significant disparities in cumulative returns for investors holding leveraged ETFs over extended timeframes.

4. Risk Factors in Leveraged ETFs: Volatility and Market Conditions

Market Volatility Amplification:

One of the primary risks associated with leveraged ETFs is the amplification of market volatility. The use of leverage can lead to more significant price swings, exposing investors to heightened levels of risk, especially during periods of market turbulence. Understanding the correlation between market conditions and the performance of leveraged ETFs is crucial for investors.

5. Tracking Error: Assessing Deviations from the Underlying Index

Challenges in Precision:

Leveraged ETFs may exhibit tracking errors, where the fund's performance deviates from the expected multiple of the underlying index's return. Factors such as transaction costs, management fees, and the daily compounding mechanism contribute to these discrepancies. Investors must be aware of tracking errors and their potential impact on returns.

6. Investment Strategies: Tactical Use in Portfolios

Strategic Considerations:

Despite their complexities and risks, leveraged ETFs can be strategically employed in certain investment portfolios. Traders and investors with a high risk tolerance and a thorough understanding of the funds' dynamics may use leveraged ETFs for short-term tactical plays, hedging strategies, or to capitalize on specific market movements.

7. Regulatory Scrutiny and Investor Education: Navigating the Landscape

Regulatory Measures:

Given the high-risk nature of leveraged ETFs, regulatory bodies scrutinize these funds to ensure they are suitable for investors and adequately disclose associated risks. Investor education plays a crucial role in mitigating risks, emphasizing the importance of understanding the mechanics, risks, and potential rewards before engaging with leveraged ETFs.

Conclusion: Balancing Opportunities and Risks in Leveraged ETFs

Striking a Balance:

In conclusion, understanding leveraged ETFs requires investors to navigate a complex landscape where amplified returns come hand in hand with heightened risks. While leveraged ETFs offer opportunities for tactical plays, hedging, and short-term strategies, investors must approach them with caution, considering their risk tolerance, investment objectives, and the potential impact of market conditions on these high-risk financial instruments. As with any investment, thorough research, due diligence, and a clear understanding of the associated risks are paramount when incorporating leveraged ETFs into an investment portfolio.

Volatility Decay Over Time

Volatility decay stands as a critical factor influencing the performance of high-risk Exchange-Traded Funds (ETFs) over extended periods. This subtopic explores the nuances of volatility decay, shedding light on how the interaction between market dynamics and the structure of these funds can lead to diminished returns over time.

1. The Mechanics of Volatility Decay: A Conceptual Overview

Understanding Volatility Decay:

Volatility decay arises from the daily compounding nature of leveraged ETFs, where the magnification of returns is recalculated daily. As market conditions fluctuate, the compounding effect may result in a deviation from the expected multiple of the underlying index's return, influencing the fund's performance trajectory.

2. The Impact of Market Volatility on Decay Rates

Volatility Amplification and Decay:

In periods of heightened market volatility, the risks associated with leveraged ETFs are accentuated. The interplay between amplified market movements and daily compounding can lead to increased decay rates, as the fund reacts more dramatically to price fluctuations. Investors must grasp this relationship to anticipate potential erosion of long-term returns.

3. The Role of Market Conditions in Decay Dynamics

Dynamic Market Environments:

Volatility decay is not a static phenomenon; its dynamics are deeply intertwined with prevailing market conditions. Factors such as sudden market shocks, prolonged volatility, or directional changes in the underlying index contribute to varying rates of decay. Investors need to consider the adaptability of leveraged ETFs to different market environments.

4. The Time Horizon Effect: Short-Term vs. Long-Term Considerations

Temporal Considerations:

The impact of volatility decay is more pronounced over extended holding periods. Short-term traders may experience less significant decay, benefiting from the magnification of daily returns. Conversely, long-term investors face the challenge of sustaining amplified returns, as the compounding effect may erode the fund's performance relative to the underlying index.

5. Tracking Error and Decay: Assessing Performance Deviations

Tracking Error in Long-Term Holding:

Volatility decay contributes to tracking errors in leveraged ETFs, particularly when held over extended durations. Investors relying on these funds for prolonged exposure should be attentive to tracking discrepancies, understanding that the fund's performance may deviate from the expected multiple of the index's return due to the compounding effect.

6. Mitigating Decay-Induced Risks: Investor Strategies and Considerations

Risk Mitigation Strategies:

Investors can employ various strategies to mitigate the risks associated with volatility decay. These may include periodic rebalancing, adjusting exposure based on market conditions, and incorporating leveraged ETFs as tactical components within a diversified portfolio. Each strategy comes with its own set of considerations, requiring a nuanced approach to risk management.

7. Investor Awareness and Education: Navigating the Challenges

Importance of Investor Education:

As volatility decay remains a complex aspect of leveraged ETFs, investor awareness and education play pivotal roles in navigating associated challenges. Regulators, financial institutions, and fund managers must prioritize transparent communication, ensuring that investors comprehend the dynamics of volatility decay and can make informed decisions aligning with their investment objectives.

Conclusion: Balancing Act of High-Risk ETFs in the Face of Volatility Decay

Striking a Balance:

In conclusion, understanding and managing volatility decay is fundamental to navigating the high-risk landscape of leveraged ETFs over time. Investors must strike a delicate balance between the potential for amplified returns and the inherent risks posed by the compounding effect. By staying informed, adopting appropriate strategies, and aligning investments with their risk tolerance and time horizon, investors can navigate the challenges posed by volatility decay in high-risk ETFs.

Rebalancing Eats Returns

In the realm of high-risk Exchange-Traded Funds (ETFs), the strategy of rebalancing emerges as a double-edged sword. While intended to align portfolios with predefined targets, the process of rebalancing introduces complexities that can potentially erode returns. This subtopic delves into the nuanced dynamics of rebalancing within high-risk ETFs, shedding light on the challenges and considerations that investors must navigate.

1. The Essence of Rebalancing: A Brief Overview

Defining Portfolio Rebalancing:

Rebalancing is a systematic process wherein investors adjust their portfolio holdings to maintain or restore desired asset allocations. In the context of high-risk ETFs, the need for rebalancing arises from the inherent volatility and leverage that can cause drift from the initial allocation.

2. The Challenge of Timing: Rebalancing Frequency Matters

Timing Considerations in Rebalancing:

The timing of rebalancing activities significantly impacts returns in high-risk ETFs. Frequent rebalancing in response to short-term market movements may lead to increased trading costs and potential losses. Conversely, infrequent rebalancing may result in portfolios deviating significantly from the intended risk profile.

3. Transaction Costs: The Silent Eater of Returns

Transaction Costs and their Impact:

Every rebalancing act incurs transaction costs, consisting of brokerage fees, bid-ask spreads, and other associated expenses. In the high-risk ETF space, where frequent adjustments may be necessary, the cumulative effect of transaction costs can eat into returns, potentially nullifying gains and even turning positive returns into negatives.

4. The Tax Conundrum: Capital Gains and Investor Pockets

Tax Implications of Rebalancing:

Rebalancing often triggers capital gains taxes, a consideration that can diminish returns for investors. High-risk ETFs, characterized by active trading strategies and leverage, may amplify tax consequences, requiring investors to carefully weigh the benefits of rebalancing against potential tax liabilities.

5. Portfolio Drift and the Need for Realignment

Portfolio Drift Challenges:

High-risk ETFs are susceptible to rapid and pronounced price movements, leading to portfolio drift. Drift occurs when the asset allocation deviates from the intended proportions due to market fluctuations. Rebalancing is employed to realign the portfolio with its original risk profile, but the process itself introduces challenges and risks.

6. Behavioral Considerations: Emotions and Rebalancing Decisions

Emotional Aspects of Rebalancing:

Investor behavior plays a crucial role in the success of rebalancing strategies. Emotional responses to market volatility, fear of losses, or the temptation to chase short-term gains can hinder disciplined rebalancing. Successful investors in high-risk ETFs understand the emotional challenges and implement strategies to overcome them.

7. Alternative Approaches to Rebalancing: Tackling the Trade-offs

Dynamic vs. Periodic Rebalancing:

Investors can choose from various approaches to rebalancing, each carrying its own set of trade-offs. Dynamic rebalancing, based on predetermined triggers or market indicators, offers flexibility but may increase transaction costs. Periodic rebalancing at fixed intervals provides stability but may lag in responding to rapidly changing market conditions.

Conclusion: Striking a Balance in the Rebalancing Act

Navigating the Rebalancing Dilemma:

In conclusion, the challenge of rebalancing in high-risk ETFs demands a delicate balancing act. Investors must carefully weigh the benefits of realigning portfolios to maintain risk targets against the potential costs incurred through transaction fees, taxes, and the impact on returns. By adopting a well-informed and disciplined approach to rebalancing, investors can navigate the complexities of high-risk ETFs while striving to achieve their long-term financial goals.

Sector Risks Like Biotech

In the high-risk ETF landscape, sector-focused funds, particularly those centered around biotechnology, introduce a layer of complexity that goes beyond general market volatility. This subtopic explores the unique risks associated with sector-based ETFs, with a focus on the biotech industry, providing insights into the dynamics that investors must navigate.

1. Biotech Sector Overview: Opportunities and Pitfalls

The Biotech Industry Landscape:

Biotechnology, known for its innovative and transformative potential, is a dynamic sector within the broader healthcare industry. Investors are drawn to biotech ETFs for the promise of high returns, driven by breakthrough innovations, drug developments, and mergers. However, the very factors that make biotech attractive also contribute to heightened volatility.

2. Regulatory Hurdles: FDA Approvals and Market Reactions

Biotech and Regulatory Challenges:

Biotech companies are heavily reliant on securing approvals from regulatory bodies, most notably the U.S. Food and Drug Administration (FDA). The process of obtaining regulatory clearance introduces uncertainty, as rejections or delays can trigger significant market reactions. Investors in biotech-focused ETFs must be attuned to regulatory developments and their potential impact on portfolio performance.

3. Clinical Trial Outcomes: A High-Stakes Game

Investing in Uncertainty: Clinical Trials and Their Impact:

Biotech companies often undergo extensive clinical trials to validate the efficacy and safety of their products. The outcomes of these trials are binary, with success leading to substantial market gains and failure resulting in steep declines. Investors in biotech ETFs face the challenge of navigating the unpredictable nature of clinical trial results and managing associated risks.

4. Market Sentiment and Speculation: Riding the Rollercoaster

Sentiment Swings in Biotech:

The biotech sector is particularly susceptible to shifts in market sentiment and speculative trading. Positive news on drug developments or successful clinical trial outcomes can trigger euphoria, driving prices to new highs. Conversely, negative news or regulatory setbacks can lead to sharp declines. Understanding and managing the impact of sentiment-driven volatility is crucial for investors.

5. Mergers and Acquisitions: Opportunities and Disruptions

Deals and Disruptions: M&A in the Biotech Space:

The biotech industry is characterized by frequent mergers and acquisitions (M&A) as companies seek to bolster their portfolios and pipelines. While successful M&A can enhance the value of biotech ETFs, unexpected disruptions or failed deals can lead to rapid and substantial losses. Investors need to stay vigilant and assess the potential impact of M&A activity on their holdings.

6. Diversification Challenges in Sector-Specific ETFs

Diversification Dilemmas:

Investors often turn to ETFs for diversification benefits, but sector-focused funds, including those in biotech, present challenges in achieving a well-rounded portfolio. The concentrated nature of these funds means that adverse events affecting a single company or a few key players can have a pronounced impact on the entire ETF. Managing diversification within the constraints of sector-specific ETFs is a critical consideration.

7. Balancing Risk and Reward: Strategies for Biotech ETF Investors

Strategies for Mitigating Risks:

Given the inherent risks in biotech-focused ETFs, investors should adopt strategies to mitigate potential downsides while capitalizing on opportunities. This may involve thorough research, active monitoring of regulatory developments, setting realistic expectations, and employing risk management techniques to navigate the unique challenges posed by the biotech sector.

Conclusion: Navigating the Biotech Landscape in High-Risk ETFs

Striking a Balance in Sector Investing:

In conclusion, investing in high-risk ETFs focused on sectors like biotech requires a nuanced approach. While the potential for high returns exists, so do elevated risks. Investors must carefully weigh the allure of innovation and growth against the sector-specific challenges, making informed decisions to navigate the complexities of the biotech landscape within the high-risk ETF space.

Avoid Holding Long-Term

In the realm of high-risk ETFs, the strategy of holding investments for the long term encounters unique challenges. This subtopic delves into the pitfalls associated with extended investment horizons, offering insights into why, despite conventional wisdom, prolonged holding may not align with the characteristics and objectives of high-risk exchange-traded funds.

1. High-Risk ETF Characteristics: Unsuitability for Long-Term Holding

Defining High-Risk ETFs:

High-risk ETFs are characterized by their exposure to volatile assets, leveraged positions, or niche markets. Unlike traditional, low-risk investments suitable for long-term strategies, high-risk ETFs often involve complex financial instruments that are not designed for extended holding periods. Understanding the nature of these funds is essential before committing to a long-term approach.

2. Volatility Amplification: Exacerbating Risks Over Time

Amplified Volatility in Leveraged ETFs:

Leveraged ETFs, a subset of high-risk funds, aim to magnify returns on the underlying assets through financial derivatives. However, this amplification works in both directions, intensifying losses during market downturns. Prolonged holding exposes investors to the compounding effects of volatility, potentially eroding the value of the investment over time.

3. Decay and Erosion: The Time Sensitivity of Leveraged ETFs

Understanding Decay in Leveraged ETFs:

Leveraged ETFs are subject to decay, a phenomenon arising from the daily resetting of their leverage. In volatile markets, the compounding of daily returns can lead to a gradual erosion of the fund's value. Extended holding periods exacerbate this decay, diminishing the effectiveness of leveraged ETFs as tools for long-term wealth accumulation.

4. Market Timing Challenges: Unpredictability and Long-Term Strategies

Market Timing in High-Risk Environments:

Successful long-term investing often requires precise market timing, a challenge in the context of high-risk ETFs. The inherent volatility and unpredictability of the underlying assets make it difficult to execute well-timed entry and exit points. Investors may find that prolonged exposure to high-risk ETFs exposes them to market movements that cannot be reliably forecasted over extended periods.

5. Deterioration of Investment Objectives: Aligning Goals with Fund Dynamics

Aligning Objectives with Fund Dynamics:

Investors holding high-risk ETFs for the long term may experience a misalignment with their original investment objectives. These funds are designed for tactical, short- to medium-term strategies aimed at capitalizing on specific market conditions. Prolonged holding can result in a deviation from the intended strategy, potentially leading to suboptimal outcomes.

6. Opportunistic Trading vs. Buy-and-Hold: A Paradigm Shift

Shifting Paradigms:

The traditional buy-and-hold strategy, successful in certain investment contexts, may need to be reevaluated when dealing with high-risk ETFs. An opportunistic trading approach, capitalizing on short-term market trends, economic events, or specific catalysts, may align more closely with the dynamic nature of high-risk assets.

7. Tactical Portfolio Management: Adjusting Positions as Conditions Evolve

Tactical Adjustments for Long-Term Success:

Investors aiming for prolonged exposure to high-risk ETFs should adopt a tactical portfolio management approach. This involves regularly reassessing positions, adjusting holdings based on changing market conditions, and incorporating risk management techniques to mitigate potential downsides associated with extended holding.

Conclusion: Reevaluating Long-Term Strategies in High-Risk ETFs

Dynamic Decision-Making for Optimal Outcomes:

In conclusion, the notion of avoiding long-term holding in high-risk ETFs is rooted in the dynamic and often unpredictable nature of these investment vehicles. Investors seeking exposure to high-risk assets should carefully consider the characteristics of the funds, align their strategies with market dynamics, and embrace tactical portfolio management to optimize outcomes over time.

Chapter 16: Junk Bonds
What Are High-Yield Bonds?

High-yield bonds, often colloquially referred to as "junk bonds," represent a distinctive corner of the fixed-income market. In this section, we explore the fundamentals of high-yield bonds, examining their characteristics, risk-reward profile, and the unique role they play in investment portfolios.

1. Defining High-Yield Bonds: Beyond Conventional Debt Instruments

Characteristics of High-Yield Bonds:

High-yield bonds are debt securities issued by corporations or entities with lower credit ratings than investment-grade issuers. These bonds offer higher yields to compensate investors for the increased risk of default. Unlike traditional investment-grade bonds, high-yield bonds are considered riskier but present opportunities for enhanced returns.

2. Credit Ratings and Risk Spectrum: Understanding the Grading System

Credit Ratings in the High-Yield Universe:

Credit rating agencies assess the creditworthiness of bond issuers, assigning ratings that reflect the likelihood of default. High-yield bonds typically fall below the investment-grade threshold, with ratings below BBB from agencies like Standard & Poor's and Moody's. Investors navigate the risk spectrum, balancing the allure of higher yields with the potential for increased default risk.

3. Issuers and Sectors: Diverse Landscape of High-Yield Issuers

Diversity Among High-Yield Issuers:

The universe of high-yield bonds encompasses a broad range of issuers, from established companies facing financial challenges to emerging entities seeking capital. Sectors such as energy, technology, and healthcare are well-represented. Understanding the diversity within the high-yield landscape is crucial for investors crafting a balanced portfolio.

4. Risk and Return Dynamics: The Trade-Off in High-Yield Investing

Enhanced Returns vs. Default Risk:

High-yield bonds offer attractive yields compared to their investment-grade counterparts. However, this enhanced income potential comes with an elevated risk of default. Investors must carefully evaluate the risk-return dynamics, recognizing that the pursuit of higher yields involves accepting a greater degree of uncertainty and volatility.

5. Market Conditions and Economic Impact: Sensitivity to Cycles

High-Yield Bonds in Economic Cycles:

The performance of high-yield bonds is closely tied to economic cycles. During economic expansions, these bonds can thrive as issuers' financial health improves. Conversely, economic downturns may pose challenges, increasing default risks. Investors should consider economic conditions when incorporating high-yield bonds into their portfolios.

6. Covenants and Protections: Navigating Bondholder Safeguards

Understanding Bond Covenants:

High-yield bonds often feature fewer protective covenants than investment-grade bonds. Covenants are contractual safeguards that aim to protect bondholders' interests. Investors in the high-yield space should carefully assess the presence and strength of covenants, recognizing their role in mitigating risk and preserving bondholder rights.

7. Liquidity Considerations: Market Dynamics and Trading Activity

Liquidity Challenges in the High-Yield Market:

The high-yield market can exhibit lower liquidity compared to more mainstream fixed-income markets. This characteristic introduces challenges related to trading and price volatility. Investors need to be mindful of liquidity considerations when entering or exiting positions in high-yield bonds.

8. Portfolio Diversification: Integrating High-Yield Bonds Strategically

Strategic Integration in Investment Portfolios:

High-yield bonds can serve as valuable components of a diversified investment portfolio. When strategically integrated, they may enhance overall portfolio returns and provide diversification benefits. Investors should approach the inclusion of high-yield bonds with a clear understanding of their risk profile and the potential impact on portfolio dynamics.

Conclusion: Navigating the High-Yield Landscape

Balancing Risk and Reward:

In conclusion, high-yield bonds offer investors an avenue to potentially augment returns, but this comes with an inherent trade-off of increased risk. Navigating the high-yield landscape requires a nuanced understanding of credit risk, market conditions, and the role these instruments play in a well-diversified investment strategy. Investors embracing the world of high-yield bonds should do so with a clear risk-aware perspective, recognizing both the opportunities and challenges these instruments present.

The Appeal of High Coupons

High-yield bonds, colloquially known as "junk bonds," captivate investors with the allure of high coupon payments. In this section, we delve into the factors that make high coupons appealing, examining the impact on investor portfolios and the considerations for those enticed by the promise of enhanced income.

1. Understanding Coupon Payments: The Core of Bond Returns

Essence of Coupon Payments:

At the heart of bond investing lies the coupon payment – the periodic interest paid by the bond issuer to the bondholder. High-yield bonds distinguish themselves by offering elevated coupon rates compared to investment-grade bonds. This heightened income component becomes a primary attraction for income-seeking investors.

2. Enhanced Income in a Low-Yield Environment: The Quest for Yield

Yield Hunger in Low-Interest Environments:

In environments characterized by historically low interest rates, investors grapple with the challenge of generating meaningful income from their portfolios. High-yield bonds, with their elevated coupon payments, become a beacon for those seeking higher yields to meet income requirements or surpass the returns offered by safer, lower-yielding alternatives.

3. Portfolio Income and Total Return: Balancing Act for Investors

Income-Driven vs. Total Return Objectives:

Investors often face the dual objectives of generating income and achieving overall portfolio growth. High-yield bonds contribute substantially to the income component, potentially offering a solution for investors prioritizing immediate cash flow. However, the trade-off involves a nuanced balance with total return considerations, encompassing both capital appreciation and income.

4. Risk-Return Profile: Navigating the High Coupon Landscape

Risk Associated with High Coupons:

While high coupons present an attractive income stream, investors must navigate the associated risks. The very nature of high-yield bonds, with their lower credit ratings, implies an increased risk of default. As investors chase higher yields, they must carefully assess and price in the elevated credit risk that comes with the pursuit of high coupon payments.

5. Interest Rate Sensitivity: A Dance with Market Dynamics

High Coupons in Rising Rate Environments:

The interest rate environment significantly influences the appeal of high-yield bonds. In a rising rate environment, bond prices tend to decline. Investors holding high-yield bonds for their income may experience capital losses. Understanding the interplay between high coupons and interest rate sensitivity is crucial for investors crafting resilient portfolios.

6. Sector and Issuer Considerations: Where High Coupons Reside

Sector Dynamics Impacting Coupons:

The sectors and issuers within the high-yield universe vary widely, influencing the coupon rates offered. Certain industries, such as energy or telecommunications, might offer higher coupons due to their perceived risk. Investors must assess not only the absolute coupon rate but also the relative risk and reward within specific sectors.

7. Duration and Maturity: Time Horizon in the High Coupon Quest

Duration Risk and Maturity Impact:

Investors seeking high coupons should be attuned to the duration and maturity of the bonds in their portfolios. Duration risk, reflecting interest rate sensitivity, and the time to maturity can impact the stability of coupon payments and the overall risk profile. Effective management of these factors is essential for aligning high coupon strategies with investors' financial objectives.

Conclusion: The Persistent Appeal of High Coupons

Strategic Considerations for Investors:

In conclusion, the appeal of high coupons in the realm of high-yield bonds persists as a compelling proposition for income-oriented investors. The quest for enhanced income, especially in low-yield environments, draws investors to the distinctive risk-reward profile of high-yield bonds. Yet, the pursuit of high coupons requires a strategic and informed approach, with investors mindful of the associated risks and the broader dynamics shaping the fixed-income landscape. As investors navigate the high coupon landscape, a thoughtful integration of these instruments into diversified portfolios can contribute both income and potential for capital appreciation, provided it aligns with their risk tolerance and investment objectives.

Credit Risk Spectrum

The realm of junk bonds is characterized by a diverse and dynamic credit risk spectrum. In this section, we explore the nuances of credit risk within the high-yield bond market, understanding the factors that contribute to this spectrum and the implications for investors seeking returns in a riskier segment of the fixed-income universe.

1. Defining Credit Risk in Junk Bonds

Credit Quality Gradients:

Credit risk in junk bonds encapsulates the probability of bond issuers defaulting on their payment obligations. The credit quality of these bonds varies widely, from the higher end of the high-yield spectrum, bordering investment grade, to the lower end where default risk is more pronounced. Investors must grasp the intricate gradations within this credit risk spectrum to make informed investment decisions.

2. Rating Agencies and Their Role

Credit Ratings as Barometers:

Rating agencies play a pivotal role in assessing and assigning credit ratings to junk bonds. These ratings, ranging from BB and B to CCC and lower, provide a snapshot of the perceived creditworthiness of bond issuers. Understanding the criteria employed by rating agencies helps investors interpret these ratings within the broader context of credit risk.

3. Factors Influencing Credit Ratings

Beyond Financial Metrics:

While financial metrics are crucial, other qualitative factors influence credit ratings in the high-yield space. Industry dynamics, management competence, and economic conditions can impact an issuer's ability to meet its debt obligations. Investors should appreciate the holistic approach taken by rating agencies in evaluating the overall credit risk of junk bonds.

4. Default Rates and Historical Patterns

Learning from History:

Examining historical default rates in the junk bond market provides valuable insights into the potential risks associated with different credit quality levels. Understanding how economic downturns, industry-specific challenges, and market conditions correlate with default rates aids investors in assessing the likelihood of future defaults within their portfolios.

5. Differentiating Between Industries

Sectoral Variations in Credit Risk:

The credit risk spectrum in junk bonds is not uniform across industries. Certain sectors, such as technology or healthcare, may exhibit more resilience and lower default risk, while others, like energy or retail, may be more susceptible to economic downturns. Diversification across industries becomes a strategic consideration for managing credit risk exposure.

6. Market Conditions and Credit Risk Dynamics

Interest Rates and Economic Cycles:

Market conditions and the broader economic cycle significantly influence credit risk dynamics. In periods of economic expansion, default rates may decline, while contractions can amplify credit risk. Investors should be attuned to macroeconomic indicators and interest rate movements to anticipate shifts in the credit risk landscape.

7. Liquidity Concerns in Lower-Rated Bonds

Market Liquidity and Trading Challenges:

Lower-rated junk bonds often face liquidity challenges in the secondary market. Investors holding these bonds may encounter difficulties in trading, especially during periods of market stress. Understanding the liquidity dynamics associated with different credit quality levels is crucial for investors seeking to manage risk effectively.

8. The Role of Covenants in Mitigating Credit Risk

Covenants as Safeguards:

Covenants in bond agreements act as safeguards for bondholders by imposing restrictions on issuers' actions. Strong covenants enhance investor protection and mitigate credit risk. Analyzing the covenants associated with junk bonds provides investors with valuable insights into the issuer's commitment to meeting its debt obligations.

Conclusion: Navigating the Credit Risk Spectrum

Strategic Considerations for Investors:

In conclusion, navigating the credit risk spectrum within the realm of junk bonds requires a nuanced and strategic approach. Investors must appreciate the multifaceted nature of credit risk, considering not only quantitative metrics but also qualitative factors that shape the risk landscape. A thorough understanding of industry dynamics, economic conditions, and the role of covenants empowers investors to make informed decisions as they navigate the high-yield market. By strategically positioning their portfolios along the credit risk spectrum, investors can seek to optimize returns while managing the inherent risks associated with junk bonds.

Recession Impacts on Defaults

The high-yield bond market, often regarded as the riskier segment of fixed-income investments, is particularly sensitive to economic cycles. In this section, we delve into the intricate relationship between junk bonds and economic recessions, exploring how downturns impact default rates and the broader dynamics of the high-yield market.

1. The Symbiotic Dance: Junk Bonds and Economic Cycles

Pro-Cyclicality of Defaults:

Junk bonds and economic cycles engage in a symbiotic dance, where the fortunes of the high-yield market are intricately tied to the broader economic landscape. During periods of economic expansion, companies issuing junk bonds may thrive, but when a recession looms, default risks escalate, testing the resilience of these riskier fixed-income instruments.

2. Economic Indicators as Harbingers of Default

Leading and Lagging Indicators:

Certain economic indicators act as harbingers of impending defaults in the junk bond market. Unemployment rates, GDP growth, and manufacturing indices are among the leading indicators that provide insights into the overall health of the economy and, by extension, the creditworthiness of junk bond issuers.

3. Industry-Specific Vulnerabilities

Sectoral Variances in Recession Impact:

The impact of a recession on default rates varies across different industries within the high-yield universe. Some sectors may prove more resilient, benefiting from countercyclical factors, while others face heightened vulnerability. Understanding these sectoral variances is crucial for investors seeking to navigate the high-yield landscape during economic downturns.

4. Liquidity Crunch: Amplifying Default Risks

Tightening Credit Conditions:

Recessions often trigger a tightening of credit conditions, creating a liquidity crunch that can amplify default risks for junk bond issuers. Reduced access to financing and higher refinancing costs contribute to a challenging environment for companies with existing high-yield debt, increasing the likelihood of defaults.

5. Investor Behavior in Times of Recession

Flight to Quality and Risk Aversion:

Investor behavior during recessions significantly influences the high-yield market. A flight to quality, where investors seek safer assets, and a general risk aversion sentiment can exacerbate challenges for junk bond issuers. Understanding how market dynamics and investor sentiment evolve during economic downturns is pivotal for effective risk management.

6. Role of Central Bank Policies

Monetary Policy Interventions:

Central banks often play a crucial role in mitigating the impact of recessions on the high-yield market. Monetary policy interventions, such as interest rate adjustments and quantitative easing, can influence credit conditions and provide a lifeline to struggling companies. Investors must closely monitor central bank actions as they navigate the challenges posed by economic contractions.

7. The Unpredictability Factor

Black Swan Events and Systemic Shocks:

While historical data and economic indicators provide valuable insights, the unpredictable nature of black swan events and systemic shocks adds an element of uncertainty to the impact of recessions on junk bonds. Investors must remain vigilant to unexpected events that can disrupt the high-yield market, causing defaults to deviate from historical patterns.

8. Preparing Portfolios for Recessionary Environments

Strategies for Risk Mitigation:

In light of the recessionary impacts on junk bonds, investors should adopt strategies to mitigate risk. Diversification across industries, thorough credit analysis, and an awareness of economic indicators can enhance portfolio resilience. Additionally, maintaining a proactive approach to risk management and staying informed about macroeconomic trends are essential components of navigating the challenges posed by economic downturns.

Conclusion: Navigating the Recessionary Landscape in Junk Bonds

Striking the Balance:

In conclusion, understanding the impacts of recessions on junk bonds is integral to effective risk management. Investors must strike a delicate balance, recognizing the inherent vulnerabilities of high-yield debt during economic contractions while leveraging strategic insights and proactive measures to navigate the challenges posed by recessionary environments. By adopting a nuanced approach, investors can position themselves to make informed decisions and potentially capitalize on opportunities within the ever-evolving landscape of junk bonds.

Bond Covenants Matter

Bond covenants play a pivotal role in the high-yield bond market, providing a framework for the issuer-investor relationship. In this section, we explore the multifaceted importance of bond covenants in the context of junk bonds, shedding light on how these contractual agreements influence risk, investor protection, and the overall dynamics of the high-yield market.

1. Defining Bond Covenants

Purpose and Scope:

Bond covenants are contractual agreements that outline the terms and conditions between bond issuers and investors. In the context of junk bonds, these covenants serve as a set of rules and obligations designed to protect the interests of bondholders, regulate the issuer's behavior, and mitigate risks associated with the inherently speculative nature of high-yield debt.

2. Types of Bond Covenants in Junk Bonds

Affirmative vs. Negative Covenants:

Junk bonds feature a range of covenants, broadly categorized as affirmative and negative. Affirmative covenants require issuers to meet specific financial targets or take proactive actions, while negative covenants restrict certain activities that may jeopardize bondholders' interests. Understanding the nuances of these covenants is crucial for investors assessing risk and return in the high-yield market.

3. Investor Protections: Safeguarding Interests through Covenants

Limitations on Additional Debt and Collateral Protection:

Bond covenants act as a line of defense for investors in the high-yield market. Limitations on additional debt issuance prevent issuers from overleveraging, while collateral protection ensures that bondholders have a claim on specific assets in the event of default. These provisions enhance investor protections in an environment where default risks are inherently higher.

4. Financial Safeguards: Monitoring Issuer Performance

Financial Reporting Requirements:

Junk bonds often come with stringent financial reporting requirements embedded in bond covenants. Issuers must regularly provide detailed financial statements, enabling investors to monitor the issuer's performance and financial health. These reporting mechanisms empower investors with the information needed to make informed decisions and assess ongoing default risks.

5. Covenant Flexibility and Negotiation Dynamics

Tailoring Covenants to Issuer Needs:

The negotiation of bond covenants involves a delicate balance between issuer and investor interests. While investors seek robust protections, issuers aim for flexibility to navigate operational challenges. Understanding the dynamics of covenant negotiation is crucial for both parties, as it sets the stage for the ongoing issuer-investor relationship throughout the bond's lifecycle.

6. Impact on Pricing and Yield

Risk-Return Dynamics:

The presence and nature of bond covenants influence the pricing and yield dynamics of junk bonds. Investors demand higher yields for bonds with fewer protective covenants, reflecting the increased risk. Conversely, bonds with stringent covenants may offer lower yields, attracting investors seeking a balance between risk and return. Assessing these dynamics is integral to constructing a well-balanced high-yield portfolio.

7. Covenant Violations and Default Triggers

Navigating the Default Landscape:

In the event of financial distress, issuers may violate bond covenants, triggering a series of events that could lead to default. Understanding the default triggers embedded in covenants is essential for investors, allowing them to anticipate and react to changes in the risk profile of their high-yield investments.

8. Legal Remedies and Enforcement Mechanisms

Protecting Investor Rights:

Bond covenants provide the legal framework for enforcing investor rights in the event of default. Investors can employ various legal remedies, such as accelerating the bond's maturity or taking control of collateral. The effectiveness of these mechanisms depends on the specificity and strength of the covenants, underscoring the importance of thorough covenant analysis for investors.

Conclusion: The Ongoing Significance of Bond Covenants in Junk Bonds

Strategic Considerations for Investors:

In conclusion, bond covenants remain a cornerstone of the junk bond market, shaping the risk and return profiles of these high-yield instruments. Investors navigating the high-yield landscape must strategically evaluate and understand the implications of bond covenants, recognizing their role in providing both protection and potential challenges within the dynamic realm of junk bonds. As the market continues to evolve, astute investors will leverage a nuanced understanding of bond covenants to make informed decisions and optimize their risk-adjusted returns.

Chapter 17: Cryptocurrencies
Blockchain and Crypto Basics

Cryptocurrencies, spearheaded by the pioneering Bitcoin, have revolutionized the financial landscape. At the heart of this digital revolution lies blockchain technology, providing the foundation for the creation, transfer, and secure storage of cryptocurrencies. In this section, we delve into the fundamentals of blockchain and essential concepts underpinning the world of cryptocurrencies.

1. The Genesis: Understanding Blockchain Technology

Definition and Structure:

Blockchain, in its simplest form, is a decentralized and distributed ledger technology. It consists of a chain of blocks, each containing a list of transactions. The decentralized nature ensures that no single entity has control, promoting transparency, security, and immutability in the recording of transactions.

2. Decentralization and Distributed Consensus

Power to the People:

Decentralization is a core tenet of blockchain technology. Unlike traditional centralized systems, blockchain relies on a network of nodes, each maintaining a copy of the entire ledger. Consensus mechanisms, such as Proof of Work (PoW) or Proof of Stake (PoS), enable these nodes to agree on the validity of transactions without the need for a central authority.

3. Cryptography in Blockchain

Securing Transactions:

Cryptography plays a pivotal role in ensuring the security and integrity of transactions within a blockchain. Public and private keys are used to sign and verify transactions, providing a robust framework for ownership verification and secure transfers.

4. Smart Contracts: Code as Law

Automating Agreements:

Smart contracts are self-executing contracts with the terms of the agreement directly written into code. These contracts automatically execute and enforce the terms when predefined conditions are met. Ethereum, a prominent blockchain platform, popularized the concept of smart contracts, opening up new possibilities for decentralized applications.

5. Consistency and Immutability

Once Written, Never Altered:

One of the key features of blockchain is immutability. Once a block is added to the chain, altering its contents is nearly impossible. This characteristic enhances the security of transactions, as historical records remain tamper-proof, providing a transparent and verifiable history of all activities on the blockchain.

6. Mining and Transaction Validation

Proof of Work and Beyond:

Mining is the process by which transactions are added to a blockchain. In Proof of Work systems like Bitcoin, miners solve complex mathematical problems to validate transactions and create new blocks. Other consensus mechanisms, such as Proof of Stake, offer alternatives, each with its own advantages and challenges.

7. Introduction to Cryptocurrencies

Digital Assets in a Decentralized World:

Cryptocurrencies are digital or virtual currencies that leverage cryptography for security. Bitcoin, created by an unknown person or group using the pseudonym Satoshi Nakamoto, was the first cryptocurrency, setting the stage for a plethora of alternative digital currencies.

8. Bitcoin: The Pioneer and Benchmark

Digital Gold:

Bitcoin, often referred to as digital gold, is the benchmark for cryptocurrencies. It introduced the concept of a decentralized, trustless, and censorship-resistant currency. Understanding the intricacies of Bitcoin, including its limited supply and halving events, is fundamental to grasping the broader cryptocurrency landscape.

9. Altcoins and Tokenization

Beyond Bitcoin:

Beyond Bitcoin, a multitude of alternative cryptocurrencies, or altcoins, have emerged. These cryptocurrencies vary in their underlying technology, use cases, and consensus mechanisms. Additionally, tokenization, the representation of real-world assets on a blockchain, has gained traction, expanding the utility of blockchain beyond currencies.

10. Wallets and Exchanges: Navigating the Crypto Ecosystem

Storage and Trading:

Cryptocurrency wallets, both hardware and software, are essential tools for storing and managing digital assets. Exchanges facilitate the buying, selling, and trading of cryptocurrencies. Understanding the security features of wallets and the functionalities of various exchanges is crucial for any participant in the crypto ecosystem.

Conclusion: Building Blocks for the Future

Embracing the Crypto Revolution:

In conclusion, blockchain and crypto basics form the building blocks of a transformative digital era. The decentralized, transparent, and secure nature of blockchain technology, coupled with the innovative concepts introduced by cryptocurrencies, opens the door to a new paradigm in finance and beyond. As the crypto space continues to evolve, a solid understanding of these foundational concepts is indispensable for anyone navigating the dynamic and ever-expanding world of cryptocurrencies.

Volatility Versus Stocks

The cryptocurrency market is renowned for its unparalleled volatility, setting it apart from traditional stock markets. In this section, we explore the factors that contribute to the volatility of cryptocurrencies and how it compares to the more stable environment of stocks.

1. Understanding Cryptocurrency Volatility

Inherent Characteristics:

Cryptocurrencies, led by Bitcoin, are known for their price fluctuations. The decentralized and relatively young nature of the market, combined with factors like limited liquidity, speculative trading, and market sentiment, contribute to heightened volatility. Traders and investors in the crypto space must navigate a landscape where prices can experience drastic swings in short periods.

2. Factors Influencing Cryptocurrency Prices

Speculation and Sentiment:

Unlike traditional stocks, cryptocurrencies are often driven more by speculation and sentiment than by fundamentals. Market sentiment, influenced by news, social media, and macroeconomic factors, can lead to rapid and sometimes irrational price movements. Additionally, the relatively small market size makes cryptocurrencies susceptible to large price swings based on individual trades.

3. Market Liquidity and Impact on Volatility

Thin Markets and Flash Crashes:

Cryptocurrency markets, compared to stock markets, are relatively thin. This thinness, or low liquidity, means that large trades can have a more significant impact on prices. Flash crashes, where prices plummet and recover rapidly, are not uncommon in the crypto space, creating challenges and opportunities for traders.

4. Regulatory Environment and Legal Factors

Uncertainty Amplifies Volatility:

The regulatory environment significantly impacts cryptocurrency prices. Statements or actions from regulatory bodies can create uncertainty and lead to market volatility. Unlike traditional stocks, which operate within established legal frameworks, the evolving nature of cryptocurrency regulation introduces an additional layer of unpredictability.

5. Comparing Cryptocurrency Volatility to Stocks

Contrast with Stock Market Stability:

In contrast to cryptocurrencies, traditional stocks are often perceived as more stable. Established companies with proven track records, regular financial reporting, and adherence to regulatory requirements contribute to a more predictable environment. Institutional participation and the overall maturity of stock markets add a layer of stability that the cryptocurrency market, in its nascent stage, lacks.

6. Historical Volatility Trends

Examining Past Performance:

Analyzing historical volatility trends provides insights into how both cryptocurrency and stock markets have behaved over time. Historical data helps investors understand the potential risks and rewards associated with each asset class, enabling more informed decision-making.

7. Investor Behavior and Risk Appetite

Psychology of Volatility:

Cryptocurrency volatility is, to a considerable extent, driven by investor behavior and risk appetite. The speculative nature of the market attracts traders seeking high returns, but it also exposes them to higher risks. Understanding how psychological factors influence market dynamics is crucial for anyone navigating the cryptocurrency space.

8. Risk Management Strategies in Cryptocurrency Trading

Navigating the Storm:

Given the inherent volatility of cryptocurrencies, risk management is paramount. Traders and investors employ various strategies, such as setting stop-loss orders, diversifying portfolios, and carefully managing position sizes, to mitigate the impact of sudden price movements. These risk management practices are crucial for safeguarding capital in the face of market turbulence.

Conclusion: Navigating the Turbulence

Strategies for Success:

In conclusion, the volatility of cryptocurrencies presents both challenges and opportunities. While the potential for substantial returns attracts many to the crypto market, understanding and navigating its inherent volatility is essential for success. As the market matures and regulatory clarity increases, the dynamics of cryptocurrency volatility may evolve, shaping a more stable and predictable landscape. Until then, participants in the crypto space must remain vigilant, employing sound risk management strategies to weather the storms and capitalize on the unique opportunities presented by this dynamic market.

Debates Over Usefulness

Cryptocurrencies have become a subject of intense debate, with proponents and skeptics arguing about their usefulness, practical applications, and long-term viability. In this section, we delve into the multifaceted debates surrounding cryptocurrencies, exploring the contrasting perspectives that shape the narrative.

1. Proponents' View: The Promise of Cryptocurrencies

Decentralization and Empowerment:

Cryptocurrency enthusiasts argue that the decentralized nature of blockchain technology empowers individuals by eliminating the need for intermediaries like banks. This vision aligns with the original ethos of Bitcoin, aiming to create a financial system that operates without centralized control.

Financial Inclusion:

One of the primary arguments in favor of cryptocurrencies is their potential to bring financial services to the unbanked and underbanked populations. Proponents believe that blockchain technology can provide a means of financial inclusion for those excluded from traditional banking systems, particularly in developing regions.

2. Skeptics' View: Challenges and Concerns

Volatility and Speculation:

Critics often point to the extreme volatility of cryptocurrencies as a major impediment to their usefulness. The frequent and sometimes unpredictable price fluctuations raise concerns about the practicality of using cryptocurrencies as a stable medium of exchange or store of value.

Regulatory Uncertainty:

Skeptics emphasize the regulatory uncertainties surrounding cryptocurrencies. The lack of clear guidelines and the evolving nature of regulations in various jurisdictions create challenges for widespread adoption and integration into existing financial systems.

3. Use Cases and Practical Applications

Digital Gold or Medium of Exchange:

Debates also center around the primary use case of cryptocurrencies. Some argue that cryptocurrencies, particularly Bitcoin, serve as a digital gold—a store of value akin to precious metals. Others advocate for their role as a medium of exchange, facilitating everyday transactions without the need for traditional fiat currencies.

Smart Contracts and Decentralized Finance (DeFi):

Blockchain technology enables the creation of smart contracts, self-executing contracts with the terms of the agreement directly written into code. Proponents highlight the potential of smart contracts and decentralized finance (DeFi) to revolutionize traditional financial services, offering more accessible and efficient alternatives.

4. Environmental Concerns and Sustainability

Energy Consumption Debate:

The environmental impact of cryptocurrency mining, particularly for proof-of-work-based cryptocurrencies like Bitcoin, is a significant point of contention. Critics argue that the energy consumption associated with mining is unsustainable and contributes to carbon emissions, while proponents point to ongoing efforts to transition to more eco-friendly consensus mechanisms.

5. The Role of Institutional Adoption

Institutional Investment:

The increasing involvement of institutional players in the cryptocurrency space has sparked debates about the asset class's legitimacy. While some see institutional adoption as a sign of growing acceptance, skeptics question the motivations behind these investments and express concerns about market manipulation.

6. Technological Advancements and Innovations

Evolving Technological Landscape:

Advancements in blockchain technology, such as the development of more scalable and energy-efficient consensus mechanisms, contribute to ongoing debates. Supporters argue that continuous innovation will address current limitations, while skeptics question the pace of progress and the ability to overcome fundamental challenges.

7. Regulatory Frameworks and Global Coordination

Harmonizing Regulations:

Debates extend to the necessity of a coherent and globally coordinated regulatory framework for cryptocurrencies. Proponents argue that clear regulations will foster mainstream adoption, while skeptics express concerns about overregulation stifling innovation or the lack of international consensus on regulatory standards.

Conclusion: Navigating the Uncertainties

Dynamic Nature of Cryptocurrency Debates:

In conclusion, the debates surrounding the usefulness of cryptocurrencies reflect the dynamic nature of this evolving technology. While there is no consensus on their role in the future of finance, it is evident that cryptocurrencies have sparked important conversations about decentralization, financial inclusion, and the potential transformation of traditional systems. As the landscape continues to evolve, participants in these debates must navigate the uncertainties with an awareness of the challenges and opportunities presented by the world of cryptocurrencies.

Cryptographic and Protocol Risks

Cryptocurrencies are built upon the foundation of cryptographic principles and protocols, essential components that ensure security, privacy, and functionality. In this section, we explore the cryptographic and protocol risks associated with cryptocurrencies, shedding light on the challenges and vulnerabilities within these fundamental elements.

1. Cryptographic Foundations: Ensuring Security

Public and Private Key Cryptography:

At the heart of most cryptocurrencies lies the use of public and private key cryptography. While this cryptographic system is robust, the security of cryptocurrencies heavily relies on the private key's secrecy. Any compromise in the confidentiality of private keys poses a significant risk to user funds.

Hash Functions:

Hash functions play a crucial role in securing transactions and creating a link between blocks in a blockchain. However, vulnerabilities in hash functions or the emergence of more advanced computational methods could threaten the integrity of the entire blockchain.

2. Quantum Computing Threats: Breaking Traditional Encryption

Quantum Resistance:

The advent of quantum computing introduces a potential risk to traditional cryptographic methods. Cryptocurrencies, which rely on current encryption standards, may become vulnerable to quantum attacks. Ongoing efforts to develop quantum-resistant cryptographic algorithms aim to address this concern and secure the future of cryptocurrencies.

3. Consensus Protocols: Balancing Security and Efficiency

Proof-of-Work (PoW) Risks:

While PoW has been a reliable consensus mechanism, it is not without risks. The environmental impact due to energy-intensive mining is a well-known concern. Additionally, the 51% attack threat, where a single entity controls the majority of the network's mining power, remains a persistent risk.

Proof-of-Stake (PoS) and Delegated Proof-of-Stake (DPoS) Concerns:

PoS and DPoS aim to address the environmental impact of PoW but introduce their own set of challenges. Questions about the centralization of wealth and decision-making power, as well as potential attacks on the network, highlight the need for careful consideration of these consensus mechanisms.

4. Smart Contract Risks: The Double-Edged Sword

Code Vulnerabilities:

Smart contracts, self-executing contracts with the terms directly written into code, are vulnerable to coding errors. Exploitable vulnerabilities in smart contracts, as witnessed in high-profile incidents, can result in financial losses and undermine confidence in the broader ecosystem.

Oracle Exploitation:

Smart contracts often rely on oracles to interact with real-world data. Manipulating or compromising these oracles can lead to inaccurate information being fed into smart contracts, potentially causing unintended and adverse consequences.

5. Network Security: Protecting Against Attacks

Sybil Attacks:

In a Sybil attack, a malicious actor creates multiple nodes to control a significant portion of a network. This undermines the decentralization principle, posing a threat to the security and integrity of the cryptocurrency network.

DDoS Attacks:

Distributed Denial of Service (DDoS) attacks, though not unique to cryptocurrencies, can disrupt network operations and affect transaction processing. Ensuring robust network security measures becomes crucial to mitigate the impact of DDoS attacks.

6. Regulatory and Compliance Risks: Navigating the Legal Landscape

Legal Uncertainties:

Cryptocurrencies operate in a regulatory gray area in many jurisdictions. The lack of clear regulatory frameworks poses risks for users, investors, and businesses operating within the cryptocurrency space. Legal uncertainties can impede mainstream adoption and investment.

Compliance Challenges:

As regulators globally grapple with how to categorize and oversee cryptocurrencies, compliance challenges arise. Cryptocurrency projects and exchanges must navigate evolving regulatory landscapes, addressing issues related to anti-money laundering (AML) and know your customer (KYC) regulations.

Conclusion: Mitigating Risks in an Evolving Ecosystem

Dynamic Nature of Cryptocurrency Risks:

In conclusion, the cryptographic and protocol risks associated with cryptocurrencies highlight the dynamic nature of this technology. While advancements and innovations continue to address existing vulnerabilities, it is crucial for stakeholders to remain vigilant, employing robust security measures and adapting to the evolving threat landscape. As cryptocurrencies strive for broader acceptance and integration into mainstream financial systems, the mitigation of cryptographic and protocol risks will be pivotal for ensuring the long-term success and security of the cryptocurrency ecosystem.

Evolving Regulatory Oversight

The regulatory landscape surrounding cryptocurrencies is undergoing continuous evolution as governments and financial institutions grapple with the challenges and opportunities presented by this emerging technology. In this section, we delve into the nuances of evolving regulatory oversight, exploring the developments, challenges, and potential impacts on the cryptocurrency ecosystem.

1. Early Regulatory Responses: Navigating Uncharted Territory

Emergence of Cryptocurrencies:

In the early days of cryptocurrencies, regulatory bodies worldwide found themselves in uncharted territory. The decentralized and pseudonymous nature of blockchain networks posed challenges for traditional regulatory frameworks designed for centralized financial systems. Initial responses ranged from cautious observation to outright skepticism.

Regulatory Divergence:

Divergence in regulatory approaches emerged globally. Some jurisdictions embraced innovation, fostering a conducive environment for blockchain and cryptocurrencies, while others opted for stringent measures, expressing concerns over illicit activities and investor protection.

2. Regulatory Challenges: Addressing Concerns and Risks

Money Laundering and Terrorism Financing Concerns:

One of the primary regulatory concerns has been the potential misuse of cryptocurrencies for money laundering and terrorism financing. Regulatory authorities sought to implement Anti-Money Laundering (AML) and Know Your

Customer (KYC) requirements to mitigate these risks and bring cryptocurrencies in line with traditional financial norms.

Market Manipulation and Fraud:

Instances of market manipulation and fraud raised alarms among regulators. Lack of investor protection mechanisms and transparency in certain cryptocurrency projects fueled the need for regulatory interventions to safeguard market integrity.

3. Regulatory Responses: Striking a Balance

Implementing AML and KYC Regulations:

Many jurisdictions started imposing AML and KYC regulations on cryptocurrency exchanges and service providers. This move aimed to enhance transparency, traceability, and accountability within the cryptocurrency ecosystem.

Licensing and Registration Requirements:

Some countries introduced licensing and registration requirements for cryptocurrency businesses, ensuring that entities operating in the space comply with established standards and undergo regulatory scrutiny.

4. Evolving Regulatory Frameworks: Adapting to Change

Recognition of Cryptocurrencies as Assets:

An evolving trend is the recognition of cryptocurrencies as legitimate financial assets. Regulatory authorities in certain jurisdictions have taken steps to define and categorize cryptocurrencies, providing a clearer legal status for their use and trade.

Development of Sandboxes:

Regulatory sandboxes have emerged as a mechanism to foster innovation while maintaining regulatory oversight. These controlled environments allow cryptocurrency projects to test their solutions under the guidance of regulators, striking a balance between innovation and risk management.

5. Global Coordination: Addressing Cross-Border Challenges

International Collaboration:

Recognizing the global nature of cryptocurrencies, regulators are increasingly emphasizing international collaboration. Forums and initiatives that facilitate cooperation among regulators aim to address challenges related to cross-border transactions, fraud prevention, and standard-setting.

Challenges of Jurisdictional Arbitrage:

The decentralized nature of cryptocurrencies poses challenges in enforcing regulations consistently across jurisdictions. Jurisdictional arbitrage, where entities choose locations with more favorable regulatory environments, remains a hurdle for global regulatory harmony.

6. Future Considerations: Balancing Innovation and Security

Encouraging Innovation:

Regulators face the ongoing challenge of encouraging innovation while ensuring consumer protection and market stability. Striking the right balance is crucial to harness the potential benefits of cryptocurrencies without compromising financial integrity.

Regulatory Certainty:

As the cryptocurrency landscape matures, market participants and investors seek regulatory certainty. Clear and comprehensive regulatory frameworks can provide the confidence needed for institutional investors to enter the space, fostering broader adoption.

Conclusion: Navigating the Path Forward

Dynamic Nature of Regulation:

In conclusion, the evolving regulatory oversight of cryptocurrencies reflects the dynamic nature of the industry. Striking a balance between fostering innovation and mitigating risks is an ongoing challenge. As cryptocurrencies become more integrated into mainstream finance, collaboration between industry stakeholders and regulators will be essential to navigate the path forward, ensuring a regulatory framework that promotes responsible innovation and protects the interests of all participants.

Chapter 18: Startup Investing
Evaluating Founders and Teams

In the realm of startup investing, perhaps nothing holds greater significance than the founders and teams behind the ventures. This section explores the multifaceted aspects of evaluating founders and teams, acknowledging their pivotal role in determining the success or failure of a startup.

1. Vision and Leadership

Visionary Leadership:

Successful founders possess a clear and compelling vision for their startup. Investors assess the ability of founders to articulate this vision, demonstrating a keen understanding of market dynamics, potential challenges, and the unique value proposition their venture brings to the table.

Adaptability and Resilience:

Equally important is the capacity of founders to adapt to changing circumstances. Startup journeys are seldom linear, and leaders must exhibit resilience in the face of setbacks. Investors look for founders who can navigate challenges with agility and maintain a steadfast commitment to their vision.

2. Track Record and Experience

Entrepreneurial Experience:

A founder's past entrepreneurial experience can provide valuable insights into their capabilities. Investors scrutinize previous ventures, examining both successes and failures to gauge the founder's ability to learn from experiences and apply those lessons to the current startup.

Industry Expertise:

In addition to entrepreneurial experience, deep industry expertise is a key consideration. Founders with a profound understanding of the market they operate in are better positioned to make informed decisions and navigate industry-specific challenges, earning the confidence of investors.

3. Team Dynamics and Diversity

Building a Complementary Team:

While founders play a central role, successful startups are built on the foundation of a cohesive team. Investors assess the dynamics within the team, looking for evidence of complementary skills, effective communication, and a shared commitment to the venture's goals.

Diversity as an Asset:

Diversity within the founding team is increasingly recognized as an asset. Differing perspectives, backgrounds, and skill sets contribute to a more robust decision-making process and enhance the startup's ability to tackle challenges from various angles.

4. Passion and Commitment

Passion for the Mission:

Investors seek founders who are deeply passionate about the mission and purpose of their startup. This passion is a driving force that sustains founders through the inevitable ups and downs of entrepreneurship and communicates a genuine commitment to the venture.

Long-Term Commitment:

Long-term commitment is a critical factor. Investors are wary of founders who might view the startup as a short-term project. Demonstrating a commitment to seeing the venture through challenges and milestones adds to the overall appeal of the founding team.

5. Communication and Transparency

Effective Communication:

Communication skills are paramount. Founders need to effectively convey their vision, strategy, and progress to both investors and team members. Clear and transparent communication builds trust and fosters a positive relationship between founders and their stakeholders.

Handling Challenges Transparently:

Equally important is the ability to communicate challenges transparently. Investors appreciate founders who openly discuss potential obstacles, demonstrating a realistic understanding of the startup landscape and a proactive approach to addressing issues.

6. Assessing Cultural Fit

Aligning Values:

Investors consider the cultural fit between founders and their investment thesis. Alignment in values and principles increases the likelihood of a successful partnership. Investors often seek founders who share a similar vision for the future and are receptive to collaboration.

Compatibility with Investor Goals:

Beyond cultural fit, compatibility with investor goals is crucial. Founders and investors should have a shared understanding of the milestones, exit strategies, and overall objectives for the startup, ensuring a harmonious relationship throughout the investment journey.

Conclusion: The Human Element in Startup Investing

In the dynamic world of startup investing, where uncertainties abound, the evaluation of founders and teams emerges as a critical determinant of success. Investors must navigate the intricate web of leadership qualities, team dynamics, and cultural alignment to make informed decisions that go beyond financial metrics. By recognizing the human element in startup ventures, investors contribute to the cultivation of a thriving entrepreneurial ecosystem.

Difficulty of Valuing Pre-Revenue Startups

Valuing pre-revenue startups is a formidable challenge in the realm of startup investing. Unlike established companies with revenue streams and historical financial data, pre-revenue startups lack tangible metrics for traditional valuation methods. This section delves into the complexities associated with valuing pre-revenue startups, exploring the unique considerations investors face in this dynamic landscape.

1. Lack of Revenue as a Valuation Metric

Traditional Metrics Inapplicable:

One of the primary hurdles in valuing pre-revenue startups is the absence of revenue, a key metric in traditional valuation models. Without a revenue track record, investors must rely on alternative indicators and qualitative assessments to determine the startup's potential for future success.

Focus on User Metrics:

In the absence of revenue, user metrics often take center stage. Investors scrutinize user acquisition, engagement, and retention data to gauge the startup's ability to attract and retain a user base. Metrics such as Monthly Active Users (MAUs) and Customer Acquisition Cost (CAC) become pivotal in this evaluation.

2. Qualitative Factors and Market Potential

Emphasis on Qualitative Assessment:

Valuing pre-revenue startups necessitates a shift toward qualitative assessments. Investors closely examine factors such as the founding team's expertise, the uniqueness of the product or service, and the startup's positioning within its market niche. The ability to articulate a compelling vision and demonstrate market understanding becomes crucial.

Total Addressable Market (TAM):

Investors often turn to the concept of Total Addressable Market (TAM) to estimate the startup's market potential. By assessing the size of the market the startup aims to capture, investors gain insights into the scalability and revenue potential, even in the absence of current revenue streams.

3. Comparable Analysis Challenges

Limited Comparable Companies:

Comparable analysis, a common method in traditional valuation, presents challenges for pre-revenue startups. The limited pool of comparable companies in similar stages of development makes it challenging to draw accurate parallels. Investors must carefully weigh the relevance and applicability of available comparables.

Adjustments for Growth Trajectory:

When comparable companies are identified, adjustments become imperative. Pre-revenue startups often exhibit high growth potential, requiring adjustments to reflect the expected trajectory. Investors assess factors such as the startup's market positioning, technology, and scalability to make informed adjustments.

4. Dynamic Nature of Startups

Inherent Uncertainties:

Startups operate in an inherently uncertain environment. Valuation at the pre-revenue stage is further complicated by the unpredictable nature of early-stage ventures. Factors such as shifting market dynamics, emerging competitors, and evolving consumer preferences introduce a level of uncertainty that traditional valuation models struggle to capture.

Iterative Nature of Development:

The iterative nature of product development in startups adds another layer of complexity. Products and services often undergo significant transformations in response to user feedback and market insights. This fluidity makes it challenging for investors to project future revenue with a high degree of certainty.

5. Investor Risk Tolerance

Alignment of Risk Tolerance:

Valuing pre-revenue startups requires a nuanced understanding of investor risk tolerance. Early-stage investors, such as angel investors and venture capitalists, often embrace higher risk levels in exchange for the potential of substantial returns. The valuation process involves aligning the startup's risk profile with the risk appetite of potential investors.

Convertible Notes and SAFE Agreements:

In many cases, early-stage startups opt for funding instruments like convertible notes or Simple Agreement for Future Equity (SAFE) agreements. These instruments delay the valuation discussion until a later funding round or significant milestone. While providing flexibility, they add complexity to the overall valuation process.

Conclusion: The Art and Science of Valuing Potential

Valuing pre-revenue startups is a delicate balance of art and science, requiring investors to navigate a landscape where financial metrics play a secondary role to qualitative assessments and forward-looking indicators. Successful investors in this space possess a keen ability to discern the potential for future revenue, market disruption, and the founding team's capacity to execute their vision. As the startup ecosystem continues to evolve, so too must the methodologies for valuing these early-stage ventures, acknowledging the dynamic and unpredictable nature of the entrepreneurial journey.

High Failure and Loss Rates in Startup Investing

Navigating the realm of startup investing is a high-stakes endeavor, characterized by the dynamic interplay between risk and potential reward. This section delves into the sobering reality of high failure and loss rates that investors must grapple with when participating in the vibrant yet unpredictable startup ecosystem.

1. Inherent Risks of Early-Stage Ventures

Inherent Uncertainties:

Investing in startups inherently involves a higher degree of uncertainty compared to more established companies. The early-stage nature of these ventures means they often operate in untested markets with unproven business models, presenting significant unknowns that contribute to the elevated risk profile.

Product-Market Fit Challenges:

One of the primary drivers of startup failure is the inability to achieve product-market fit. Even with a compelling idea, startups may struggle to resonate with their target audience or face unexpected challenges in aligning their product or service with market demand.

2. Market Dynamics and Competitive Pressures

Dynamic Market Conditions:

Startups operate in a dynamic environment where market conditions can change rapidly. External factors such as shifts in consumer preferences, technological advancements, or the emergence of new competitors can disrupt even the most promising ventures, contributing to higher failure rates.

Intense Competition:

The startup landscape is often fiercely competitive, with numerous ventures vying for attention and market share. The intense competition places additional pressure on startups to differentiate themselves, execute flawlessly, and adapt swiftly—a challenging task that not all can accomplish.

3. Execution Challenges and Team Dynamics

Execution Risks:

Even with a groundbreaking idea, successful execution is a formidable challenge. Many startups face hurdles in product development, scaling operations, and navigating unforeseen obstacles. The inability to execute effectively contributes significantly to the failure rates observed in early-stage investments.

Team Dynamics and Leadership:

The role of leadership in startup success cannot be overstated. Disruptions in team dynamics, lack of experience, or inadequate leadership skills can derail a promising venture. Investors must scrutinize the founding team's ability to navigate challenges, make strategic decisions, and pivot when necessary.

4. Financial Considerations and Burn Rates

Cash Burn and Runway:

Financial mismanagement is a common pitfall for startups. High burn rates, where startups spend more money than they generate, can deplete available funds quickly. Investors must assess a startup's financial health, scrutinizing its runway—the time it can operate before running out of funds.

Lack of Profitability:

Many startups prioritize growth over short-term profitability. While this strategy can lead to market dominance in the long run, it also exposes investors to the risk of prolonged periods without returns. Balancing growth objectives with financial sustainability is a delicate act for startups.

5. External Factors and Regulatory Risks

External Economic Conditions:

The macroeconomic environment significantly impacts startup success. Economic downturns, recessions, or global crises can create challenging conditions for startups to secure funding, meet customer demands, or navigate regulatory landscapes.

Regulatory Challenges:

Regulatory uncertainties pose a specific risk to startups, especially in industries subject to evolving legal frameworks. Changes in regulations can require significant adjustments to business models, impacting a startup's viability and potentially leading to failure.

6. Investor Expectations and Due Diligence

Realistic Investor Expectations:

Investors entering the startup space must maintain realistic expectations. Acknowledging the inherent risks and understanding that a substantial portion of investments may not yield positive returns is crucial. A diversified portfolio approach can help mitigate losses by balancing potential failures with successful exits.

Thorough Due Diligence:

Conducting comprehensive due diligence is an investor's first line of defense against high failure rates. Thoroughly assessing a startup's business model, market fit, competitive landscape, and the experience of the founding team enhances the investor's ability to make informed decisions and minimize risks.

Conclusion: Navigating the Rollercoaster of Startup Investing

Startup investing is akin to navigating a rollercoaster, with exhilarating highs and challenging lows. Acknowledging the high failure and loss rates inherent in this landscape is a crucial step for investors seeking to capitalize on the potential rewards of successful ventures. By understanding the multifaceted risks, conducting thorough due diligence, and maintaining a realistic outlook, investors can navigate the unpredictable terrain of startup investing with greater resilience and strategic acumen.

Lack of Liquidity in Startup Investing

Startup investing, while offering the allure of high returns, is often accompanied by a significant challenge – the lack of liquidity. Unlike publicly traded stocks, where investors can easily buy or sell shares on the open market, startup investments are characterized by a lack of readily available buyers or sellers. This section explores the various dimensions of this illiquidity challenge and its implications for investors in the startup ecosystem.

1. The Nature of Illiquidity in Startup Investments

Non-Tradeable Securities:

The core of the illiquidity issue in startup investing lies in the nature of the securities involved. Unlike stocks listed on public exchanges, startup investments often take the form of private securities, making them non-tradeable on open markets. This lack of secondary market infrastructure restricts the ability of investors to easily convert their investments into cash.

Extended Investment Horizons:

Investing in startups requires a mindset geared towards the long term. Illiquidity often translates into extended investment horizons, as startups typically take years to develop, mature, and potentially exit. Investors must be prepared for a patient approach, understanding that liquidity events, such as acquisitions or IPOs, may be years away.

2. Implications for Investor Portfolios

Portfolio Lock-In:

The illiquid nature of startup investments can lead to a lock-in effect. Once capital is committed to a startup, it is tied up for an extended period. Investors may find themselves unable to easily reallocate funds based on changing market conditions, limiting their ability to adapt their portfolio to new opportunities or risk factors.

Diversification Challenges:

Illiquidity poses challenges to the principles of portfolio diversification. With a significant portion of capital tied up in illiquid assets, achieving a well-diversified portfolio becomes more complex. Investors must carefully consider the allocation of funds across various startup investments to manage risk effectively.

3. Exit Strategies and Liquidity Events

Limited Exit Avenues:

Exiting a startup investment is a critical aspect of realizing returns. However, illiquidity limits the avenues available for exits. Investors are often reliant on specific liquidity events, such as the startup going public or being acquired, to convert their investment into cash. The unpredictable nature of these events adds an element of uncertainty to the exit strategy.

Challenges in Valuation:

Illiquidity complicates the valuation of startup investments. The absence of a public market price makes it challenging to determine the current value of the investment. Valuation often relies on periodic assessments or external funding rounds, introducing subjectivity and potential discrepancies in determining the worth of the investment.

4. Mitigating Illiquidity Challenges

Strategic Portfolio Management:

Investors can mitigate the challenges of illiquidity through strategic portfolio management. Diversifying across different startups, industries, and investment stages can help balance the portfolio's risk and enhance the chances of participating in successful exits.

Access to Secondary Markets:

While secondary markets for private securities are not as robust as those for public stocks, they do exist. Investors can explore platforms that facilitate the trading of private company shares, providing a limited avenue for liquidity before a formal exit event.

5. Regulatory Considerations

SEC Regulations and Investor Protections:

Regulatory frameworks, such as those established by the Securities and Exchange Commission (SEC), play a crucial role in protecting investors. Understanding the regulatory landscape surrounding private investments is essential, as compliance requirements and investor protections vary.

Potential Regulatory Changes:

Ongoing discussions and potential regulatory changes may impact the liquidity landscape for startup investments. Investors should stay informed about evolving regulations that could influence the liquidity options available to them.

Conclusion: Balancing Risk and Reward in Illiquid Ventures

Startup investing's lack of liquidity adds a layer of complexity to the risk-reward equation. While the illiquidity challenge is inherent in this asset class, investors can navigate it successfully with careful consideration, strategic planning, and a thorough understanding of the implications. By adopting a patient investment approach, exploring diversification strategies, and staying informed about regulatory dynamics, investors can strike a balance between the potential rewards of startup investing and the inherent challenges posed by illiquidity.

Diversification Challenges in Startup Investing

Diversification, a fundamental principle in investment strategy, takes on a distinctive dimension in the realm of startup investing. This section explores the challenges associated with achieving meaningful diversification in a startup portfolio, considering the unique characteristics and risk factors inherent in this asset class.

1. Limited Investment Opportunities

High-Quality Deal Flow:

One of the primary challenges in startup diversification is the limited pool of high-quality investment opportunities. Identifying promising startups with strong growth potential is a competitive process, often requiring significant research, networking, and due diligence. Investors may find themselves grappling with a scarcity of suitable deals, hindering efforts to build a diversified portfolio.

Concentration of Capital:

The limited availability of attractive investment opportunities can lead to a concentration of capital in a few select startups. Investors may face the dilemma of either deploying capital into fewer deals than desired or compromising on the quality of investments to achieve diversification. Striking the right balance becomes a delicate exercise in risk management.

2. Sector and Industry Concentration

Overlapping Industries:

Startups tend to cluster around specific industries or sectors, driven by prevailing trends, technological advancements, or market demands. Achieving sector diversification becomes challenging when the investment landscape is dominated by startups operating in overlapping or closely related industries. This concentration amplifies sector-specific risks.

Technology and Innovation Focus:

Many startups operate in the technology and innovation space, contributing to an inherent sector bias. While technology-driven ventures offer significant growth potential, they also share common risks. Investors may find it challenging to diversify across industries without deviating from the technology-centric focus prevalent in startup ecosystems.

3. Stage-Specific Risks

Early-Stage Dominance:

Startup investing often involves participation in the early stages of a company's development, where the risk of failure is the highest. While early-stage investments offer the potential for substantial returns, they also introduce a concentration of risk. Achieving diversification across different stages of startup development—early, growth, and late stages—requires careful planning.

Follow-On Investments:

Investors may face challenges in diversifying their portfolios across different stages due to the inclination towards follow-on investments. When early investments show promise, investors may be tempted to allocate additional capital to the same startups, increasing exposure to a particular stage and reducing overall diversification.

4. Geographical Constraints

Localized Startup Ecosystems:

Startup ecosystems often exhibit geographic concentration, with certain regions becoming hubs for innovation and entrepreneurship. While these hubs offer access to vibrant networks and opportunities, they also present challenges in achieving geographic diversification. Investors may find themselves unintentionally concentrated in startups from a specific geographic area.

Global Market Dynamics:

Investors seeking international diversification in startup portfolios face additional complexities. Navigating diverse regulatory environments, cultural nuances, and market dynamics requires a nuanced approach. The pursuit of global diversification may be impeded by barriers such as limited access to information, time zone differences, and regulatory hurdles.

5. Exit Strategy Considerations

Dependency on Few Exits:

The successful exit of startups, whether through acquisitions or initial public offerings (IPOs), is a pivotal aspect of realizing returns. Diversification challenges emerge when a portfolio's success is contingent on a few startups achieving successful exits. Limited exit options can compromise the diversification benefits intended by investors.

Unpredictability of Exit Timelines:

Startup exits are inherently unpredictable, making it challenging for investors to time their exits and rebalance their portfolios. The lack of a clear timeline for exit events introduces uncertainty and may disrupt diversification plans.

6. Mitigating Diversification Challenges

Strategic Allocation:

Investors can strategically allocate capital across different industries, stages, and geographies to enhance diversification. Balancing the allocation based on risk-return profiles and recognizing the limitations of overconcentration is essential.

Portfolio Monitoring and Adjustments:

Regularly monitoring the startup portfolio and adjusting allocations based on the evolving risk landscape can help investors address diversification challenges. Staying agile and responsive to changing market conditions is crucial.

Exploring Specialized Funds:

Investors can explore specialized funds or investment platforms that focus on specific sectors, stages, or geographic regions. These funds may provide access to diversified opportunities aligned with the investor's preferences.

Conclusion: The Art of Balancing Risk and Diversification

Startup investing demands a nuanced approach to diversification, acknowledging the unique challenges posed by limited opportunities, sector concentrations, and geographic constraints. While achieving perfect diversification may be elusive, investors can navigate these challenges through thoughtful allocation, vigilant monitoring, and a willingness to adapt strategies in response to the dynamic startup landscape. Balancing the pursuit of high returns with the imperative of risk management remains the art of successful startup portfolio diversification.

Conclusion
Key Takeaways on Risky Investing

As we conclude our exploration into various realms of risky investments, it's crucial to distill key takeaways that encapsulate the nuances, challenges, and opportunities inherent in venturing into high-risk financial instruments. Whether delving into cryptocurrencies, startups, penny stocks, or other unconventional assets, understanding these key takeaways can serve as a compass for investors navigating the complex landscape of risk.

1. Risk Is Inherent, but Manageable

Understanding that risk is an inherent part of investing is the foundational principle. Rather than avoiding risk altogether, investors should focus on managing and mitigating it. Diversification, thorough research, and strategic asset allocation are powerful tools for managing risk across various investment categories.

2. Thorough Research Is Non-Negotiable

In the realm of risky investments, the importance of thorough research cannot be overstated. Each asset class comes with its unique set of risks, and a deep understanding of these risks is critical. From scrutinizing financial statements to evaluating market trends, informed decision-making is rooted in comprehensive research.

3. Diversification as a Risk Mitigation Strategy

Diversifying a portfolio remains one of the most effective strategies for mitigating risk. Spreading investments across different asset classes, industries, and geographic regions can help cushion the impact of underperformance in any single investment. Achieving a balance between risk and return involves a thoughtful approach to diversification.

4. Long-Term Perspective

Risky investments often exhibit volatility and short-term fluctuations. Adopting a long-term perspective can help investors weather the storms of market volatility. Patiently holding onto investments through market cycles allows for the potential of value appreciation and recovery from temporary downturns.

5. Adaptive Strategies in Evolving Markets

Markets evolve, and so should investment strategies. Remaining agile and adapting strategies to changing market conditions is crucial. Whether it's adjusting allocations, exploring new opportunities, or reevaluating risk tolerance, investors who stay nimble are better positioned to navigate the dynamic landscape of risky investments.

6. Risk and Reward Are Inextricably Linked

The fundamental principle of finance holds true: higher potential returns come with higher levels of risk. Investors should be cognizant of the risk-return tradeoff and align their investment decisions with their financial goals, risk tolerance, and time horizon. Balancing the desire for returns with an understanding of associated risks is central to successful investing.

7. Importance of Risk Management Strategies

Implementing risk management strategies is paramount in the world of high-risk investments. Setting stop-loss orders, having exit strategies in place, and employing hedging techniques can act as safeguards against significant losses. Prudent risk management empowers investors to protect their capital while participating in potentially lucrative opportunities.

8. Continuous Learning and Adaptation

The landscape of risky investments is dynamic and influenced by various factors, including technological advancements, regulatory changes, and market trends. Embracing a mindset of continuous learning and adaptation is crucial for investors seeking to thrive in this ever-evolving environment. Staying informed and open to new insights enhances decision-making capabilities.

9. Importance of Regulatory Awareness

Navigating risky investments requires a keen awareness of regulatory environments. Different asset classes operate within distinct regulatory frameworks, and understanding these dynamics is essential. Investors should stay abreast of regulatory developments that may impact their investments and adapt their strategies accordingly.

10. Psychological Resilience in Volatility

The world of risky investments can be emotionally charged, with the potential for significant highs and lows. Developing psychological resilience is a key takeaway. Remaining disciplined, unswayed by short-term market movements, and maintaining a rational approach in the face of volatility contributes to long-term investment success.

Conclusion: Navigating Risk for Financial Success

In conclusion, venturing into risky investments demands a combination of knowledge, strategy, and resilience. While the potential for substantial returns exists, so too does the prospect of significant losses. Investors who approach risky investments with a clear understanding of the key takeaways outlined here are better equipped to navigate the challenges and seize opportunities in this dynamic financial landscape. Balancing risk and reward is not just a financial strategy; it's a mindset that guides investors towards financial success in the world of high-risk investments.

Balancing Risks and Rewards

At the heart of every investment decision lies the delicate equilibrium between risks and rewards. Achieving a harmonious balance between these two fundamental elements is the essence of successful investing. In this concluding exploration, we delve into the art and science of balancing risks and rewards, examining the principles that underpin this crucial aspect of financial decision-making.

1. Risk-Reward Ratio: The Foundation of Decision-Making

The risk-reward ratio is the linchpin of investment strategy, representing the proportion between the potential for profit and the exposure to loss. Investors meticulously evaluate this ratio to make informed decisions. Striking the right balance involves assessing not only the magnitude of potential gains but also the level of risk acceptable within the context of individual financial goals.

2. Tailoring Risk to Objectives

One size does not fit all when it comes to risk. Investors must tailor their risk exposure to align with their unique financial objectives, time horizons, and risk tolerance. Understanding personal financial goals is crucial in determining the level of risk one can comfortably bear. A balanced approach involves harmonizing risk with the pursuit of specific financial milestones.

3. Diversification Strategies: Spreading Risk, Maximizing Returns

Diversification is a cornerstone of balancing risks and rewards. By spreading investments across a range of asset classes, sectors, and geographic regions, investors can mitigate the impact of poor performance in any single investment. The art lies not only in diversifying but in doing so thoughtfully to optimize the risk-reward profile of the overall portfolio.

4. The Psychological Aspect: Emotions and Decision-Making

Balancing risks and rewards extends beyond numbers; it involves managing emotions. Emotional resilience is crucial in navigating the peaks and valleys of the market. Fear and greed can tilt the delicate balance, leading to impulsive decisions. Investors who cultivate emotional intelligence and discipline are better equipped to maintain equilibrium in the face of market fluctuations.

5. Aligning Risk Tolerance with Investment Horizon

An investor's tolerance for risk should harmonize with their investment horizon. Long-term investments may withstand short-term market volatility, allowing for a more aggressive risk profile. Conversely, short-term goals may require a more conservative approach to safeguard capital. Aligning risk tolerance with investment horizons is pivotal in maintaining equilibrium.

6. Comprehensive Risk Assessment: Beyond Financial Metrics

Balancing risks and rewards necessitates a comprehensive risk assessment that extends beyond financial metrics. Environmental, social, and governance (ESG) factors, regulatory landscapes, and macroeconomic trends are integral components. Investors must consider the holistic risk landscape to make informed decisions that align with their values and long-term sustainability.

7. Leverage: A Double-Edged Sword

While leverage can amplify returns, it equally heightens risks. Balancing the allure of potential gains through leverage with the associated risks requires a nuanced approach. Prudent use of leverage involves understanding its implications and incorporating risk management strategies to prevent outsized losses.

8. Active Monitoring and Adjustment

Maintaining balance is an ongoing process that demands active monitoring and adjustment. Market conditions evolve, and so should investment strategies. Regularly reassessing the risk-reward dynamics of a portfolio enables investors to adapt to changing circumstances, optimizing the balance to reflect current market realities.

9. Learning from Setbacks: Turning Challenges into Opportunities

In the pursuit of balancing risks and rewards, setbacks are inevitable. However, these setbacks can serve as valuable learning experiences. Successful investors view challenges as opportunities to refine their approach, strengthen risk management strategies, and emerge more resilient. Adapting and learning from setbacks contributes to a more robust and balanced investment approach.

Conclusion: The Art of Financial Equilibrium

In conclusion, the art of balancing risks and rewards transcends financial metrics; it embodies a holistic approach to investment decision-making. Investors who master this art harmonize the quantitative and qualitative aspects of risk, align risk exposure with personal objectives, and remain adaptable in the face of a dynamic market. The delicate equilibrium between risks and rewards is not a static destination but a continuous journey that requires vigilance, resilience, and a strategic mindset. As investors navigate this intricate dance, they are poised to achieve not only financial success but a sense of equilibrium in their broader financial journey.

Clear Goals and Risk Tolerance

At the heart of every successful financial journey lies the clarity of purpose encapsulated in clear goals and an unwavering understanding of one's risk tolerance. In this exploration, we delve into the profound impact that having clear goals and a realistic assessment of risk tolerance can have on shaping a resilient and successful financial strategy.

1. Defining Clear Financial Goals

The foundation of any financial plan is a set of well-defined goals. These goals act as guiding beacons, providing direction and purpose to every financial decision. Clarity in defining short-term objectives, such as buying a home or funding education, and long-term aspirations, such as retirement or generational wealth creation, enables investors to tailor their strategies to meet specific milestones.

2. Aligning Goals with Personal Values

Beyond mere financial metrics, clear goals should align with an individual's values and aspirations. Investments that resonate with personal values not only contribute to a sense of purpose but also reinforce a commitment to long-term objectives. The intersection of financial goals and personal values fosters a more profound connection to the wealth creation journey.

3. The Role of Time Horizon in Goal Setting

Having clear goals necessitates a realistic assessment of the time horizon associated with each objective. Short-term goals may require more conservative and liquid investments, while long-term goals can accommodate a more growth-oriented strategy. Understanding the interplay between time and goals is instrumental in crafting a well-rounded financial plan.

4. The Power of Specificity in Goal Setting

Vague goals can lead to ambiguous strategies. The power of specificity cannot be overstated in goal setting. Instead of aspiring to "save for retirement," specifying a target retirement age and desired lifestyle provides a more concrete foundation for planning. Clarity in goal specificity facilitates a more accurate assessment of required financial resources.

5. Risk Tolerance: The Cornerstone of Investment Strategy

Understanding and acknowledging one's risk tolerance is the cornerstone of a robust investment strategy. Risk tolerance is a deeply personal metric, influenced by factors such as age, financial situation, and emotional temperament. A candid appraisal of one's ability to withstand market fluctuations empowers investors to tailor their portfolios in alignment with their comfort levels.

6. Balancing Ambition with Realism

While ambitious goals can be motivating, they must be balanced with realism. Clarity in understanding the potential risks and challenges associated with each goal ensures that expectations remain grounded. Balancing ambition with a pragmatic assessment of the journey ahead contributes to a more sustainable and achievable financial plan.

7. The Dynamic Nature of Risk Tolerance

Risk tolerance is not static; it evolves with changing circumstances. Life events, market experiences, and shifts in financial situations can influence an individual's risk appetite. Acknowledging the dynamic nature of risk tolerance underscores the importance of periodic reassessment to ensure that the investment strategy remains in harmony with evolving comfort levels.

8. Psychological Resilience: Navigating Market Volatility

Clarity in risk tolerance is as much about psychological resilience as it is about financial metrics. The ability to navigate market volatility, stay disciplined during downturns, and resist the temptation to deviate from the plan is integral to long-term success. Investors with a clear understanding of their risk tolerance are better equipped to weather the inevitable storms.

9. Professional Guidance: Augmenting Clarity

Navigating the terrain of clear goals and risk tolerance can be complex, and seeking professional guidance can be invaluable. Financial advisors bring expertise, experience, and an objective perspective to the table. Collaborating with professionals ensures that the goals are realistic, the risk tolerance is accurately assessed, and the strategy remains aligned with broader financial aspirations.

Conclusion: The Empowerment of Clarity

In conclusion, the empowerment that comes from having clear financial goals and a realistic assessment of risk tolerance cannot be overstated. These anchors not only provide direction and purpose to financial journeys but also serve as resilient foundations during market uncertainties. As individuals gain clarity on their goals, align them with personal values, and navigate their risk tolerance, they embark on a journey that transcends financial success – it becomes a profound and purposeful expedition towards a future they have consciously crafted.

Limit Speculation to Small Allocations

In the intricate landscape of investments, the notion of limiting speculation to small allocations emerges as a prudent approach. This strategy is grounded in the principles of risk management, portfolio diversification, and the acknowledgment of the unpredictable nature of speculative endeavors. In this exploration, we delve into the rationale behind restricting speculative investments to modest portions of a portfolio and the potential benefits it can offer to investors.

1. Understanding Speculation in Investment

Before delving into the limitations of speculation, it's crucial to understand what speculation entails in the context of investments. Speculation involves taking positions in assets with a high degree of uncertainty and risk, often with the expectation of significant short-term gains. While speculation can yield lucrative returns, it is inherently volatile and exposes investors to the possibility of substantial losses.

2. The Appeal and Risks of Speculation

Speculative investments often carry an allure due to the prospect of quick and substantial profits. However, this appeal is counterbalanced by inherent risks, including market volatility, lack of fundamental analysis, and susceptibility to external factors. Acknowledging both the potential rewards and risks is the first step in adopting a measured approach to speculation.

3. The Role of Diversification in Risk Mitigation

Diversification is a fundamental tenet of modern portfolio theory, and its importance is magnified when dealing with speculative assets. By spreading investments across different asset classes, industries, and geographic regions, investors can mitigate the impact of poor-performing assets on the overall portfolio. Limited speculation ensures that the potential losses from speculative positions do not unduly affect the entire investment portfolio.

4. Pragmatic Risk Management Strategies

Speculative investments are often characterized by higher volatility and uncertainty. Implementing pragmatic risk management strategies becomes imperative when engaging in such ventures. This may include setting strict stop-loss orders, regularly reassessing risk tolerance, and staying informed about the factors that could impact the speculative assets. These measures contribute to a more controlled and calculated approach to speculation.

5. Aligning Speculative Allocations with Risk Tolerance

The size of speculative allocations should be aligned with an investor's risk tolerance. While the allure of potential gains may be tempting, allocating a proportion that exceeds one's risk appetite can lead to anxiety, emotional decision-making, and potentially significant financial losses. Striking a balance that allows for participation in potential upside while preserving emotional well-being is a key consideration.

6. The Pitfalls of Overcommitting to Speculation

Overcommitting to speculative investments can have detrimental consequences. Large allocations to speculative assets increase the overall risk profile of the portfolio, making it more susceptible to market downturns. Furthermore, excessive speculation may lead to a departure from a well-thought-out investment strategy, as emotional reactions and attempts to recoup losses become more prevalent.

7. Long-Term versus Short-Term Perspectives

Limiting speculation to small allocations inherently aligns with a more long-term perspective on investments. While speculative assets may offer short-term gains, the emphasis on long-term wealth creation requires a more stable and diversified portfolio. Investors adopting this approach prioritize sustainability and resilience over the allure of quick but volatile returns.

8. Speculation as a Complementary Strategy

Rather than constituting the core of an investment strategy, speculation is positioned more effectively as a complementary element. Small allocations to speculative assets can add an element of dynamism to a portfolio, potentially enhancing overall returns. However, maintaining a disciplined and diversified core remains paramount for long-term financial success.

9. Professional Guidance in Speculative Endeavors

Navigating the terrain of speculative investments can be challenging, and seeking professional guidance becomes especially relevant. Financial advisors bring expertise, market insights, and an objective perspective to the table. Collaborating with professionals ensures that speculative endeavors are approached with due diligence, aligned with broader financial goals, and integrated into a comprehensive investment strategy.

Conclusion: Navigating the Spectrum of Investments

In conclusion, the strategy of limiting speculation to small allocations stands as a rational and prudent approach in the vast spectrum of investments. By acknowledging the risks associated with speculation, adopting diversified portfolios, and aligning speculative allocations with risk tolerance, investors can navigate the complexities of the market with greater resilience. This measured approach not only safeguards against potential pitfalls but also positions investors for sustainable, long-term success in their financial endeavors.

Conduct Proper Due Diligence

In the dynamic realm of investments, the practice of conducting proper due diligence emerges as a cornerstone for safeguarding capital and making informed decisions. This comprehensive process involves scrutinizing potential investments, assessing risks, and gaining a profound understanding of the underlying assets. As we navigate through the significance of due diligence, this exploration sheds light on the multifaceted aspects of this critical practice.

1. Understanding Due Diligence in Investments

At its core, due diligence is a systematic investigation and analysis of an investment opportunity. It transcends a cursory review, delving deep into the financial, legal, operational, and strategic aspects of the investment. This meticulous process is designed to uncover risks, validate claims, and provide investors with a comprehensive view of what they are committing to.

2. Financial Due Diligence: Beyond the Balance Sheet

Financial due diligence constitutes a pivotal component of the overall process. Beyond merely scrutinizing balance sheets and financial statements, it involves a nuanced examination of cash flow patterns, revenue projections, and the sustainability of earnings. Investors seek to understand the financial health and viability of the investment, ensuring alignment with their financial objectives.

3. Legal Due Diligence: Mitigating Legal Risks

Legal due diligence is indispensable in evaluating the legal standing of an investment. This entails a thorough examination of contracts, regulatory compliance, litigation history, and any potential legal pitfalls. Identifying and mitigating legal risks is crucial to avoid unforeseen complications that could jeopardize the investment's success.

4. Operational Due Diligence: Assessing Efficiency and Stability

Operational due diligence focuses on the efficiency and stability of the business operations underlying the investment. It involves evaluating the management team, operational processes, supply chain dynamics, and the overall scalability of the business. A robust operational foundation is indicative of a resilient investment that can weather market fluctuations.

5. Strategic Due Diligence: Aligning with Investment Goals

Strategic due diligence revolves around assessing whether the investment aligns with the investor's broader financial goals and objectives. It involves evaluating the business model, market positioning, competitive landscape, and growth potential. Investors seek assurance that the investment fits cohesively into their overall portfolio strategy.

6. Technological Due Diligence: Embracing the Digital Era

In an era defined by technological advancements, technological due diligence has gained prominence. This involves scrutinizing the technological infrastructure, cybersecurity measures, and the adaptability of the business to emerging technologies. For investments in tech-driven sectors, this facet of due diligence is particularly critical.

7. Environmental, Social, and Governance (ESG) Due Diligence: Responsible Investing

The paradigm of responsible investing has propelled the importance of ESG due diligence. Investors recognize the significance of assessing a company's environmental impact, social responsibility, and adherence to governance principles. Beyond financial returns, this form of due diligence aligns investments with ethical and sustainable practices.

8. Quantitative and Qualitative Due Diligence: Balancing Analytical Rigor

Due diligence encompasses both quantitative and qualitative dimensions. While quantitative analysis involves numerical assessments and statistical models, qualitative analysis delves into the softer aspects, including management competence, corporate culture, and industry trends. A balanced approach that combines both quantitative and qualitative due diligence provides a holistic understanding of an investment opportunity.

9. Continuous Due Diligence: A Dynamic Process

Due diligence is not a one-time affair; it's a dynamic process that evolves with the investment landscape. Investors must stay vigilant, continuously monitoring changes in market conditions, industry dynamics, and the overall economic environment. This proactive stance ensures that investments remain aligned with evolving objectives and market realities.

10. Professional Advisory in Due Diligence: Leveraging Expertise

Navigating the complexities of due diligence often necessitates professional advisory services. Financial analysts, legal experts, and industry specialists bring their expertise to the table, augmenting the investor's ability to conduct a thorough and objective assessment. Collaborating with professionals enhances the due diligence process and contributes to well-informed decision-making.

Conclusion: Empowering Investors Through Informed Choices

In conclusion, the practice of conducting proper due diligence empowers investors to make informed and strategic choices in the dynamic landscape of investments. By thoroughly examining financial, legal, operational, and strategic facets, investors can mitigate risks, identify opportunities, and align investments with their overarching financial goals. As a continuous and evolving process, due diligence stands as a safeguard against unforeseen challenges, ensuring that investments remain resilient and well-positioned for sustainable success.

THE END

Wordbook

Welcome to the glossary section of this book. Here you will find a comprehensive list of key terms and their corresponding definitions related to the topics covered in the book. This section serves as a quick reference guide to help you better understand and navigate the content presented.

Key Terms and Definitions

1. Due Diligence: The systematic investigation and analysis of an investment opportunity, encompassing financial, legal, operational, strategic, technological, and environmental, social, and governance (ESG) aspects.

2. Financial Due Diligence: A process of evaluating an investment's financial health, involving a detailed examination of financial statements, cash flow patterns, revenue projections, and overall financial viability.

3. Legal Due Diligence: The comprehensive assessment of the legal standing of an investment, including contracts, regulatory compliance, litigation history, and potential legal risks.

4. Operational Due Diligence: An examination of the efficiency and stability of the business operations underlying an investment, involving assessments of management, operational processes, and scalability.

5. Strategic Due Diligence: The evaluation of an investment's alignment with an investor's broader financial goals, analyzing the business model, market positioning, competitive landscape, and growth potential.

6. Technological Due Diligence: The scrutiny of an investment's technological infrastructure, cybersecurity measures, and adaptability to emerging technologies, particularly relevant in tech-driven sectors.

7. ESG Due Diligence: An assessment of an investment's environmental, social, and governance factors, focusing on responsible and sustainable investing practices.

8. Quantitative Due Diligence: Analysis involving numerical assessments and statistical models to evaluate various aspects of an investment, such as financial performance and market trends.

9. Qualitative Due Diligence: An examination of softer aspects of an investment, including management competence, corporate culture, and industry trends, providing a holistic perspective.

10. Continuous Due Diligence: The ongoing and dynamic process of monitoring changes in market conditions, industry dynamics, and economic factors to keep investments aligned with evolving objectives.

11. Professional Advisory Services: Expert guidance provided by financial analysts, legal experts, and industry specialists to enhance the due diligence process and contribute to well-informed decision-making.

12. Risk Mitigation: Strategies and actions taken to identify, assess, and manage risks associated with an investment, ensuring the protection of capital and achievement of financial objectives.

13. Investment Portfolio: A collection of investments owned by an individual or entity, including stocks, bonds, real estate, and other asset classes, designed to achieve specific financial goals.

14. Responsible Investing: An investment approach that considers environmental, social, and governance factors to align investments with ethical and sustainable practices.

15. Market Conditions: The prevailing economic and financial circumstances that impact the performance and value of investments, including factors like interest rates, inflation, and overall economic stability.

Supplementary Materials

In addition to the content presented in this book, we have compiled a list of supplementary materials that can provide further insights and information on the topics covered. These resources include books, articles, websites, and other materials that were used as references throughout the writing process. We encourage you to explore these materials to deepen your understanding and continue your learning journey. Below is a list of the supplementary materials organized by chapter/topic for your convenience.

Introduction:
Bodie, Z., Kane, A., & Marcus, A. J. (2018). "Investments."
Malkiel, B. G. (2003). "A Random Walk Down Wall Street."

Chapter 1: Naked or Uncovered Options:
McMillan, L. G. (2011). "Options as a Strategic Investment."
Natenberg, S. (2015). "Option Volatility and Pricing."

Chapter 2: Digital or Binary Options Trading:
Cofnas, A. (2013). "Trading Binary Options: Strategies and Tactics."
Crouch, D., & Furnell, S. (2019). "Digital Trading and the 'New Economy.'"

Chapter 3: FOREX Rollover Arbitrage:
Lien, K. (2016). "Day Trading and Swing Trading the Currency Market."
Douglas, M. (2007). "Forex Essentials in 15 Trades."

Chapter 4: Initial Coin Offerings (ICOs):
Casey, M. J., & Vigna, P. (2018). "The Truth Machine: The Blockchain and the Future of Everything."
Narayanan, A., Bonneau, J., Felten, E., Miller, A., & Goldfeder, S. (2016). "Bitcoin and Cryptocurrency Technologies."

Chapter 5: Futures Contracts:

Hull, J. C. (2017). "Options, Futures, and Other Derivatives."
Kolb, R. W. (2015). "Futures, Options, and Swaps."
Chapter 6: Options Trading:
McMillan, L. G. (2011). "Options as a Strategic Investment."
Thomsett, M. C. (2011). "The Options Trading Body of Knowledge."
Chapter 7: Forex Trading:
Lien, K. (2016). "Day Trading and Swing Trading the Currency Market."
Dicks, T. (2018). "Forex For Beginners."
Chapter 8: Newer Cryptocurrencies:
Tapscott, D., & Tapscott, A. (2016). "Blockchain Revolution."
Mougayar, W. (2016). "The Business Blockchain: Promise, Practice, and Application of the Next Internet Technology."
Chapter 9: Microcap Stocks:
Anderson, J. (2010). "The Complete Guide to Investing in Microcap Stocks."
Schell, C. (2014). "Microcap Magic: Why the Biggest Returns Are in the Stocks You've Never Heard Of."
Chapter 10: Ultra High-Yield Bonds:
Altman, E. I., & Riddick, L. A. (2013). "Corporate Financial Distress and Bankruptcy: Predict and Avoid Bankruptcy, Analyze and Invest in Distressed Debt."
Bragg, S. M. (2016). "The New CFO Financial Leadership Manual."
Chapter 11: Penny Stocks:
Leeds, D. M. (2013). "Invest in Penny Stocks: A Guide to Profitable Trading."
Babin, T. (2016). "Investing in the Next Big Thing: How to Invest in Startups and Equity Crowdfunding Like an Angel Investor."

Chapter 12: NFTs:
Haun, K., & Williams, A. (2021). "Crypto: How Bitcoin and Blockchain Are Challenging the Global Economic Order."
Casey, M. J., & Vigna, P. (2018). "The Truth Machine: The Blockchain and the Future of Everything."
Chapter 13: Offshore Private Placements:
Mazzucchelli, F. (2012). "Offshore Investments that Safeguard Your Cash: Learn How Savvy Investors Grow and Protect Wealth."
Siegel, J. J. (2017). "The Offshore Renminbi: The Rise of the Chinese Currency and Its Global Future."
Chapter 14: Unregulated Online Lending:
Casey, M. J., & Vigna, P. (2018). "The Truth Machine: The Blockchain and the Future of Everything."
Brown, A., Minnick, M., & Rezaee, Z. (2018). "The Handbook of Board Governance: A Comprehensive Guide for Public, Private, and Not-for-Profit Board Members."
Chapter 15: High Risk ETFs:
Fabozzi, F. J., & Kizer, J. R. (2010). "Exchange-Traded Funds and the New Dynamics of Investing."
Sullivan, T. (2018). "A Random Walk Down Wall Street."
Chapter 16: Junk Bonds:
Altman, E. I. (2015). "Corporate Financial Distress and Bankruptcy: Predict and Avoid Bankruptcy, Analyze and Invest in Distressed Debt."
Bragg, S. M. (2016). "The New CFO Financial Leadership Manual."
Chapter 17: Cryptocurrencies:
Tapscott, D., & Tapscott, A. (2016). "Blockchain Revolution."
Antonopoulos, A. M. (2014). "Mastering Bitcoin: Unlocking Digital Cryptocurrencies."

Chapter 18: Startup Investing:

Blank, S. G., & Dorf, B. (2012). "The Startup Owner's Manual: The Step-By-Step Guide for Building a Great Company."

Ferriss, T. (2017). "Tools of Titans: The Tactics, Routines, and Habits of Billionaires, Icons, and World-Class Performers."

Conclusion:

Swedroe, L. E., & Kizer, J. R. (2008). "The Only Guide to Alternative Investments You'll Ever Need."

Malkiel, B. G. (2003). "A Random Walk Down Wall Street."

www.ingramcontent.com/pod-product-compliance
Lightning Source LLC
LaVergne TN
LVHW012031070526
838202LV00056B/5468